Stay Safe My Grenadier

Stephen Leslie Pearmain

Stay Safe My Grenadier
Stephen Leslie Pearmain

ISBN 9781912821235

A CIP catalogue record for this book is available
from the British Library.
Published 2019

The letters within this book have been lightly edited
to improve their accessibility, yet remain true to
the originals, including turns of phrase and some
spellings.

Every effort has been made to contact the original
owners of the postcard designs in each instance they
have been used.

Tricorn Books
Aspex Gallery, 42 The Vulcan Building
Gunwharf Quays
Portsmouth PO1 3BF
Printed & bound in the UK

Contents

Acknowledgements

I would like to start by thanking my mother Maureen and late father Graham for keeping the letters and handing them down to me when the time came. I would also like to thank my fiancé Sally for her extreme kindness and patience. It has been an epic journey bringing this book to life, one which I could not have done without her.

Special thanks to Dan Bernard at Tricorn Books, your creative graphic design and organisation has been fantastic. Your belief in my book and your enthusiasm has been exceptional, along with your dedication to ensure that the book does the letters justice. This means a lot to me. Thank you.

Thanks to Liz Bourne for proofreading the book. For your kind words of encouragement and interest in the people behind the letters, and for your respect to keep the letters as authentic as possible, while keeping my great-grandparents' personalities alive.

I would also like to thank everyone not mentioned who have been involved in producing the book. You have all made my dream possible.

Introduction

This book is about my great-grandparents in World War One. It draws from my collection of over 500 letters, including postcards and photos, which my great-grandmother kept in her trusty old suitcase. The letters span over four years of correspondence, from the trenches to the home front, between them both during the war. I decided to write this book as it tells the story of my great-grandparents' lives, taking part in the Great War and doing their bit for King and country.

I was never really interested in the letters, so stored them away in the loft, where they stayed for many years. It was during 2013 while I was up in my loft, sorting stuff out that I had noticed were getting damp, when I came across my great-grandmother's suitcase once again. I brought it down from the loft fearing that it had been damaged. I slowly opened the lid to make sure the letters were not damp and to my amazement they were not. I was so relieved.

I was quite inquisitive and started to go through the case, reading some of the letters. I found as I was reading them that they were describing the War and some of the places where the battles had taken place. This interested me, so I read some more, looked at some of the photos and noticed that there were letters from both of them. Letters which my great-grandmother had written to my great-grandfather, and those that he had written to her from the trenches. I was hooked. I could not put them down. I thought to myself, I had to find out more about what was happening in their lives, so I decided to sort the letters into years, then months and I noticed they ran from 1914 to 1919. While putting the letters into order I counted over 500 of them. I was amazed that they were all in fantastic condition, considering their age, and just the thought that they must have meant so much to my great-grandmother made me feel quite emotional. As I started to go through the letters and type them up on my computer, things just got more and more interesting. I never met my great-grandparents, but by going through their letters it was like being able to travel back in time and experience what their lives had been like. While piecing together the facts and finding out new things each time, it gave me a real sense of what they were like and I felt that I got to know them. I had to write a book and share this story.

After completing what, I would like to point out, was the mammoth task of putting all the letters together, with some of them having no dates, I finally finished. I also had to find out my family history so I would know who was who. I was fortunate that my mother helped me in identifying some of the relatives and placing the names to the faces in the photos. The research was huge. I read many books, carried out research on the internet and watched documentaries to see what went on in the Great War, all so I could piece together the events which happened in the letters accurately.

Meet the family

Mary Josephine Hazeltine (Phine) was my great-grandmother. She was 15 years of age in 1914 and was the eldest of two sisters and one brother. Her sisters' names were Madgie (aged 8) and Mona (aged one year old). Freddy, her brother, was 13 in 1914. Josephine's mother was also called Mary so she used her middle name Josephine, and also a shortened version – Phine – to her friends and family. Phine and her family lived in the county of Essex in a village called Warley, just south of Brentwood. She was born and lived in Warley Barracks with her family, in the married quarters where her father was a drummer in the 3rd Battalion Essex Regiment.

Phine's mother, Mrs Hazeltine, was a housewife. In between looking after the children, she undertook part-time work at home washing and ironing clothes for soldiers, and also making alterations to their uniforms.

Phine had two Uncles from her mothers' Irish side, Mick and Pat. Before the outbreak of war Uncle Mick was serving as a drummer in The Queens regiment and Uncle Pat was serving in the 15th Hussars.

Albert Leslie Cox was my great-grandfather. He was known by his middle name, Leslie. Leslie joined the Grenadier Guards in 1908 as a boy soldier, after leaving school at the age of 15. He was trained as a drummer – his trade of calling was a musician in the Guards. He was a talented individual who played several other instruments, including the piano and trumpet, and had a great love for music. Leslie was also a keen sportsman and had particular success as part of the regimental swimming team. On 16th of June 1913, he achieved adult service, leaving the drums behind, and was appointed as a Lance Corporal of the Grenadier Guards.

Leslie was bought up at his mother and father's home in south-east London in the borough of Southwark at 125 New Kent Road. Leslie was 21 years of age in 1914, had one 16-year-old sister called Mabel and a 14-year-old brother called Bruce. Leslie's mother was a housewife and had several full-time lodgers living in her house. Most of her time was spent cleaning and cooking for them. Leslie's father worked as a commissioner at a bank in London.

When and where did Phine and Leslie meet?

Phine and Leslie first met each other when Phine's parents lived at Warley Barracks. Leslie was stationed there and he was friends with Phine's father who was a bandsman himself. Socially at the Barracks there were hockey matches and music hall dances put on as entertainment for the soldiers and their families. Leslie and Phine used to play hockey together and also would go to dance lessons held on Tuesdays at the 'Old Tin Hut' at the Barracks. This memory always stayed with them, as the Tin Hut was where they first set eyes on each other. They both were passionate about dancing, music and having a good time, and this is when their love for each other began.

Setting the scene

The letters start in May 1914, in a time of peace in Great Britain. The population was just getting on and living their lives.

Phine and Leslie had only just started their relationship together, so writing love letters to each other was quite new; it was one of the common forms of communication in those days.

At the time, Leslie was undertaking a normal soldiering routine, attending training and guarding military camps in different locations with his regiment. In May 1914, Phine's father decided to retire from the army at the age of 40, after soldiering for 24 years. His overseas career included fighting in the South African Boer War in 1899–1902, so having a civilian working life was a change from a long career in the army.

Phine's mother and father were also looking for a house to rent, as their married quarters were no longer available to them. They both decided to look for a house in the nearby village of Brentwood, as Phine's father had a new job secured at the Palace Cinema, working as a doorman. Phine at the time was also looking for a job. She was helping her mother to make shirts and wanted something different for herself. She was hoping to start at the Palace Cinema as a chocolate girl, and so the story begins…

1914 first love

Purfleet Camp,
Essex
17th May 1914

Dear Josephine

Just a line to let you know I am still alive. It is an awfully quiet place down here at Purfleet, not a house in sight.

We pass the evenings sitting on the side of the Thames watching the boats passing by, quite an exciting pastime. I would sooner be playing hockey or donkey. I thought Warley quiet enough, but this place beats it.

I am going up to London, to the house with the two stone dogs, next weekend for a little rest, the gay life down here is too fast.

I saw you when we came back from London on Tuesday, I tried to catch your eye but I don't think you noticed.

Please thank your mother for me for the sandwiches she sent over, they were very nice. Tell her I am properly on "tack" now, I have had no beer since I left Warley.

We are camped alongside of the Irish Guards, and by the time it comes for us to move to London I am sure I shall be speaking with an accent myself, instead of my beautiful cockney talk.

I suppose you are starting to make your fancy aprons & caps now for that job as "chocolate girl". Of course when I go to the pictures I shall not have to pay to go in & to buy chocolates. Shall I?

Well I must close now to catch the post. Give my kind regards to Mother & Father, hoping they are in the best of health. So goodbye for the present.

With love, Leslie

6 Block married quarters,
Warley Barracks,
Brentwood,
Essex
21st May 1914

Dear Leslie

I received your letter and was so pleased to hear from you and also to hear you are still alive. So am I, but I am not busy making caps and aprons, I am busy helping to make shirts, as they don't need a chocolate girl at the Palace so you won't be able to have any chocolate. But Dad said that you can go in for nothing if you tip him with a bob. I did see you on Tuesday, but I did not like to take any notice as there was such a lot of men. Dad might go down to see you. I wish I could come, but Dad won't let me because there are all men there.

I went out with Mam and Dad on Sunday for a nice walk but I would rather play hockey. Mam is pleased to hear you are on the <u>JACK</u>. She said look at the money you can <u>SAVE</u>.

We did miss you on Sunday, also our hockey match. Don't mention donkey the horrible game. I hope you will enjoy your little residence with the two stone dogs. I wish you were coming here but people are too nosey.

Mam said we will soon have our own house where you can come when you like and they can't say nothing. I can't think of any more news just now. Mam and Dad send their respects and hope to see you soon. I will now bring my first letter in scribble to a close. Hoping to hear soon, goodbye for the present.

With love from Josephine

Excuse my letter as I can't write like you.

28th May 1914

Dear Leslie

I received your letter safe and I was so pleased to hear from you and to know you are quite well. Did you catch cold on Saturday when you got wet? You are very unlucky in getting wet.

Dad started work on Monday, suppose you won't be sorry to get to London. As you will be near home we might go up for the holidays but we are not sure. Mam has been busy looking for a house. It is such a job to get one but we got one now. I suppose you know we have only got three weeks in barracks now, you won't be too proud to come and see us when we get outside in our new house will you?

Dad did not go down because he thought you were going home and he can't get this week as he is at work. Dear Leslie, mam said she will let you know when we are settled and then you must come down and have a weekend with us.

I tried to set fire to myself on Saturday. I put some oil on the fire. I of course burnt my hand but it is better now. I suppose you will say donkey. I don't think there is any more news now. Mam and Dad send their best respects, hoping to see you soon, so goodbye for present.

With love from Josephine

X

Excuse my bad writing.

Wellington Barracks,
London S.W.
1st June 1914

Dear Josephine

I received your letter quite safe. I was sorry to hear you burnt your hand. I will not say you were a donkey. But-a, well, a little barmy. I hope it is quite well by now.

I am pleased to get back to London again. I came home on Saturday to spend the holidays here but found everybody in the house gone away except my Father so I am housekeeper until tonight.

I thought I might have had the chance of coming back to Warley next Wednesday. Half of our company and six corporals are coming but it is not my luck. I am consoling myself with what they told me, that the <u>smart corporals</u> are to stay in London. Don't think I am swanking.[1]

How does your Dad like his place? I expect he finds it a bit different to being a soldier.

I suppose you are looking forward to your change of quarters, do you think you will like living out of barracks, after so long?

I shall certainly not feel too proud to come and see you in your new home; I am looking forward to the time when I may come down. No I did not catch cold last Saturday week, in fact I lost one, because I have not had one since then.

Well Phine dear I must make this a short letter as I have got to cook my Father's supper and get back to barracks. You ought to see me here dodging around trying to cook, it makes me think of that saying "What is home without a Mother?". Give my best respects to your Mam and Dad and I hope they are quite well.

Hoping to see you soon (although it will be a long month yet), mind you do not burn yourself again.

With best love Les Xxx

5th June 1914

Dear Leslie

I received your letter and am pleased to hear you are quite well. We went to the sports on Monday after tea, they had dancing there. I had one with Charlie, you know who I mean as I don't know his other name, and he told me that some of your company was coming in. He said he bets Leslie would like to be here. It did seem funny at a dance without you, I did not want to dance.

Dear Leslie, Dad does not care for his job but he said he will soon get used to it. I suppose I would like to have seen you busy cooking, if I had been near I would have helped you. I suppose you are kept very busy now you are in London. Don't you wish you were not so smart, then they would have sent you to Warley, but I am pleased to hear that you should feel proud of it. Mam said of course you are swanking, of course she would but I don't, that is only her fun.

Dear Leslie, we shall be pleased to see you roll on not a long month. We have got a nice house near the palace,[2] we are looking forward to when we get there so it is much nicer than barrack life. Mam will feel a bit lonely but I am pleased we are going as I never did like being here, so will Dad. I don't think there is any more news now. Hoping to see you soon. Goodbye for the present. Mam and Dad send their best respects and hope to see you soon.

With best love, from Josephine
XXX

Wellington Barracks,
London S.W.
8th June 1914

Dear Josephine

I received your letters quite safe. I would like to have been at the sports with you last Monday. I heard you was there from Cpl[3] Parkinson. He told me when he came up here last week. I was very nearly going, Cpl Pickering wanted to run in some races, & he asked me to go with him, but we had to cancel it because of returning to London & you see we did not know if we should be for any duty or not.

I've got a new job now, Caterers in the Corporal's mess. I have to stick in here all day, from reveille to ten at night. I cannot get out for a month, not till the 1st July, so you can guess how I keep saying "roll on". I thought at first that being behind the bar would make me go off the "tack" again, but the awful smell of the stuff all day is quite enough.

I am sorry to hear your Dad does not care for his new job, I suppose it comes a bit strange to him. Still as you say he may get used to it soon, I hope so anyhow.

I hope you will not be offended with me or think it cheeky what I am going to ask you, but I should very much like to have a photo of you, if you have one to spare. You see it is such a long time since I saw you last & I have got to wait another month yet.

You must excuse my letter being short this time, as I am continually being interrupted for something or another, so I will say goodbye for the present. Hoping your Mam & Dad are in the best of health & give them my best respects, with love & kisses Leslie.

XXX

17 King Edwards Road,
Brentwood, Essex

Dear Leslie

I received your letter and pleased to hear you are quite well. I am so sorry to keep you waiting for a letter but we are in such a muddle. We shifted yesterday but it is so nice. I am sending a photo but they are not nice you know but I will have one taken later on, now we want a nice one of you for our parlour.

Dear Leslie, I suppose you will be surprised to hear that I have got the job you chaffed me about. I am going to be a chocolate girl tonight, 6/1 week and commission. I suppose we won't see you until the 4th as that is on a Saturday. We have not had a game since you went. Don't you like being in the mess? It must be a tie but it will soon pass by. Now I hope you will excuse this short letter as we are so busy getting straight and of course I have got to work tonight. I don't think I shall like it. I have not more news to tell now. Mam and Dad send you their best respects and hope you are well. I will close now so goodbye for the present. With best love, from Josephine.

XXXX

Wellington Barracks,
London S.W.
17th June 1914

Dear Josephine

I was very pleased to get your letter, thank you very much for the photo.

I thought perhaps you was moving when I did not hear from you at first. I expect all of you have been very busy getting straight. How do you like your new home? I suppose your Mam likes it better than the other place; it must seem strange at first. I do not suppose the lights go out at ten-fifteen, like they used to do in barracks, in the midst of our hockey games.

I was surprised to hear you had started work, how do you like it? You must write and tell me all about it. I bet you will eat more chocolates than you sell. I know I do in the mess here; I eat the cakes and things all day long.

I expect next week you will have the pictures showing at your place of our battalion trooping the colours on the King's birthday, they are practising every day. I remember one year when I was a drummer trooping colours, I went to a music hall the same night and saw myself on the pictures, it was quite amusing. Still I am very glad I am missing it this year, it is much too like work for my liking.

I have just done something similar to what you did the other day when you tried to burn your hand. I was lifting some boxes and put my thumb out. It is nothing much, only rather painful. Don't have your own back and call me donkey will you?

Well I must close now, I cannot think of any more to say now, you know I am a terrible letter writer, when I start to write I don't know what to put down. I think I shall have to employ a clerk.

Give my kind regards to your Mam and Dad, hoping they are quite well. So goodbye for the present, with best love, Leslie.

XXXX

Dear Leslie

I received your letter and pleased to hear from you. I was wondering why I did not hear but I forgot I was late with my letter. Mam had a game with me and said I should not hear from you again but she got had. I am sorry to hear you hurt your thumb. You say it is not much but I expect it is. I won't call you donkey because you got to work with it and I done nothing so I feel sorry for you.

Dear Leslie, there is nothing to tell you about my job only I don't care for it. I don't get a chance to eat the chocolates for they are counted out to me, so your job is better – you can eat what you like and I got to look at them, I suppose I will get used to it presently. You won't forget your photo will you? We want it for our parlour. If you don't, Mam is going to pull your nose for you when you come down, so you know what to expect.

I suppose you are kept very busy this hot weather as they want more beer. Don't you want a barmaid to help you or shall I be your clerk because I am an expert at letter writing, you can see.

Dear Leslie, we do like our new home. Mam thought she would feel lonely but it is quite a treat a nice house, it gives you pleasure to clean it, something different to the other, see what you think of it, it is rather good rent 9/. a week but we go into the parlour dressed out of the block gate about 100 yards and the station is opposite us.

Dear Leslie, I don't think there is any more news now. Hoping you are quite well. Mam and Dad send their best respects and hopes, I will close with best love and kisses, from Josephine.

Six this time XXXXXX

21st June 1914

Dear Josephine

I received your letter, I was pleased to hear from you so soon, I did not expect your letter till Monday morning. You see we don't have a post on Sundays in London. That was why I was late with my letter last week, because I did not get yours till Monday, and I was very busy Monday and Tuesday. Still I am punctual this time to make up for it.

I have not a photo to let you have at present. I have never had it taken properly yet, I've always been afraid to. When I come out of this hole, I will have it done, (if the photographer will chance it) and let you have one.

You are right about the fellows wanting more beer now the weather is hot. Yesterday they drank every drop in the place, so today I'm having an easy time sitting down and telling them there isn't any. Thank you for your offer of Barmaid, but you see I do not require one just now. My thumb is much better now, it is still a little stiff, that's all.

My Father was in here yesterday talking to me. When I received your letter. Of course, being rather inquisitive, he wanted to know who it was from and all about it. So I had to tell him, and show him your photo. He wants to know when he is going to be introduced, so I told him soon.

I started to write this letter at seven o'clock and got as far as this when some chaps came in with these friends and demanded that I should play the piano for them, so I had to oblige.

They made a fine old row too, singing and dancing till ten o'clock. It reminded me of our practice dances we used to have in the Mess at Warley. I don't suppose I shall have such decent times as those again, especially the Corporals dances and the old tin hut.

Well I must close now, it is just on "lights out", so goodbye for a little while now (I'm counting the days, roll on). Give my best respects to your Mam and Dad, with best love, Leslie.

XXXXXXX

I've gone one better this time. <u>Seven</u>.

This letter will be a bit late now because I cannot post it till the morning.

Dear Leslie

I received your letter early this week, Monday. I was pleased to hear your thumb was better. I suppose you have quite a lively time in the mess serving beer, too lively for you. I suppose you must not play the piano too much for them for we want you to play for us when you come down. Fancy your Father being there when you got my letter. Were you proud to tell him? I suppose he teased you about it.

Mam said you can bring him down with you if you like. He will be welcome with both Mam and Dad, if it suits you make your own arrangements and let us know when you are coming won't you. Thank you for promise of photo, shall be pleased to have one. Are you tired of being shut in and can't go home? The weather is very warm too.

Dear Leslie, I forgot to tell you that we live next door to Mrs Highte, you know the old lady you see Mam with at the dances. She does play the piano nice, I wish I could, I must have some lessons off you.

You must write and tell us your arrangements. You know your Dad will be welcome don't you? Of course you will come if he does not.

Dear Leslie, I don't think there is any more news now, not many more letters before we see you so goodbye for the present.

With best love, from Josephine.

XXXXXXXX

I beat you this time. If I put any more I shall want another sheet of paper.

Wellington Barracks,
London S.W.
28ᵗʰ June 1914

Dear Josephine

I received your letter quite safe. My Father wishes to thank your Mam and Dad for their invitation to him to come down. He would have been pleased to come, only his work prevents him, as he has to work on Sundays as well.

I shall come down sometime this weekend, if it will be convenient for you. I am not sure quite certain, but I am afraid in the Mess a day or two longer yet. Then when I do come out I expect I shall be for piquet⁴ or guard, so I will write you again during the week and let you know for certain.

I am going to ask for three or four days' leave, but I don't know if I shall get it, because there is so much duty to do up here. I have been properly run down the last day or too, hardly able to move, it is because I cannot get out into the fresh air. Still I don't suppose I am too wicked.

How are you getting on with your place now? Have you got used to it yet?

You frighten me when you say the lady next door to you plays the piano well, I should not dare to play if anybody was about who could play a piano properly. I would not mind to play that small one you have at home, you know, the one you have to blow with one hand and play with the other.

Well I will close now, give my kind regards to your Mam and Dad, hoping to see you very soon now.

    With best love and kisses, Leslie.

    XXX

    All I can spare this time, I'm saving them up till I see you.

    P.S. I will write again when I come out of the Mess.

Dear Leslie

I received your letter and so sorry to hear you are not well. You did not say what was the matter. I hope you feel better by now, if you can get three or four days down here it will do you good in the nice fresh air, try and get it. I am sorry your Father can't come but his work comes first. If you are for guard you must try and get someone to do it for you.

    The weather is enough to kill anyone it is so hot and of course it is much worse in London. Pity you could not stop in Warley. You say you are too wicked to die, good job you are wicked I don't want you to die yet, I want some more dances and games and to hear you play our piano. You will be alright when you get out of that horrid place away from the smell of beer.

    Dear Leslie, I don't mind my job so much now I am getting used to it. I have got a nasty cold, I suppose it is eating so much chocolates, don't you? I am anxious to hear when you are coming as we will be pleased to see you. Mam said if it is only to pull your nose.

    There is no more news. Mam and Dad send their respects and hope you are better. I will close now with best love, from Josephine.

    XXX

    Only three this time, can't spare no more.

Prepare for War

Wellington Barracks,
London S.W.
8th July 1914

Dear Josephine

You must excuse me not writing you before now. But I have had so much to do that I have not had time to write. I do not know when I shall be able to come down again, not till we go to the Tower[5] anyhow, you see it takes us for duty so often. I am on piquet again today and guard tomorrow. It was a good job your Mam made me busy on Sunday night as the train was waiting when I got on the station. I feel a lot better for the weekend change; I am saying roll on the next one now.

I can't say when it will be because I come in waiting for the drummers next Tuesday week for three weeks whilst they are firing their annual course at Purfleet. Just my luck, because I have been a drummer myself I am supposed to know all about it.

I have been sitting here for about ten minutes trying to think of something to write about. I don't know what to put, I am such a duffer when it comes to writing letters, so you must excuse me and let it be a short letter this time. I know one thing, I wish I could have had those few days leave. I quite envy Violet with her week's holiday with you. Give my best respects to your Mam and Dad. Hoping to see you again soon, with best love and kisses, Leslie.

XXXXX

Tower of London,
16th July 1914

Dear Josephine

I was pleased to receive your letter, but I was extremely sorry to hear your Dad had been ill. I hope it was nothing serious and that he is quite well by now.

I am sorry I have not written you before now, but we have been so busy here in London, with guards and now shifting to the Tower. When you write again address your letter to the Tower, you will see this by this letter. I live in a small room in a tower with the drummer boys. They say it is the room where Queen Elizabeth was imprisoned and where several other people have died, so I cannot say that I like the idea of living there. I have got to stay here in waiting till the 6th July, and I am not allowed out except on occasional Sunday afternoons, so it will be another long month nearly before I can see you again.

I have got one consolation though, the drum Major has gone home to Warley on poulo[6] and left me in charge, and he asked me if I would take over his schools where he teaches the lads on drum and bugle. Of course, I agreed as it means a matter of 10/- or so a week. So, I don't mind so much having to step in, although I would rather be him on furlough down at Warley.

Well Phine, I must close, I am very busy. I have a lot of writing to do tonight, you must excuse me saying such a thing when I am writing you, but I know you will understand, so goodbye for the present. Give my best respects to your Mam and Dad and hope to hear your Dad is well again when you write me next time. So, goodbye for the present.

With lots of love and kisses, Leslie.

XXXXXXXX

P.S. Excuse my bad writing but I am writing all day long now.

XXXX

Write soon.

18th July 1914

Dear Leslie

I received your letter and so pleased to hear from you. Dad is better now, it was something upset him. I am pleased to hear you get paid for your job, you must not grumble about being shut in for a little while, some more money for your Bank Book, you will be too rich to come and see me presently, me with my 5/- a week. I am very rich, I would not like your job in that horrid place. Mam has been in there, you must not think of it, it must seem lonely to be shut in there but what about me? I never go out, I never want to. I would not mind going out to a dance somewhere if you were here. Don't tell Mam I said so, will you? Not that she would mind because she thinks such a lot of you, so does Dad. I am sorry you can't get away before the 6th of August but it cannot be helped. You will come down then, won't you?

I might go up for a Sunday before then, perhaps I will be able to see you. I will let you know.

Dear Leslie, you said write soon so I am answering your letter tonight hoping you are quite well. I will close now. Mam and Dad as usual send their best respects and so goodbye for now, with very best love, from Josephine.

XXXXXXXXXXXX

Baker's dozen

P.S. don't forget the photo.

24th July 1914

Dear Leslie

I received your letter and so pleased to hear from you, also to know that you are coming on Sunday. Mam said of course it is convenient for you to come down when you like and pleased to see you.

Dad is quite alright now.

Dear Leslie, Mam and Dad will be very pleased if your Mother will come down in August, we will be pleased to see her. I will make this letter a short one as I will see you on Sunday. I suppose you got to go back Sunday night. I am busy ironing with mam so I will close for now, hoping you are quite well & don't have to go to bed when you come down. Mam and Dad send their best respects so goodbye.

  With best love, from Josephine

  XXXXXX can't spare no more

Tower of London E. L.
28ᵗʰ July 1914

Dear Josephine

Just a line to let you know I arrived home quite safe on Sunday night.

I do not know if I shall be able to see you if you come up on Sunday. We have just been ordered to Edinburgh. We go tonight at seven o'clock, it must be something very serious because we have been served with full ammunition. We don't know what it is all about, but we might be there two days or two months. When you write again address the letter to the Tower, as I expect they will forward it on.

  Well Phine dear, I must close as I have only an hour to pack up and get ready and there is plenty today, everybody flying about. The men think we are going on a picnic or something. Give my best respects to your Mam and Dad; I must close, yours in haste, with best of love, Leslie.

  XXXXXXXXXX

Invergordon, Scotland

Dear Phine

Just a line to let you know where I am. We are in a little place right in the north of Scotland about twenty miles north of Ferness. It is a pretty little place on the sea.

A detachment of fifty men and two officers of the Grenadier Guards had been rushed from London to guard the Admiralty oil tanks at Invergordon, Leslie was one of the fifty men sent.

30ᵗʰ July 1914

Dear Leslie

I received your letter and I am so sorry to hear you are gone away; I hope nothing will happen to you, I feel so upset about it.

  Mam said you will be alright. For goodness sake write and let me know what you are doing or if you get your food alright. Let me know if I can send you anything, I will be only so pleased to do so, if there is anything you would like as we don't know how you are placed.

  Dear Leslie, I won't go to London on Sunday now, I will wait until you come back. Pray be careful nothing does not happen to you. I suppose your poor mother is upset about you going but I hope it is not for long or nothing serious.

  Dear Leslie, be sure and drop me a line won't you to know how you are and what you are doing. There is no more news now, you got all the news to tell. Mam and

Dad are very sorry you had to go and send their best respects hoping you will soon be back. I will close now Leslie dear, with very best love and kisses, from Josephine.

XXXXXXXXXXXXXXXX

1st August 1914

My dear Leslie

Just a line hoping you are quite well. Did you get my letter on Saturday? I hope you are not cross with me for sending that card. Freddy brought it home and said that is you and Leslie so I thought I would send it for a bit of fun, but I was sorry after I sent it. I wondered if you would like it, but you are not cross are you Leslie? I expected a letter this morning from you and I feel worried because I did not get one. I hope you are not gone.

Dear Leslie, Mam wrote to your Mother but she has not had an answer. She hopes your Mother is alright. I expect she is very busy now. Do write soon, I will close for present.

With fondest love and kisses, Josephine

XXXXXXXXXXXXXX

17 King Edwards Road,
Brentwood

Dear Leslie

I received your cards this morning and you don't know how pleased I was to hear from you. I have been so anxious all the week as we could not hear where you were or what you were doing. I am pleased you are alright, you are supposed to be back in Warley Tuesday so they say here, some went to Newcastle and came back Saturday, I wrote to the Tower but I suppose you did not get it.

Dear Leslie, the cards you sent me are very nice indeed. I am going to keep the postcards as a token of where you have been, they are making preparations to call our third up.

Dear Leslie, I won't worry you with any more news now. Mam and Dad send their best respects. I hope you will be back soon and that you keep well, look after yourself. I will close now with very best love and kisses, from Josephine.

XXXXXXXXXXXXXXX

Let me know if I can send you anything. I shall be pleased to send it.

4th August 1914 Britain declared war on Germany

Tower of London,
London
3rd August 1914

My dear Phine

You must excuse me not answering your letter before now but I only received your letter last night (Sunday) when we came back from Scotland. I thought perhaps they would have sent your letter on, but they did not know where we were exactly. I expect you received my postcard alright. I would have wrote you last night but I only had a hour spare so I went home to let them know I was alright.

Goodness knows what is going to happen now. I am on guard to day, and I feel just about fed up after being tied up in a train for 21 hours, travelling.

Our last order now is to be ready to mobilise at any moment, and if we do we shall have to come to Warley. My Company is in readiness to come to Warley now, we might come at any minute, in fact we expect to be there by tomorrow night. If we are allowed out I will come down and see you when we get there, if not I must ask you to come up to the gate and ask for me, I know you will not mind for once, considering how I am placed.

I will close now, as I am feeling very tired, and it has turned one o'clock, so I will say goodbye, give my best respects to Mam and Dad, hoping to see you within the next day or two, with best love and kisses, Leslie.

XXXXXXXXXXX

Wellington Bks,
London SW
22nd August 1914

Dear Josephine,

Just a line to let you know we arrived here safe I have just come off guard, mounted directly we came from Warley. We are a bit busy here, batches of troops leave every night for Southampton, but I think our battalion will stay here a week or two yet. I know we shall not go before Tuesday as we are finding all the guards in London up till Monday. We are having rather a good time here, we are allowed out every night till 12 o'clock and all the buses, trams and underground railways are free to us.

My Mother came along by the gate yesterday morning, and was going to ask the corporal of the guard if our battalion was still in Warley, when to her surprise she found it was me on guard. She told me when I saw her again last night that your Mam had written her, saying I had come to London.

I am waiting for tomorrow now to see my brother Bruce, he is coming home for the day. I suppose I shall have to keep him in his place as he is swanking a bit now, about doing an eleven miles' march and not falling out.

We are just off for a route march this morning around London, so I will close for now. Give my best respect to your Mam and Dad. I will write you again soon, so au revoir (not goodbye). With best love and kisses, Leslie.

XXXXXXXX

Please excuse pencil and scribble as I am in a terrible hurry.

Wellington Bks,
London SW
26ᵗʰ August 1914

My dear Phine

I have just received your letter; I was glad to hear you arrived home safe. I am pleased to say my arm is quite well, I cannot feel anything at all.

From what I can see of things, we shall be very lucky if we ever see France. We are about as far off from going as we were before the war started. They have taken our ammunition away from us. I think it is because the Irish Guards tried to mutiny because they were sent to Warley instead of to the Front, and they are afraid of our battalion doing the same. A draft was sent out tonight from over 3ʳᵈ Battn, but we are still standing by. I believe I was very nearly crying myself watching them march away with the band playing and people cheering.

Don't worry if we do have to go because you can be sure they will not put us anywhere where the Prince of Wales is likely to get hurt.

We had a fine time this morning, our Company marched to Mr Rothschild's, the millionaires place, where he invited us to lunch. We had a great time, and he allowed us to walk through his gardens and orchids afterwards and told us to pick what we wanted. I believe he had a few left when we had finished.

I will let you know when we do go, but I am afraid it will be sudden when we do. We had orders to shift last Monday night, but they were cancelled at the last minute. All the men's leave was stopped, and if I had stopped in another quarter of an hour, I should not have been able to come out. I don't know what I should have done if they had gone, missed it altogether perhaps.

I will have a photo taken as soon as I can. I am for guard tomorrow, so it will be the next day. As soon as they are done I will send one.

Well Phine dear, I will close now, give my best respects to your Mam and Dad and cheer up, don't get upset, it won't be long now before I shall be coming down to see you again, like I used to.

With very best love and lots of kisses, Leslie.

XXXXXXXXXXXXXXXXXX

29ᵗʰ August 1914

My dear Leslie

I received your letter and I was pleased to hear your arm is quite alright. I am also pleased you are not gone yet. What do you think of it? The papers is looking very bad indeed, very heavy losses on our side. Mam is very worried about it, she thinks my two uncles might be in the wounded as there is no names yet. I hope they are not.

Dear Leslie, I expect you will have to go by tonight's paper there is a lot more to go out and Dad fully expects to be called up now.

I am pleased to hear you had a nice outing. Where is my share, it has got to come. I suppose that is only my fun. Leslie, I am pleased you are having a photo taken. It will be something to look at. We are having a lively time down here. Freddy has just come in 9 o'clock. He has been watching some of the Irish Guards giving the sergeant of the police a good thrashing for pulling him out of the pub, they say the Scots Guards are coming here tomorrow so I will be able to have one of those. I won't have one of the Irish.

Dear Leslie, I won't worry. Dad said they won't put the Prince in danger but I would rather see him in danger than you. I will close now as it is 10 o'clock. Mam and Dad send their best respects. I will close, hoping to see you soon, with very best love and kisses, Josephine.

XXXXXXXXXXXXX

Mam said she won't answer your letter. She thinks you got enough to do to write mine.

Wellington Bks,
London S.W.
1st September 1914

My dear Josephine

I was very sorry I could not answer your letter before now, because on Sunday I went to see my brother at St Albans, and then Monday morning I went on guard on the docks down the river and I have just come off.

I received your letter and card alright. You ask me who the P.C.[7] reminds you of, well I think it reminds me of a nice young lady I met last Sunday and Monday. Anyhow I know she was doing what the girl on the picture is doing – sitting on a soldier's knee. You say the Scots guards are coming to your place, I would not have one of them if I was you, they are far worse than the Irish, take my advice and have a Grenadier, they are the best of the lot.

I suppose you have not had any news of your uncles yet have you? I expect they are alright, though there have been a lot wounded. Our Major told us a day or two ago that our 2nd Battn and the Middlesex Regt had suffered very heavy indeed. We are expecting to go any day now, we sent out a draft on Sunday, Corp Pickering and I was going, but we were kept back afterwards. You should have heard Pickering grouse when he could not go.

We were told this morning that according to the way events were going on, the war would only last two months. Let us hope so, although I should like to get that medal. I feel ashamed of myself, having to stay quietly at home, like we are, whilst others are out there doing all the work.

We are having another outing tomorrow at Highgate. Don't trouble about your share, I will eat it for you, and think of you at the same time.

We are allowed to go out of London on leave now, but have to be in at twelve, so I might be able to come down and see you one evening, I will let you know.

Give my best respects to Mam and Dad, I hope they are in the best of health.

So, au revoir, with best love and lots of kisses, Leslie.

XXXXXXXXXXXXX

Wellington Bks,
London S.W.
3rd September 1914

My dear Phine

I received your letter alright, our letters must have crossed in the post. I did not receive your other letter till Sunday afternoon, so you must excuse me not answering it. As I told you in my letter, I went off to see my brother and I had to hurry to be in barracks by twelve o'clock.

Fancy you thinking that I was cross because you sent that postcard, as if I would be – barmy! I knew you sent it for fun, I was glad you did send it.

Don't worry thinking I have gone away, I will write you discreetly I hear we have to go, which will not be yet awhile.

I did not go on the outing yesterday, after all I had to go to Purfleet ranges marking for the reservists and again today, in fact I am writing this letter to you now in the butts,[8] because I shall not be back till late, so please excuse me writing in pencil.

I am for guard again tomorrow over the German prisoners at the Olympia, I think I shall have to shoot one or two, just for luck, as I cannot go to the Front yet.

I am not sure but I think I shall be clear of duty on Saturday so I will come down in the afternoon if it will be convenient for your Mam. Of course I shall have to be back by 12 o'clock I will let you know if I cannot come.

Well Phine dear, I cannot think of anymore to say just now, I will conclude, hoping you can understand this awful scribble, with best respects to Mam and Dad, and hoping they are in the best of health.

So, au revoir with fondest love and kisses, Leslie.

XXXXXXXXXXXXXXXXXX

3rd September 1914

My dear Leslie

I received your kind letter and was pleased to hear from you. Now I am waiting for you to come down, I hope it is soon. I shall be pleased to see you, it seems months.

Dear Leslie, you need not tell me to have a Grenadier, I hope I will. They are the best in my eye at least you I hope you won't have to go. Dad said he will give you one of his medals instead as there is such a lot killed you know it is very risky.

I will make this a short letter as I expect to see you soon please God. Mam and

Dad send their best respects to you and hope you don't go. I will close now, with fondest love and lots of kisses, Josephine

XXXXXXXXXXXXXX

P.S. Dear Leslie, Mam and Dad said you can bring CPL Pickering down with you for the evening if you like, he will be company for you going back.

With love, Josephine.

XXXX

Wellington Barracks,
London SW
8th September 1914

My dear Josephine

I received your letter alright, it seems that we are both in hot water with your Mother. I blame it on to you, should not have said anything. I expect I shall get my nose pulled now for it.

I was home to barracks last Saturday night, the train did not get to Liverpool station until twelve o'clock and it was twenty past when I reached barracks. Still I knew the Sergeant on guard and with the aid of a bob I was not reported, so it was alright.

Tell your Mam my Mother was very pleased with her present, she said it was just the thing that she wanted.

I have got a new job now instructing the recruits down at Purfleet every day. We have long hauls from six in the morning till six at night, still I do not have to do guards, so I shall be able to come down and see you next Sunday. I will try and come early discreetly after church parade, if I may.

I suspect I shall be bad again for a day or two now, as I have just been inoculated again. What they call the second dose, 14 instead of 2 as before. It pained a bit while he was doing it, nothing much, still I hope I shall not feel so queer this time.

Well Phine dear, I will close give my best respects to your Mam and Dad, hoping to hear from you soon. With fondest love. Heaps of kisses, Leslie.

XXXXXXXXXXXXXXXXXX

P.S. Please excuse this awful scribble and dirty paper, it is all I have just now.

Don't forget photo.

9th September 1914

My dear Leslie

I received your welcome letter. Sorry to hear you have been inoculated again. I hope you don't feel bad like you did before.

Dear Leslie, you said you are coming down Sunday, if you may Mam said she won't have you now for your sauce. Let us know what time, we will wait dinner for you if it is not too late. Try and come early won't you, because you will have to go back about 10 o'clock being Sunday. I will close now.

Dear Leslie, hoping you don't feel ill. Give our best respects to your Mam and

Dad hoping they are quite well. Roll on Sunday. Mam and Dad send their best respects, so I will close with best and fondest love, lots of kisses Phine.

XXXXXXXXXXXXXXXXXXXXXXXXXXXXXXXXXXXXXXXXXXXX
XXXXXXXXXXXXXX

P.S. excuse this envelope.

On 15th of September Leslie's Battalion left London by train to Lyndhurst camp, located near Southampton.

Lyndhurst Camp,
Nr Southampton
16th September 1914

My dear Phine

I have arrived here safe and sound. We found the battalion at 7:30 this morning, we had to sleep on a big empty tent we found about 2 o'clock this morning and it was perishing cold and wet. From what I can understand we do not cross over until the 26th of this month, we are waiting for some more battalions from Malta; there is already 27,000 men here.

What time did you get here last night, was you tired? I bet you are this morning after walking around London saying goodbye. I think of yesterday. Tell your Mam I sympathise with her making those shirts. I wish I could come and help her, you with the button holes. Do you think we should get many finished?

When you write, my address will be 13959. Copl L. Cox 2 coy. 1st battalion Grenadiers gds, 20th (guards) brigade

7th Division British ex force

But until we shift from here you could put Lyndhurst camp, near Southampton instead of British Exp. Force.

I will have to make this a short letter as it is so late now, so give my best wishes to your Mam and Dad, hoping they are in the best of health. With my best and fondest love and kisses, Leslie.

XXXXXXXXXXXXXXXXXXXXXXXXX

Excuse bad pen.

18th September 1914

My dearest Leslie

I received your letter this morning and you don't know how pleased I was to hear you were alright and got away from those fellow's safe. We have done our shirts after a struggle, it was a job but we stopped up and darned them, we did not get home until twelve o'clock, we were tired. I was stiff the next day and Mam could not move her arm coming home, but we got over it now. I did not think much of mine I was thinking of you, wondering if you were alright and where you would sleep. My dear Leslie it does seem miserable now to think you are not coming down

Sunday. It seems to me as if someone is dead in the house but I suppose it will wear off in time. I must look forward for when you come back, please God hoping God will spare you to return if only wounded. That is all we do now, you must cheer up.

Leslie dear, perhaps it won't be for long. How nice it will be to come and meet you when you come back. My dear Leslie, I suppose we will be in London soon. Mam and Dad are so unsettled. I don't think there is any more news now. I wish I could go to Southampton to see you once more, but I can't. Mam and Dad sends their best respects and good wishes for a safe return. I will close with best love from Phine, to my own dear Leslie.

P.S. Dear Leslie, Mam said she did want to kiss your before you went but she did not like to as there was so many there so she sent XXXX

Lyndhurst camp,
Nr Southampton
20ᵗʰ September 1914

My dear Phine

I received your letter this morning. I was wondering what was the matter when I did not hear from you but I suppose the post office is rather crowded now. I was so pleased to hear from you, I don't think I even looked forward for a letter so much before; it cheers a chap up to get news from those he loves, when we are waiting about like this. We go sometime this weekend, I shall be pleased, the sooner it is over the better. Roll on when we come back. I am going to have the time of my life, if God spares me, which I am confident he will do. If he does not, well – still that's not it, I am getting a bit melancholy with this letter, so I will write about something else.

I was thinking about last Sunday when I was doing my washing this afternoon. I can't recommend washing; I don't see how your Mam prefers washing to making shirts and towel it nearly broke my back. What made it worse, several of the fellow's wives who had come down stood and smiled at us trying to scrub. I think that was enough to endure.

We don't have much time to spare, we are out marching and training every day from 8 o'clock till 4 in the afternoon, so when we are finished you can bet we are tired out.

I have not heard from home yet, I wrote to them, but then it always does take good old Mother about a week to answer anybody. I have asked her if she has got my photos, I hope they are good this time. I had them taken again this afternoon in a group so if they come before we go I will send you one. What is the weather like at Brentwood? It is awfully cold down here at nights, we huddle up together like rabbits to keep warm.

Well Phine dear, don't get thinking there is someone dead in the house, think of when I shall be back. I will soon bug around and liven you up, even if you do get Mam to help you on that stick. Well I will say goodnight now, with best wishes to your Mam and Dad and thanks for their kind thoughts for my safe return. I will now close with best and fondest love and kisses to my dearest Phine, from Leslie.

XXXXXXXXXXXXXXXXXX

P.S. Tell your Mam I will return her kiss when I return home which will not be long now sweetheart.

Lyndhurst camp,
Southampton
24ᵗʰ September 1914

My dearest Phine

I was awfully pleased to receive your letter, it was not delayed in coming this time, I think it is safe enough to send letters; we receive them alright as long as they are addressed properly. I cannot understand why Charlie Gransden does not receive his letters. When we leave, Southampton put British expeditionary force instead of Lyndhurst camp and I shall receive them safely.

I am writing to you at Brentwood this time as I do expect you will be in London yet according to your letter, after this I will ask Mother to send them on, as you told me to.

What is your Dad going to do? Join his old regiment or is he going on the transport? Has he tried to join the motor reserve? Tell him they get good pay on that, about 50/- a week, during war time and £4 a year during peace times. I do not know how they join but I know it is genuine enough. Still I hope for your Mother's sake that it will not be necessary for him to go up at all.

I am glad you have got the photo. I have just heard from my Mother and she says they are not at all good, she says I look so cross, no so now you can tell what an awful bad-tempered beast I am.

I think we go Sunday. From the rumours that are going around we have a forty hours' sea journey and are supposed to be going to Bordeaux, which is miles from the firing line. Still I hope we shall be having a go at them very soon.

Well I have no more news yet to write about, except to say I am the best of health and quite happy so I will close. Give my best wishes and kind regards to your Mam and Dad, and hoping they are quite well. So, for the present, au revoir, with best and fondest love to my own dearest Phine, from Leslie.

XXXXXXXXXXXXXXXXXXXXX

My dear Leslie

I received your letter this morning and so pleased to hear from you also to know you are quite well. Dad is going up tomorrow. They won't have him on the motor job because he draws a pension. I am pleased to hear you are not going in the firing line just yet.

Dear Leslie, Mam is not at all well. Don't know what is the matter, I expect she is run down with the blessed shirts. I got the hump of them, I shall be glad to get to London and get a nice job as there is nothing here, only service and the laundry and Dad and Mam won't let me do either of those. I shall be in a nice job when you come back please God and then I will be too proud to speak to you (<u>Swank</u>).

Dear Leslie, I don't think there is any more news, you got all the news to tell you.

I am anxious to hear soon. I will close now.

    With best and fondest love to my own dear Leslie, from Phine.

    XXXXXXXXXXXXXXXXXXXXX

    GOD BLESS YOU.

Lyndhurst Camp
27th September 1914

My dearest Phine

    I received your letter and also the cigarettes, thank you so much, they are the kind I generally smoke and it is so hard to get them down here. I was so pleased to have such a nice present from you.

    I am awfully sorry to hear your Mam is very bad, I hope it is nothing very serious. I expect that is what it is, overtired, working at those blessed old shirts, still suppose they have to be done.

    Well you see we have not gone yet, it is supposed that we are going Tuesday, but I think myself that nobody really knows yet and it might be days yet before we go.

    If we are here next week I am going to try and come up for the weekend, but of course it is only a faint hope then.

    We are allowed out of camp, and yesterday afternoon, Cpl Pickering and I went to Bournemouth for an hour, and it was a bit of a change after such a hard week. It was quite like being at home, sitting down to tea at a table with a cloth on.

    I suppose you have not heard any news of how your uncles are getting on out at the Front. I hope they are still well.

    Well Phine dear, I will say au revoir once again, with my best respects to your Mam and Dad, and hoping that your Mam will soon be better again.

    With best and fondest love and kisses to my own darling Phine, from Leslie.

    XXXXXXXXXXXXXXXX

29th September 1914

My dearest Leslie

I received your letter and pleased to hear you are quite well, also to know you are not gone yet but I suppose you will go before the end of the week no such luck, for you to come up it would be nice to see you once more. I am glad you liked the cigarettes I did not think you would get them. Dear Leslie, Dad went up Saturday to pass the doctor and what do you think, he passed unfit because of his shoulder. He put it out some time ago and it is a bit stiff so he can't go now so we will have to stop where we are for the present. Mam is a bit better. She has given twenty of the shirts up and only doing twenty that is quite enough to do. We have not heard from my uncles, I suppose they are alright. Dear Leslie, I had a card from your Mother. I don't think there is any more news now.

    I will live in hope to see you so I will close with best and fondest love to my dearest Leslie, from Phine.

    XXXXXXXXXXXXXXXXXXXXX

Lyndhurst camp,
Southampton
1ˢᵗ October 1914

My darling Phine

I received your letter quite safe and I was glad to hear your Mam is a bit better, I hope she will soon be quite well.

We are still here, no news of when we are going, we keep on getting scares about going but nothing comes of them. Still there is no doubt we shall be off very soon now. We are getting quite fed up with waiting, in fact we are afraid the war might end before we get out there. If it did I should desert. I should be ashamed to walk out in uniform again.

I don't think I shall be able to get leave, if we do stop over the weekend you see twenty per cent of the men had leave last week and so many stayed absent that I am afraid it spoilt it for the remainder. I could have come myself but a reserve Corporal who is married wanted to go home so I let him have my leave as he wanted it more than I did.

Where we are stationed here, the place was only a small village now with the thousands of troops here, and most of them home from abroad it has jumped in to a big town. There are hundreds of relatives and friends down here, the place is crowded out. It reminds one of London on a Saturday night. I had a nice experience one night last week, a woman who come down from London to see her husband found it was out of camp and she asked me to help find a lodging for her. Well I walked about till two in the morning looking for a place and then I went to the Catholic Priest and he told me of a place she could sleep on a couch in the kitchen. I was dead tired when I got back to camp. I was nearly five hours absent but I slipped in without anyone seeing me, so I was alright and nothing was said, but if anyone asks me again I shall run away and not stop to answer, I was properly fed up.

Well Phine dear, I think this is all I have to say now, so with my best respect to your Mam and Dad and fondest and best love to my own dearest Phine, from Leslie.

XXXXXXXXXXXXXXXXXXXX

Please excuse scribble.

3ʳᵈ October 1914

My dearest Leslie

I received your letter and pleased to hear you are quite well, also to know you are not gone although you are anxious to go. Dear Leslie, I know you will be pleased to hear Mam had a letter yesterday morning from Mick her youngest brother, and this morning she had a field service card. She ought to have had the card first. He is quite well but he begs of Mam to send him some cigarettes, so she sent him some this morning and some socks and chocolates. It cost Mam 6/4 but she doesn't mind what it costs if he gets them. She said she won't forget you when you go out there.

Dear Leslie, I did laugh when I read your letter. Fancy you being about with a woman till that hour of the night. I bet you felt happy, but you were trying to do good.

Dear Leslie, Mam had a letter from your Mother at last. She said she has been busy. Mam feels a bit better now she has heard from my uncle, but he did not give her any news. His address was scratched out. What do you think of the war, do you think it will soon be over? Mam said we will be at war with Russia before long, they will want everything I suppose. I don't think of any more news now, Leslie. I am disappointed you're not coming but it can't be helped, so I will close now with best and fondest love and lots of kisses to my dear Leslie, from Phine.

XXXX
XXX
XX
X

Dear Leslie, I left this letter as I thought you might come.

Field service postcards

Field service postcards were issued to troops so that they could inform loved ones and relatives that they were still well and alive. The soldier filled them out by deleting the pre-written sections, which for example included "I am quite well" or "I have been admitted into hospital", and putting their name and signature on the card. Any other information would result in the card being destroyed by the censor. The cards were issued to soldiers to be used in times when they were busy or involved in or around a battle as the soldier did not have any time to write a letter. It was also intended so little information would reach back home, thus speeding up the time for censorship.

Overseas for King and country

After an eight-hour march, Leslie arrived at Southampton docks awaiting his voyage.

4th October 1914

Dear Phine

Just a line to let you know that at last we are off. I am writing this at the docks so perhaps when you get this card we shall be there. I will write again as soon as possible, so once again au revoir, with fondest and best love, Leslie.
XXXXXXXX
Let Mother know please as I have not time.

Leslie's voyage started on 4th October. The journey took longer than normal due to the ship having to avoid the enemy's mines and submarines. The 7th Division finally landed at their destination at Zeebruge on 7th October. After the Battalion disembarked, they then went on to several locations in Belgium, until they were engaged at the First Battle of Ypres.

My dearest Phine

I suppose you received my postcard alright. We had a very good voyage across, it was rather cold at night, but that was of course you know we must not write about where we are, or what we are doing, so I can send you no news of any sort.

I cannot tell you how your uncles are, as we are miles from them, but if I do hear from them I will write as soon as possible.

We have not received any letters since we left England, and it does not seem likely we will yet, as we are always shifting about from place to place, sometimes billeting in buildings or sleeping out.

We have not seen any of the German Army but I do not think we are far from them. We only see lots of refugees every day. They are mostly on foot with their animals and their goods on small carts. I do not know if they will allow what I have just written so I will write no more, but tell you all when I return. Please let Mother know I am quite well and the best of health. Give my best respects to your Mam and Dad, so au-revoir once again, with fondest love, Leslie.

The First Battle of Ypres

This was Leslie's first engagement with the enemy. The First Battle of Ypres was where the Germans fought with large numbers of troops, outnumbering the Grenadiers by four to one. The Battalion managed to dig in and hold the line, but not without losing a lot of men, either killed or becoming casualties. Out of the 1 st Battalion only 4 officers and 200 men survived the awful battle. Leslie was one of those wounded in the battle in late October/November,

suffering an injury to his head caused from an explosion from a shrapnel shell burst. Leslie first wrote to his Mother informing her that he had been wounded which he had sent on the 2nd November.

C.O. Details
Boulogne Base France

My dear Phine

Just a line to let you know I am quite well, although I have been slightly wounded in the head with a piece of shrapnel shell. I went to hospital but I am out now, and I am doing guards over the German prisoners at the base. I have not heard from you yet because I am not with the Battalion and they cannot send my letters on because they do not know where I am, so do not write again till I tell you. But if you do, ask my Mother. I am writing to her and she will have the address of where I am (if the censor passes the letter) I have not much news to tell you, except that the battle I was in was simply awful, beyond description. Roll on when I can come and see you again.

When you write, address the letter "details" No. 4 base and not as I told my Mother but only write one letter because I may shift again.

Well Phine dear I will close now. Hoping your Mam and Dad are quite well and my best wishes to them. With fondest and best love to my dearest Phine, from Leslie.

XXXXX
XXXXX
XXXXX

The censor was part of the security measures which the military had in place, to censor all letters written by the troops so that important information regarding what was happening at the Front could not be used by the Germans.

9ᵗʰ November 1914

My dearest Leslie

I received your letter this morning and was delighted to hear from you and to know you are getting on, but Leslie dear I don't like to hear you are going back to the Front. For goodness sake try not to go back yet, if you can manage it stay a little while longer, then perhaps the worst will be over, it is too terrible. I am really pleased you are wounded if you were up there you might have been killed so I hope it has happened for the best, I do hope you will get this letter I have sent ever so many but you know it is not my fault.

I have sent you some cigarettes also but I don't suppose you will get them now, never mind, so long as you are all right.

Dear Leslie, let me know is there anything you would like and I will send it now you are there you might get it. I don't think there is any more news now. Mam and

Dad send their best respects and pray for your safe return so I will close now with best and fondest love to my own dearest Leslie, from Josephine.

XXXXXXXXXXXXXXXXXXXX

P.S. Dear Leslie, don't forget to put the date when you write.

C.O. Details,
Boulogne Base
France
12ᵗʰ November 1914

My dearest Phine

Pleased to say I am quite well, my wound is almost well now, so I will soon be with the Battalion again now. I have not had any letters from you yet, or from home, still I expect I shall get one soon, it is awkward being away from the Battalion. Well I have no news to tell you except to let you know I am still alive. I will say au revoir, hoping your Mam and Dad are in the best of health, with fondest love and kisses to my dearest Phine, from Leslie.

XXXX
XXXXX
XXXX

21ˢᵗ November 1914

My dear Phine

Blessed to say I am well and my wound has properly healed. I am now at the base, waiting to go back to the Front with the next reinforcements. I have not heard from you yet, but I expect to soon. Address your letters the same as at first and put "base" on as well and I shall get them sooner. Do not send any parcels, only letters. Hoping your Mam and Dad are quite well, and give my best wishes, so au revoir once again.

With best and fondest love to my dearest Phine, from Leslie.

XXXXXXXXXXXXXXXXXX

Write soon.

27ᵗʰ November 1914

My dear Leslie

I just had a card and letter from you, your Mother sent them and I was so delighted to hear from you again. I had not heard for two weeks. I am so glad you are better and still at the base as you are out of this terrible fighting that is going on, it is just your luck and I hope you will stop there longer.

Dear Leslie, I am very sorry you have not had any letter from me. I have written dozens. I wonder why you have not received any. I have wrote quite a dozen to the hospital, so it is not my fault Leslie. I hope you will get this one, if you don't I will write to the evening news.

Dear Leslie, I hope that your wound is quite well by now. I suppose you got a nice mark on your head, but we must not mind that. It's wonder you were not killed. I will be thankful when it is all over, it is terrible I do think it is a shame they do not send you home for a while.

Dear Leslie, I don't think there is any more news now, you got all the news. I am quite well so is Mam and Dad and they send you their best wishes and prayers for your safe return, so I will close now dear Leslie, with best and fondest love to my dearest Leslie, from Phine.

XXXXXXXXXXXXXXXXXXX

God bless you dear.

7th Division, The base,
Rouen
France
28th November 1914

My dear Phine

I received a letter from Mother this morning, the first I have had since we landed. I was very pleased to hear from her that you was quite well. She told me you have written many times, but of course though having to change from one hospital to another I have never received them yet. Still I hope to have one from you soon. Mother mentioned Cpl Gransden, is he alright? Because when the battalion reorganised he was among the missing, thought to be captured. Poor old "Ginger" Pickering was killed; he had been made sergeant too. I was glad to hear that Mick was alright. It is rather cold where we are, still we are all well and happy. The little corporal of the drums is here with me, he was wounded in the leg. So (au revoir), fondest with best wishes to your Mam and Dad.

Love Les
XXXXXXXXX

A sad loss for Leslie and the Battalion
Corporal J.W. Pickering 13982 1st Battalion Grenadier guards was killed in action on the Klein-Zillebeke ridge on 7th November 1914, age unknown.

29th November 1914

My dearest Leslie

Just a line hoping you are quite well, and I do hope you will get these letters. It does worry me you not getting even one or two. I hope you are not gone to the firing line yet. I don't think it will be long now before it is over. The Russians are giving them beans. I don't feel like writing much when you don't get them. Let me know if you do get these and I will write a long letter. I do wish they would let you come home, they are letting some of the men home for ten days, why don't you try? They might let you come being as you were wounded. Mam and Dad send you their best wishes for your safe return. I will close now dear Leslie. With very best and fondest love to my own darling Leslie, from Phine.

XXXXXXXXXXXXXX

4th December 1914

My dearest Leslie

I received your card this morning and pleased to hear you are well, also to know you are still at the base and hope you will stop there longer and are glad you got a letter from your Mother. I do hope you will get mine. This is three I have wrote to where you are now. I sent you a few cigarettes in a letter, did you get them? If you did I will send some each time I write. I am sorry to hear about poor old Pickering. I suppose you would have gone too if you were up there, thank God you are not.

Dear Leslie, I shall be glad to hear you got my letter. I know how you feel. I expect one every post but I get all your letters, so don't miss to write when you can, will you? Dear Leslie, I don't know of any more news now so will close dear Leslie.

With very best and fondest love to my own dear Leslie, from Phine.

XXXXXXXXXX

2nd Company 1st Battalion Grenadiers Guards
20th Guards Brigade
7th Division
6th December 1914

My darling Phine

At last I have received one of your letters. I was awfully pleased to hear from you, and thank you so much for the cigarettes. I expect you received my card saying I had joined the Battalion. We are having a fairly easy time now, only a rifle fired at us now and again to make us keep down in the trenches.[9] It is a bit cold to the feet now and again, the only thing to grumble about is the rain. When it rains, there is nothing but thick mud.

Whilst writing this I have just received another letter from you which you posted on the 9th Nov. The last one you posted on the 27th Nov. So probably I shall get all your letters back soon. I think I shall receive all your letters now, as they come straight from the trenches, that is why I did not receive your other letters because no one knew which hospital I had gone to. So write as often as you can since I have had four letters, two from a cousin of mine.

I don't suppose it will be long before the war is ended now. I know the Germans are fed up with it. When I was at Boulogne I had 80 prisoners to look after and they were all really sick of it all. Some could speak English and they were so pleased as punch because they were going to England and knowing the war was finished for them.

Well Phine dear, this is all the paper I have so please excuse this short letter and I will write a longer one next time. Hoping your Mam and Dad are in the best of health. With fondest love to my dearest Phine, from Leslie.

XXXXXXXXXX

P.S. Don't forget my address, it's <u>not</u> the Base now.

11th December 1914

My dearest Leslie

I got a letter and card this morning, your Mother sent them. I was delighted to hear you got a letter from me at last. I began to think you would be cross and wonder if I wrote, but Leslie I have written dozens. I know how you felt getting no letters as I expect one from you every post and wonder what is wrong when I don't get one. I am greedy, aren't I?

Dear Leslie, I am sorry you have gone back to the firing. I was hoping you would be left at the base for Xmas but I do hope and trust in God you will be alright. I don't mind writing now as I know you will get them, but each time I write I thought what is the use of writing when you don't get them. I suppose it is of no use sending you a parcel, your Mother said she has sent you some cigarettes in each letter and will be sure to get them.

Dear Leslie, it is miserable here wondering how long it will last. A day seems a month, but we must be thankful it is no worse. You are safe so far, thank God. Dear Leslie, this letter I cut out of the evening news and it is from Charlie, his young lady wrote for his letter. By the letter he must be badly wounded. His young lady has not heard from him now for six weeks. I feel sorry for her as she has got no parents and she thinks a lot of him I hope he will pull through alright for her sake, so I thought you would like to see it.

Mam and Dad send you their best respects and hope sincerely for your safe return, so I will close now dear, hoping God will spare you.

With very best and fondest love to my dearest Leslie, from Phine.

XXXXXXXXXXXXXXXXXXXXXXXXX

P.S. I have just had a letter returned what I sent you when you were first wounded said cannot be traced, it was on his Majesty's service envelope.

12th December 1914

My dearest Phine

I have just received the fourth letter from you which you wrote on the 4th Dec. So pleased to hear from you, I am getting all your letters regularly now, they have followed me up from the Base. We are having a very quiet time now, although it is awfully wet and terribly muddy in the trenches.

You must excuse my short note as paper is so scarce, I have asked Mother to send me some and then I will write you a long letter, so do not worry if you do not hear for a day or two, will you?

I know some of the men are having a day or two's leave but do not trouble, we shall all be home for good soon, we are sure winners, and shall soon have the enemy beat to the wide, they will soon realise they are beaten. Have had a piece of luck and been promoted to full Corporal. Well I will say au revoir once again with best wishes to your Mam and Dad.

With fondest and best love to my own darling Phine, from Leslie.

XXXXXXXXXXXXXXXXXXX

15th December 1914

My dearest Leslie

Just a line hoping you are quite well as I am quite well myself. I see by the papers that you have been very busy again. I hope you are alright. Write as often as you can, won't you, as it lets me know you are alright, when I don't hear for a week I make sure there is something wrong.

Dearest Leslie, I wonder what sort of Xmas you will have. We are not thinking of Xmas this year, everything seems upside down. The Irish Guards had the cheek to have a dance last Thursday with the sergeants.

Mam had an invite but she would not go for pounds. If you had been here I would have gone with you, but I hope to go to some before the season is out. You will be back by then with the help of God as it can't last long, you have given them a good beating this time by the papers.

Dear Leslie, Sgt East's young lady wants to know if you know anything about him. Would you be so kind as to let her know? She has not heard from him for six weeks. They are letting some of the men home on leave, I hope you will be lucky enough to come, don't forget to try. They ought to let you come being as you have been wounded.

Dear Leslie, Mam and Dad send you their very best respects and hope for your safe return. She has not heard from Mick since 28th of October. She has wrote to the war office and the depot but they said they have not heard. Well dear Leslie, I can't think of any more news just now. Wishing you a very happy Xmas which I know you won't have, but never mind, it is not for ever so I will close.

With very best and fondest love to my own dearest Leslie, from Phine.

XXXXXXXXXXXXXX

Mam has just had a card from Mick and he is wounded and a prisoner by his address, this is where he is

Reseve Lazarett

Loge Deutchland Laxe

Do you know if that is in Germany?

Dear Leslie, your name was in the paper yesterday.

Mam said have you been near the 15th Hussars, you might see something of Uncle Pat.

A letter to Leslie regarding Sgt East from Miss Connie Thorne

3 Avenue Road,
Warley
Essex
14th December 1914

Dear Cpl Cox

I am writing to you at the same time hoping you will forward the great liberty I am taking. I was talking to Mrs Hazeltine on Saturday night and she told me you are in 2nd company. Of course you must remember Sgt East, well how could you do me the favour of telling me if he is still with you, or anything you know about him, it is seven weeks come Tuesday since his Mother or myself had any news from him. His last letter was dated the 28th Oct and as you may guess his dear Mother is terribly upset over it. We have written to the war office, but had no reply. I also wrote to the record office and their reply was as far as they know he was still with his regiment. Since then his cousin came home and told us he was wounded on the 29th Oct, also missing, would you if possible get to know what has happened, and I know you don't have much spare time.

Could you send to Mrs Hazeltine and she will forward it OK to my home. Both herself and Josephine are quite well and know I am writing to you. Sincerely trusting your wounds have completely healed and are quite well again. Thanking you in anticipation I remain, yours sincerely, Connie Thorne.

18th December 1914

My dearest Leslie

I received your letter this morning and so pleased to hear you are well and also promoted.[10] You will soon be Sgt and then we won't speak surely. I had a nice letter from your Mother. She is so pleased you are promoted and also to hear you are so cheerful. I suppose it is no use being otherwise. I do hope what you said is true that you will be home soon, it is very miserable here wondering each day what news we are going to hear,

Dear Leslie, you will be pleased to hear Mam had a card last evening from her brother Mick and he is wounded and a prisoner of war but she is so pleased as she gives up she thought he was killed. She had not heard for seven weeks, not since you wrote to your Mother about him, so that is good news. Mam met Hall of the transport, he is home and he told her it was awful out there but we must look on the bright side.

Dear Leslie, I wish you a very happy Xmas which I know you won't have but never mind you will make up for it when you come back, if God will spare you. Mam and Dad wish you the same and hope for your safe return.

Dear Leslie, I will close now with very best and fondest love to my own darling Leslie, from Phine.

XXXXXXXXXXXXXXXXXXXXXXX

Dear Leslie, your Mother said she has had several things to send you so I will send you one later on as you don't want them all at once, with love Phine XXX

19th December 1914

My dearest Phine

Just a line to let you know I am still well and happy. I have received your letter of the 11 Dec, also Miss Thorne inquiring after Sgt East. I have just answered it although it was bad news. He was wounded and probably captured. Hoping all are well at home.

With best wishes for Xmas, fondest love to my dearest Phine, from Leslie.

XXXXXXXXXXXX

P.S. letter following.

**20th Brigade,
7th Division
21st December 1914**

My dear Phine

I received your letter which you wrote on the 15th. I was glad to hear from you again. I was sorry to hear Mick had been wounded and captured. I hope his wound is not very bad. Yes I think that awful long name you mentioned is in Germany.

I heard from Sgt East's young lady inquiring after him. I have answered her letter, although it was very bad news. I did not much like the idea still it had to be done and I sincerely hope she hears from him soon.

We have not been near the 15th Hussars yet to have a chance of finding out about your Uncle Pat. I met a fellow when I was in hospital and he said he was alright there but of course that is a long time ago.

Hell, I suppose Xmas will be a bit slow at home this year. I expect nearly everybody will be thinking of someone out here, although you soon can bet we will make the best of it out here. In fact our Xmas has started, we are having dozens of parcels arriving daily full of Xmas fare.

I have received a letter from Mother in which she says you are quite downhearted because I am not getting your letters. There is no need to be because I have had six or seven in the last fortnight.

Do you get my letters? Because I always say in them when I receive one from you.

Well dearest, I will close now. Excuse my short letter as I must write two more before it gets dark. I expect when you get this, Xmas will have passed. I hope it has been a merry one for you.

With fondest and best love to my own darling Phine, from Leslie.

XXXXXXXXXXXX

P.S. roll on I hope the dancing season is not over before we all return.

27th December 1914

My dearest Leslie

I received your card dated the 19th. Pleased to hear you are still well and happy. I hope you had a pretty fair Xmas but I don't expect you did. We were very quiet, Mam was quite miserable. She did not have a card from anyone, only one from Aunt Lizzie. It was quiet everywhere. I am sorry to hear about Sgt East. I suppose he has gone. It is very cold and wet here so I don't know what it must be like for you in the trenches, it must be awful.

Dear Leslie, I sent you a card. I don't know if you got it. Mam has not heard from Mick, I suppose they won't let them write very often but she is thankful for what she has heard.

I can't think of more news now, roll on when this beastly war is over, it makes me miserable to write.

Mam and Dad send you their very best wishes for a happy new year and hope for your safe return. Excuse this short letter. I hope to have one from you soon so I will close.

With very best love and kisses to my own darling Leslie, from Phine.
XXXXXXXXXXXXXXXXXXXX

Letter from Miss Connie Thorne

3 Avenue Road,
Warley
Essex

28th December 1914

Dear Cpl Cox

I now take the pleasure of writing to you a few words to thank you for your kindness to me and for the information regarding Sgt East. You will agree with me it was a relief to know. So much about him back to his Mother and myself, but I am very sorry to say we have now heard the worst. From the war office poor Ben passed away on the October 31st two days after being wounded. He was captured by the Germans and died in co 5 field hospital. 15 German army corps, all that I can say is thank God he never lived long in the hands of the Germans or he may have suffered terrible. It is reported he died from blood poison, but I hardly think it had time to develop. Being only wounded on the 29th Oct. Now I wonder if you by chance know if his wounds were very bad, and if Sgt Moore bound his legs up as we heard from his cousin he did and would you send him my thanks for his goodness to him as you know he was a lot to me. And it was nice to know all was done that was possible for him. I sincerely trust you had a peaceful Xmas and hope it will be a better and brighter beginning of a new year than the ending of this one. Once again, thanking you and with thought for your health and safe return remain, yours sincerely C Thorne.

Sergeant B. East 13549 1ˢᵗ Battalion Grenadier Guards died 31ˢᵗ October 1914, aged 25 years.

29ᵗʰ December 1914

My dearest Phine

Just a card to let you know I am still quite well. I received your letter and cigarettes on Xmas morning.

We have been having a quiet time since then, hardly any firing.[11] It is awfully wet and muddy otherwise things are going on well and we are all happy and cheerful. I shall not have time to write a letter for two days so do not get annoyed if you do not hear from me. Hoping your Mam and Dad are in the best of health.

With fondest and best love to my own darling Phine, from Leslie.

XXXXXXXXXXXXXXXX

30ᵗʰ December 1914

My dearest Phine

Just a line to tell you I am alive and kicking. We are having rather chilly weather, but things are fairly easy here now, hardly any fighting around our quarter. Things are looking rather easy according to the papers. I think it will be over now by Easter. Anyhow I write you again when we go into billets, hardly any time to spare in the trenches. Hoping all are well.

With fondest and dearest love to my own darling Phine, from Les.

P.S. How is the hockey now, do you still play?

31ˢᵗ December 1914

My dearest Phine

I received your letter and cigarettes which you sent on the 27ᵗʰ.

Glad to hear everyone is quite well I was sorry to hear you had such a quiet time at Xmas, never mind the war will soon be over and when Uncle Mick and Uncle Pat come home you will be able to live all the good old times over again.

Your letter was quite miserable, it made me feel quite downhearted. Buck up dear, why the chaps are having some trying times out here but we are all cheerful and happy and just waiting for the day when we come home. I had a letter from Miss Thorne thanking me for writing her. I was sorry to hear Sgt East eventually died, he was a very nice chap.

Well Phine, I will write you a larger letter when I get more time, just a line now to let you know I am quite well, thanking yours Mam and Dad for their period greetings and hoping they will also have a happy and prosperous new year.

With best and fondest love to my own darling Phine, from Leslie.

XXXXXXXXXXXXXXX

Notes 1914

1. Swanking, or to swank, is to display one's wealth, or knowledge or achievements in a way that is intended to impress others.
2. Palace Cinema Brentwood.
3. CPL – Corporal.
4. Piquet – to go on guard duty or fire watch.
5. Tower of London.
6. Poulo – leave of absence.
7. P.C. – postcard
8. Butts – firing practice range.
9. Leslie's position in the trenches was in the region of Fleurbaix near Armentiéres, France.
10. Leslie was promoted to full Corporal.
11. Leslie is in the trenches, still in the area near to Fleurbaix in the Sailly–Fromelles road area, France.

New Year, new trench 1915

4ᵗʰ January 1915

My dearest Leslie

I received your letter this morning, also two cards yesterday. I am so pleased to hear from you are quite well, but Leslie dear I am sorry I told you I was miserable at Xmas. Fancy me being the cause of making you downhearted, but I did not mean to do so, never mind I won't tell you any more. I might have a little more thought. I shall be glad when it is all over, you said wait until Mick and Pat come back, what about when you come back? Dear Leslie, I had a nice card from Mabel and Mam had a nice letter from your Mother. They are quite well. It is your birthday on Saturday and I wish you very many happy returns.

I am sending you just a little present. It is not much as I do not know what to send you out there. Wait until you come back please God I will pull your nose for a present. You must not think of what I said, will you? I am not miserable now, but you know that nobody could feel very happy when we know what you all are going though out there, but I don't think it can be long by the papers, they look very bright so we will soon have you all home.

Well Leslie dear, I hope this letter will find you in the best of health and not downhearted. Wishing you a happy new year and also a safe return. Mam and Dad send their very best wishes and hope for your safe return, so I will close now dear with very best of love and kisses to my own darling Leslie, hoping you don't think no more of that letter.

From Phine

XXXXXXXXXXXX

P.S. Aunt Lizzie and Violet came down yesterday.

9ᵗʰ January 1915

My dearest Phine

I received your letter and the nice parcel you sent, thank you so much. We are going to have the cake at my birthday party this afternoon. I wish I could invite you to it as well, never mind I will come to your next one, the War will be over by then I am sure. I like the cigarette holder very much, I hope I shall not damage or lose it, as I shall "think the world" of it, when I get back to England.

Mother also has sent me a parcel of good things, so you may guess my party will be a good affair, although it is in an old barn. My luck again you see, we came out of the trenches yesterday for our usual four days' rest.

As for having my nose pulled when I get home well, we will see about that, I am afraid you will have to get your Mam to help to keep you.

I am sorry I said anything about being downhearted now, when I received your other letter, I did not mind so much. But it hurt me to think that you were unhappy at all. Got to be cheerful just now, you know the fellows are always thinking of their people at home and it makes it hard for them if they think they are miserable at home. Still I am very happy and contented, and just say to myself "roll on" when I can get back to you Phine and Mother and all my people and then ruffle your hair and tease you all day.

I don't know but this letter seems to be a rotten miserable one for anyone to write on their birthday, especially to his young lady, so please excuse me, and put it down to the weather or anything like that. I suppose getting sad in my age.

I hope your Dad likes his new job alright, and that it is better than the one before. I expect he prefers being back at the old Barracks again. I wish I was, especially if it was Tuesday night at the old tin hut.

Well Phine dear, I will say au revoir once again. Thank your Mam and Dad for their kind wishes, hoping they are both in the very best of health, with best and fondest love to my own darling Phine, hoping it will not be long before I can see you again, with lots of kisses from Leslie.

XXXXXXX

9th January 1915

My dearest Leslie

I received your kind letter on Monday and also the card this morning. So pleased to hear you are quite well, thank God. Dear Leslie, I hope you will forgive me not writing this week until now as I have been so busy. We got extra shirts for a week or two. This is your birthday and many happy returns. I sent you a little parcel Monday and I silly put my letter in it. I hope you get it by now but you would have got the letter sooner, never mind dear Leslie, you know I have not forgot you if I did not write for a few days not like Miss Thorne. I see she soon forgot poor Sgt East. Mam see her with a Cpl of the Irish Guard, it is a shame.

Dear Leslie, Dad likes his new job much better. He is kept busy, he does not like standing about. Mam had a nice letter from your Mother, she is quite well and she had asked Mam to go up there, she might go up next Sunday. I wish you were there then I should like to go, but it won't be long now and I shall be able to swank with my Sgt and his medal. You said in your letter you knew someone else would swank, of course you mean me, of course I shall swank, why not? Especially if you come home like one of our married men did with a beard. I expect you are frozen at night. I sit doing button holes and look at the nice fire, if only I could send it out to you I would.

Dear Leslie, let me know if you got that little parcel. I don't think there is any more news, you got all the news to tell. Miss Thorne told Mam she had another letter from you, I begin to feel jealous. Charlie's young lady has not heard from him since the 28th of October. Don't know where he is. Mam has not heard any more from Mick. Dear Leslie, fancy asking me if I went to a dance! I should never go, for this is not the time for dancing. I do not care much for it. I went because you went and I am sure Mam would not let me go if I did want to. Mam and Dad send you their very best respects and hopes for your safe return, so I will close now with very best of love and kisses to my own darling Leslie, from Phine

13th January 1915

My dearest Phine

I received your letter and the cigarettes, that you sent on the 9th, thank you very much. I had a very nice tea party on my birthday. I invited my section, there were nine of us, and we had quite a royal time.

We had bread, butter, jam a small tin of sardines (it was a case of the 5,000 people and the 5 small fishes with the sardines), and afterwards the lovely cake that you sent. It was very nice, so you see we did not do bad for wartime, did we? Oh, and we also had milk in our tea as well. I should like to have been able to invite you, but there, roll on when we have finished off the Kaiser, this little job won't take long now, and then we will make up for it.

The weather out here is still a bit too moist for our liking, but from what I can see from the papers, it is quite as bad in England.

You mentioned about writing to Miss Thorne the second time, I meant to tell you, in fact I thought I had, I must have forgot. You see she wrote me the second time enquiring for further information, and also sent me the paper and envelope to answer her with, so I was compelled to answer her letter out of courtesy. Still I know you do not mind, always I am sorry I did not tell you anything about it. I feel sorry for Charlie Grandsons' young lady receiving no news of him, I expect she is cut up about it. I hope it will not be long before you hear again from Mick, although in a way, he is safe.

Well Phine dearest, this is all for now, roll on when I can sit by the fire watching you make those button holes, and your Mam sewing on my medal ribbon (which she promised me). With best wishes to your Mam and Dad and best and fondest love to my own dearest Phine from Les.

XXXXXXXXX

17th January 1915

My dearest Leslie

I received your letter this morning and pleased to hear you are quite well and happy. Don't think I meant it when I told you about writing to Miss Thorne, that was my fun to make you laugh. I am delighted to hear you had such a nice birthday party under the circumstances, we will make up for it when you come back, please God.

Dear Leslie, your letter was quite cheerful. I can't see anything in it to excuse but I won't want Mam to help me pull your nose as I shall be quite as big as you by then and look I am quite young and you said you are an old man, staid in your old age so I shall be quite able you see. Dear Leslie, you don't want to think so much about the cigarette holder as I sent it to you to use out there. I thought if your cigarettes got wet or dirty that would save you putting them in your mouth, you see I want to look after you. When you come back Mam is going to give me the money to buy you a nice one to keep so use that out there. I am rather late again with my letter but I have been so busy with the shirts. I will be glad when you can come and see me button hole but you won't be able to look on as I will give you the job of sewing the buttons on.

Dear Leslie, I can't think of any more news now. Mam and Dad send their very best respects and hopes for your safe return. I will close now dear Leslie, with very best of love and kisses to my darling Leslie, from Phine.

XXXXXX

20th Brigade, 7th Division
18th January 1915

My dearest Phine

Just a line to let you know I am still as well as ever. We are still having bad weather, we had a heavy fall of snow yesterday, and it is very cold.

We are still in the same trenches, the same old thing over and over again, nothing of any importance happening. It is becoming rather monotonous, I shall be glad when we make a change, although we are cheerful and happy enough.

I have got a piece of good news, although it will be a long time yet before it comes off. The Sergeant Major told me he had my name on the list for a furlough. Of course, there are a lot senior to me to go yet, and they only go two in a battalion at a time, so it will be a long time yet. Still the weather will be better, and it will be all the sweeter for waiting, so there look out Miss Phine for a rough time.

I had a long letter from my brother yesterday. I am glad he is getting on so well, I wish he was out here with me, I am sure we would have a good old time together.

I suppose your Mam has not heard from Mick yet. I hope he is alright.

Well Phine dear, this is a short letter this time. I am anxiously waiting one from you. Hoping your Dad likes his new job still. With best respects to your Mam and Dad and fondest love and kisses to my own dearest Phine, from Leslie

XXXXXXXXXX

My dearest Leslie

I received your letter yesterday and card I am pleased you are keeping well, thank God, hope you will remain so. We got a terrible fall of snow, we could not go outside the door today we had to clear it all away so I don't know what it is like out there, simply awful I bet, never mind.

Dear Leslie, I don't think it will be so very long now before the whole job is over and a good job too, then we will give you a good old welcome home that will pull up with it. I wish it was tomorrow. I have been very busy with shirts this last few weeks, we got extra so I did my best to help Mam and she has spent most of the money on me. I could not get shoes to fit me as usual so old Dad said I will have some made so he did, thick lady's washing shoes with flat heels so they will last.

Dear Leslie, you said you would like to go to the old tin hut, so would I, if you were here, but we shall go again soon. You see I am quite ready to pull your nose and give you a good old shacking, but of course it won't be in temper. This Sunday night, how I wish you were here. Still, as you say, it is sweeter by waiting – absence makes the heart fonder.

Dear Leslie, Mam had a nice card from Mick last evening asking her to send him something to eat and some money, so Dad found out if she could send it so she is sending him 10/- tomorrow. I hope he will get it, poor boy. I think this is all now Leslie. Dear Mam and Dad send you their best wishes and hopes for your safe return, so I will close now dear. With the very best of love and kisses to my own darling Leslie, from Phine.

XXXXX

22nd January 1915

My dearest Leslie

I received your letter and card this morning dated the 18th. I am so pleased to hear from you that you are quite well and more than pleased to hear you are coming home. I shall be looking for when that time I shall be prepared. I am sorry to hear you got snow out there as it is worse than rain but we have got quite a bout of it here. Mam could not take the shirts back today, Dad had to take them.

Dear Leslie, you will be sorry to hear Mr Chadwick is killed. Mam is so sorry for her, with her little children, it is a bad job, I hope God will spare you. Mam has not heard yet from Mick. She had a nice letter from your Mother yesterday. She said you told her all about your party. I do wish I could have been there. I would have made you warm with a good chasing.

Dear Leslie, four hundred of the Irish guards went out to the Front today, hear them cheer.

I see the Germans have had another raid on the east coast[1]. Roll on when it is all over. Everything is gone up, we will have to go on half rations soon. I can't think of any more news now. Dear Leslie, Mam and Dad send you their very best respects so I will close now dear with very and fondest love my darling Leslie, from Phine.

XXXXXXXXXXXXXX

31st January 1915

My dearest Leslie

I received your card and so pleased you are alright and I know you have been hard at work by the papers hard fighting.

I wish it was all over. Roll on when it is and I shall be able to see you again. Please God we have lost all our snow now but I expect you still got some out there.

Dear Leslie, there is not much news to tell you in Warley. It is still the same by day, but night time, well, it would give you the creeps. It is pitch dark, no lights, whatever they are afraid of an air raid. Roll on when they are all raided out of it. I feel I could shoot a German if I see one.

Dear Leslie, you did not say that you received my letters. I sent you one on the 22nd also one on the 27th and hope you got them by now. I am still very busy with the shirts, not a minute to spare. Roll on when you come home to put the buttons on, then I can have a rest and watch you work. It will be a change for you as you have not known what work is lately, I mean rest don't I? Have you heard any more about coming home? I hope you have. I hope it is soon. I don't think there is any more news now, dear Leslie. Hoping to see you soon. Mam and Dad send you their very best respects, so I will close with very best of love and kisses to my own darling Leslie, from Phine.

XXXXXXXXXXXX

2nd February 1915

My dearest Phine

I received your letter of the 27th I am sorry I have not written you before, but we have had so much to do lately, hardly a minute to sleep what with digging, sand bagging and bailing water out of the trenches. We are still having a fairly quiet time, the Germans are about 400 yards away from us, but there are not many shots fired during the day, it is mostly artillery duels that do all the damage. We have had slightly better weather this last week, still it is very cold and damp, and plenty of mud.

I was awfully sorry to hear about poor Mr Chadwick being killed, how unfortunate for his poor wife and children. It seems a shame that married men have to fight, still I suppose it must be done, if we are to win, let us hope it will not be long now before it is ended.

So, it is a case of having to have your shoes made for you now, good heavens, what size do you take now, 19s or what. I have got a big pair of rubber jack boots that we wear to wade through the water in, I could bring them home with me for you, if you think they will fit, but they are only tens. Still I think I had better keep quiet or I shall have a warm time when I get on leave.

Well Phine dear, I must close now to catch the post. I will write you again soon. Hoping your Mam and Dad are in the very best of health and give them my best respects. Hoping to see you again very soon, with fondest and best love to my own dearest Phine, from Leslie.

XXXXXX

6th February 1915

My dearest Phine

I received your letter of the 31st also the cigarettes, thank you very much. I also had your letters of the 22nd and the 27th. I am sorry I did not let you know before, still better late than never. I get all your letters in three days, sometimes even in two days. So you think I have not been doing any work lately, do you? Right you are miss, I will remember it all when I do come home, so look out. I have not heard any more about coming on leave yet, I think I shall forget about it, and wait till the time comes. I don't suppose I shall have to wait so long now.

We have been having some beautiful weather the last two or three days. The sun has been shining lovely, still it is awfully muddy and damp yet.

Now the fine weather has started, I expect we shall be leaving our rabbit warren soon, and be at it again hammer and tongs, the same as before the winter set in.

We have been preparing for weeks and I shall not be sorry when we make a move. The sooner we shift them out of it, the sooner we shall be back to England, so roll on.

Well Phine dear, I cannot think of any more to say now. I am quite well, suffering a little from the damp weather, but perfectly happy so I will say au revoir. With best respects to your Mam and Dad, hoping they are quite well, and the best of fondest love to my own darling Phine, from Leslie.

XXXXX

13th February 1915

My dearest Phine
I received your letter and the cigarettes quite safe, thank you very much.
I was sorry to hear your Mam has such a bad cold I hope she will soon be rid of it, and better again.

I heard from home that your Mam had been up to see my Mother. Now I come to think my ears did burn. I expect they had a proper good old washerwoman's gossip, that's done it. I expect you will show this letter to them, to show I am still saucy, like you did the other. I can see what it is, you want my Mother to help you to pull my ears when I come home. Still I shall expect I shall find you have forgot all my complimenting insults by then.

We are having beastly weather still, sometimes sunshine, then torrents of rain, and awfully cold all the time.

We had quite a grand time in billets this time, we had a gramophone and singing, a proper singsong and all the time outside you could hear the Germans firing, and sending up their illuminating rockets, but we are used to the noise now, and took no notice and went on singing "Home sweet home" and "Tipperary". I thought of the dance, when the chap sang "He's a long time gone for the wood" still I should like to hear him sing it now, what do you say? Well, Phine dearest I must close now, time is short and we are off back to the trenches again for four days, so I will say au revoir once again. Hoping your Mam will soon be better and that your Dad is in the best of health. With fondest love and kisses to my own dearest Phine, from Leslie.

XXXXXXXXXXXX

19th February 1915

My dearest Phine
I received your letter of the 15th yesterday; sorry to hear you are all laid up with colds now. I hope you will soon be better. We are having fairly cold weather, but it

is improving, now and again we have quite fine days, it is quite a treat to see the sun.

I have no news to tell you, we are still at a deadlock, living comfortably in our little underground room. The thing we complain of is the rain will persist in dripping down our necks whilst we are sitting at meals, and that is rather uncomfortable. As we are leaving now I am suited right down to the ground. I have never felt better in my life. I have not had a day's illness since I have been out here, except for that slight wound.

We do most of our own cooking. My chum and I carry a small saucepan about with us everywhere we go. With a bit of luck I shall bring it home after the war. I think it will make a good souvenir. I can picture it now, a rotten battered, old iron saucepan resting in all its glory on the top of a piano. I had a narrow escape the other day, I was crossing a field on my own to reach the dressing station, when I stooped down to pick up a piece of an exploded shell, and just as I bobbed down a bullet whistled just over my back. I thought about keeping the piece of shell as a mascot. But it was too heavy.

Well Phine dearest, I will close now, as you say we are getting very busy working day and night, so I will say au revoir. With best wishes to your Mam and Dad, hoping they are in the best of health, and with fondest love and kisses to my darling Phine, from Leslie.

XXXXXXXXX

22nd February 1915

My own dearest Leslie

I received your letter this morning and I am so pleased to hear from you. You are so well and cheerful I hope and trust you will remain so. My word, what a narrow escape you had, what a good job you stooped down, you would have bound to be hit perhaps killed.

My dearest Leslie, don't forget to bring the saucepan home. What a novelty it will be, you will be able to get a job as cook when you come home. I see we have had another air raid on Essex towns, but no lives lost. They are trying to have their own back.

My cold is much better now, so is Mam's. I am sorry to hear the rain drops down on your neck. I wish I could alter it, I would. Never mind, I suppose you will have to stick it now.

Mam had a card from Mick and he has not received the money she sent him.

Dear Leslie, is there anything you would like that I could send you? I don't know what to send you as your Mother sends such a lot to you. I am glad you don't want for anything, if you do, say so won't you? I think I will close now, dear Leslie. Mam and Dad send their very best wishes and hope to see you soon. So I will close with very best of love and kisses to my own darling Leslie, from Phine.

XXXXXXXXXXXXXX

Bombs are dropped over Essex

On 21st February, the Germans flying a Friedrichshafen FF.29 aeroplane dropped several bombs over Essex.

26th February 1915

My dearest Phine

I received your nice letter of the 22nd yesterday, also the cigarettes. Thank you so much.

I was waiting for your letter, as we had the news that they had dropped the bombs over Warley, and I was worrying they were not near there. Still I think it is just as dangerous in England as it is over here.

I am glad to hear your Mam is much better, also yourself. I was pleased to hear you had heard from Mick. I hope he will receive the money alright, I expect he will.

Dear Phine, thank you for your offer of anything I want, but I have all I require, all I want is the war to end quickly so I can come home and see you dearest, and then look out for yourself. We are having some awful cold weather again and snow and frost, we will be pleased when warm weather comes.

I am sorry to say the leave has been cancelled, still never mind, the war will be over soon and I shall be home for good. Then I will sit by the fire and tell you all about the gay times we are having out here. I wish I was doing it now. Still roll on.

Well Phine dearest, I have not much news, nothing exciting has happened, so I will close, with my best respects to your Mam and Dad, hoping they are in the best of health and also yourself, with best and fondest love to my dearest Phine, from Leslie.

XXXXXX

28th February 1915

My dearest Leslie

I received your letter on the 23rd and also three cards this week. I am pleased to hear you are quite well and cheerful, hope you will keep so. I have not much news to tell you, you get all the news. Make hast and finish the blessed war and tell me then I will be pleased. I can't forget the narrow escape you had crossing that field.

Dear Leslie, don't laugh but I must tell you this. I dreamt about you the other night. You came to see us and Mam made some tea for you and you would not have any – you said I can't stop, I only come down to see a great friend of mine in the town, and you went out, never spoke to me or took any notice and we did not see you again. I felt quite upset next morning. What do you think of yourself, I can see you doing it.

Dear Leslie, our colds are nearly better, there are such a lot of people ill. I suppose it is the weather. You must be frozen out there at times, the fine weather is coming now, let us hope it will end soon.

Dear Leslie, I can't think of any more news just now. Mam and Dad send you the very best respects so I will close dear.

With very best of love and kisses to my own darling Leslie, from Phine.

XXXXXXX

5th March 1915

My dearest Phine

I have just received your letter, you must excuse me not answering before but we have had our letters delayed for three days, on account of us moving from our old position,[2] back behind the firing line for a week or so rest, and of course we had no opportunity of writing before.

What an awfully funny dream to have, what did you have for supper that night? I don't know about "can't stop" when I come, I think it will be "can't go" once I get there. Still it was only a dream, and you know they say reverse your dreams, for them to come true.

Glad to hear you are nearly better with your colds, let's hope they will be soon quite better.

Well Phine dear, I will close now as we are still very unsettled. I will write you again soon, so once again au revoir, with best respects to your Mam and Dad, hoping they are in the best of health, and fondest love and kisses to my darling Phine, from Leslie.

XXXXXX

7th March 1915

My dearest Leslie

I received your letter dated the 26th. I was pleased to hear as I had not had a letter for a week, I had cards. I expect you have been busy. I am pleased you are quite well but I am disappointed you are not coming home but I must be thankful to think you are alright and well these times. Let us hope it won't be very long before you are home for good, with the help of God, it would be very miserable for you going back if you had come home, as you know now what you were going back to so you must buck up and don't think about it. Wait until you come home, you will soon forget it, I will torment you all day, I have not forgot my 19 they will do to pay you with if I find I am not all to myself, that is how I am going to welcome you home, but as you say I suppose I will forget it by then.

Dear Leslie, Mam had a nice letter from your Mother last evening and they are all quite well. Don't I wish I could take you a nice pie out there to warm you, it must be very cold as it is so cold here where we got fires and beds. Never mind, it is not forever. I don't think of any more news now, dear Leslie. Mam and Dad send you their best respects and hope for your safe return, so I will close dear with very best of love and kisses to my own darling Leslie, from your loving Phine.

9th March 1915

My dear Phine

Just a line to let you know I am still in the link. We have started off on the move again, shifting every day,[3] so you must excuse me if my letters do not arrive so often. We are having some awful freezing weather but there is nothing to really complain about. Hoping to hear from you soon, with fondest and best, love to my own dearest Phine, from Leslie.

XXXXX

Leslie's Battalion moved to the Estaires–La Bassée Road area in France, preparing for the forthcoming battle of Neuve Chappelle.

12th March 1915

My dearest Leslie

I received your letter and was pleased to hear you were sent for a rest out of the firing line. I suppose it won't be long. I see by the papers you are busy fighting again, let us hope it won't be long now before it will be all over. We have had a few nice days here but I suppose it will rain six for it. Dear Leslie, I wish you were here next Wednesday the 14th, it is St Patrick's day, the Irish Guards are giving a ball. I expect it will be a grand affair. I would like to go if you were here, but I must wait until the next one, please God you will be home then. Expect you are still on the move no rest, we have had some wounded come in this week, poor fellows, they were all on sticks. I did wish you were there but I hope you will come home without a stick.

Dear Leslie, I don't think there is any more news. Mam and Dad send you their best respects and thank you for your card, and I will close now dear with very best of love and kisses to my own darling Leslie, from your loving Phine.

XXXXX

17th March 1915

My dearest Phine

I received your letter of the 7th, I was so pleased to hear you are well. I could not answer your letter before, as you will see by the papers we have had an awful fight in taking the village of Neuve Chapelle, but thank God, I came out of it safely. We were at it four days and four nights and now we are resting, so you can guess how thankful we are for the rest. I had a narrow escape, one bullet went in the back of my right shoulder across my back, and then out under my left shoulder, it cut all my under clothing, but did not even graze my skin. Don't you think that God was watching over me? I do. Still I am trying to forget that now, and trusting in the lord for the future.

Do you remember this date a year ago, where we were? I should like to be there now, I hope we shall be together this next year anyhow, in fact a long time before then.

We have had a nice change in the weather, it is not nearly so cold as it was and hardly any rain for the last few days.

I don't think the war will last much longer now, with the fleet in the Dardanelles and Russia and ourselves attacking, I think they will soon realise they are beat.

Well Phine darling, I have no news of any interest to tell you, I am fairly well, rather a bad headache from the awful din of the guns, but shall be alright in a day or two, so I will say au revoir once again, with the best of wishes to your Mam and Dad, hoping they are still in the best of health, and fondest and dearest love and many kisses to my sweetheart Phine, from yours lovingly Leslie.

XXXXXXX

The Battle of Neuve Chappelle was the first British large-scale offensive whilst being in the trenches. There were over 11,000 British and Allied casualties.

Leslie struck with trench fever

20th March 1915

My dearest Phine

I received your letter of the 12th and the cigarettes, thank you so much. You will be surprised to hear I was admitted to Hospital yesterday with Influenza and Rheumatism in the legs. I expect to be out again soon, so please do not write me again dearest, until I let you have another address. Letter follows, with fondest love and kisses, Les.

2nd Station Hospital, Boulogne, B5 Ward
24th March 1915

My dearest Phine

You will see by the above address where I am and I expect I shall stay here for a few days. I am in bed with Enteric[4] and am feeling rotten, but I do not feel like writing letters. Hoping your Mam and Dad are quite well. My fondest and dearest love to my dear Phine, from Leslie.

XXXXX

26th March 1915

My darling Leslie

I received your letter this morning dated 24th I am very grieved to hear you are ill with Enteric but with the help of God you will soon be better.

I must pray hard for you, it does seem a shame after what you have been through and then to think you must suffer, but cheer up dear, perhaps God knows best as you are bound to be sent home now Dad said, so you must think to yourself I will soon be home to England to my people and of course you will be pleased to see me as I shall you.

My dear Leslie, don't write a letter if you don't feel well enough. I am indeed quite satisfied with cards just to know how you are and knowing they are from my own Leslie. Now surely you fancy something nice now, you must let me know what you must have and I will send it, won't you dear. Mam had a nice letter from Mother this morning and she said as soon as she knows you are in England she will take me to see you as she knows we will do you more good than medicine. How nice of her. Now dear Leslie, cheer up and think I will soon see Mother and Phine, won't it be nice. Mam and Dad are sorry to hear you are ill but Dad said you were taken in time so you will be alright. He said you will be a stronger man than before, so I will close dear with very best love and kisses with all my love.

Love to my own darling, loving Phine

XXXXX

My dear Leslie, put this Badge of the Sacred Heart on your neck and he will watch over you. XXXX

2nd Station Hospital, Boulogne
29th March 1915

My dearest Phine

I was awfully pleased to hear from you so soon, I received your letter last night. I am getting well very quickly, although of course I am still in bed and I am not allowed anything to eat yet, although the Doctor said I could start a milk diet tomorrow.

I am very much afraid I shall not come to England, when I am much better I shall go to the convalescent camp and afterwards back to the Batt.[5] I think it is only extremely bad cases that come, those will never get properly well. I do not want to be like that, do I. I shall soon be fit again, I have an awfully strong constitution.

Then if I join the Batt, well the War won't last much longer now and then I shall be home for good.

Thank you very much, but I am sure there is nothing I require, the Sisters and Orderlies are very patient and kind with us. Well cannot wish for more.

Give my wishes to your Mam and Dad and thank them for their kind thoughts, with lots of kisses and fondest love to my own darling Phine,from your ever loving Leslie.

XXXXXXXXX

28th March 1915

My darling Leslie

Just a few lines trusting in God you are getting better. I thought if I sent you a few lines it would cheer you up, but don't write letters until you feel quite able. Look after yourself and don't worry, you will soon be home now and I am going to see you and then look out, I will soon make you well. I will be able to pull your nose quite easy, take a mean advantage while you are ill.

Dear Leslie, there is no news to tell you dear and I don't want to worry you so cheer up dear. Mam and Dad send you their very best wishes and pray for you that you may soon be better. So I will close dear with very best of love and kisses all my love to my darling Leslie, from your loving Phine.

XXXXXXX

God bless you dear.

2nd Station Hospital, Boulogne
1st April 1915

My dearest Phine

I received your nice letter last night, and am pleased to say I am getting on splendidly.

I was told I have not Enteric as I was treated for the first week, and today I was allowed up for the first time. I am feeling awfully weak of course, but with the chicken they are giving me and a week or so at the Convalescent Camp and I shall be my old self again, ready to go back to the Batt.

I am awfully sorry they will not send me home, because you will not have your chance of a mean advantage, you will have to wait till the War is over, and then I shall be quite well enough to take my own part.

Well Phine darling, I am feeling fatigued already so I will close, with best wishes to your Mam and Dad and yourself for a happy Easter tide, as far as possible, and fondest and very best of love to my own darling sweetheart Phine.

From Leslie

XXXXXXX

4th April 1915

My dearest Leslie

I received your letter this morning dated the 1st and I was very pleased to hear you have not got Enteric, Dad said you are sure to be sent home. Mam had a nice letter from your Mother. In the war she said your Father went to somebody and found out that you will sure to be sent home. I hope you will.

Dear Leslie, Mam and I went out on Saturday and we see Darky, he has been sent home to go under an operation so I don't see why you shouldn't come home.

Madgie has put her shoulder out but it is getting better now.

Dear Leslie, excuse this short letter, so I will close now with fondest and very best love to my own darling Leslie, from Phine.

XXXXXXXXXXXXXX

Convalescent Camp, Boulogne
6th April 1915

My dearest Phine

Just a line to let you know I am almost well now. I am still weak and suffer with headache, but I am leaving Hospital today for the Convalescent Camp, where I think the open life by the seaside will soon put me right.

I think the above address will find me, if it is different when I get there I will let you know at once.

We had awful wet weather for Easter, but this morning it was perfect, a glorious day.

I have not much time to make this a long letter as we are just off, so I will write you later.

Hoping your Mam and Dad are still in the best of health and with best and fondest love to my dearest Phine from your ever loving Leslie.

XXXXXXX

Excuse paper as I have no other.

7th April 1915

My dearest Phine
Just a line to let you know my address for the next few days is
A Company
No. 1 Convalescent Camp
Boulogne

It is very comfortable here, right up on the cliffs looking over the sea. We are in big Marquees which are heated with coke stoves and we also have bedsteads, so it is practically the same as being in Hospital.

We are up to date here, we have a cinematograph, and during this week we have a theatre on the go which is seen by the officers, it almost makes one forgets there is a war on at all.

Have you received my last two letters yesterday and a few days previous? I have not heard from you since the letter you wrote on the 28th. Still I suppose your letters will follow on, if not you will have them returned, so you will know if I receive them or not.

Give my best wishes to your Mam and Dad, hoping they are still the same as ever, with fondest and dearest love to my own darling Phine from your ever loving Leslie.
XXXXXXXXXXXXXXXXXX

8th April 1915

My darling Leslie
I received your letter this morning and so pleased to hear you are getting better and sent down to seaside. I do hope and trust it will do you good, you are bound to feel weak dear after what you have been through all the winter months, but with the help of God they will send you home. I do hope so, then you will be alright when we get you home. For goodness sake, try and come, don't feel bitter as you have done your share towards the war. I think it is a shame if they don't send you home with your poor head, don't say it is better, there are plenty of others to go.

My dear Leslie, I wrote to you but you did not say you got my letter. I suppose they will follow you up. I hope you will get this one as I know how anxious I am for a letter. I suppose there is nothing I could send you. Let me know, don't be afraid. I hope this letter will find you much better, please God, but don't say so. Mam and Dad send their usual hoping to see you soon so I will close now dear Leslie with very best of love and kisses to my own darling Leslie, from Phine.
XXXXXXXX
God bless you.

A Company, No. 1 Convalescent Camp, Boulogne
11th April 1915

My dearest Phine

I received your letter of the 4th, it was forwarded on from Hospital, I received it Friday, and yesterday I had your letter of the 8th. I was sorry to hear Madgie had put her shoulder out, I sincerely hope she is quite well by now.

I am glad to say I am feeling much better, although I can still feel the effects, and still have beastly pains from rheumatism. It makes me feel it will be weeks after the War before I shall be properly well again. Still I hope not, and with God's help I shall come home well and strong

You made me smile when you said I must try and come home. Why, I have a lot more to do yet before I have done my bit, as you say. What would you think of me if I come home and there was hardly anything wrong with me. Not much I am afraid. Think of your Uncle Pat, he has been out longer than me, and he is still sticking it. No dear, it seems hard but we must stick it to win, so I shall join my Batt as War will soon be ended now.

Who did you mean by Darky? It is Cpl Payne or Tom Porter, they are both in England, but Payne has been there about four months now I think and Porter is a Corporal.

Thank you again for asking if I want anything, but there is nothing I require, only to be able to see you again very soon.

We were out for a walk this morning along the Cliffs, it is a fine place here at Boulogne. We all gazed out to sea, to see if we could spot the coast of old England, but it was a bit too misty. We saw the Hospital ship sail out and I think we all wished we were on her, wounded or very sick, so that we could get home, then the mail boat came in and of course we all wondered if there was a letter on there for us.

Well dear, I must close as I must write home to Mother and the post goes in half an hour. Give my best respects to your Mam and Dad, hoping they are still in the very best of health. With fondest love and kisses to my own darling Phine, from your ever loving Leslie.
XXXXXXXXX

12th April 1915

My dearest Leslie

I received your letter dated the 7th and I am so pleased to hear they have sent you to the seaside. I do hope it will make you better. I have wrote to you four times since the 28th, how funny you did not get this one as it is miserable when you don't get a letter. I suppose they won't let you home, for goodness sake try and come. There are plenty of men home not so bad as you are, they could not get about.

My dear Leslie, Aunt Lizzie was down to see us yesterday and Dad has got a day off today and he has gone up to his sister's on the bike. I wish I could have gone but Mam's old bike is no good or I would have gone and see your Mother, but I will wait now dear until you come home, then I will be off to see you, that will be a good day's outing. Write dear and let me know how you are. Mam and Dad send you their very best wishes, so I will close dear with fondest and dearest love and kisses to my darling Leslie, from Phine.

XXXXXXXX

15th April 1915

My dearest Leslie

I received your letter on Tuesday dated the 11th and was so pleased to hear from you, also to hear you are feeling better. Dear Leslie, Mam had a letter from Mick in the week which was dated the 1st of March and he got the money, he asked Mam to send him out something to eat.

Dear Leslie, when I said Darky I meant Tim Porter. I hope they will send you home. I suppose when you saw the Hospital ship sail out you wished you were on it. Dad said you are sure to be sent home. I would not care if there was not anything the matter with you long as you were sent home.

Dear Leslie, Madgie's shoulder is getting better now. Dad has got the job in the pay office[6] for good now, and he will have to wear uniform and boots so he will be working under the government again.

Dear Leslie, there has been another great air raid on Newcastle. I don't think there is any more news so I will close with very best of love and kisses to my own darling Leslie, from your young Phine.

XXXXX

April 16th

My dearest Phine

I have just arrived at the Base so my address for the time being is

7th Division

Infantry Base

Harfluer

I have not heard from you since the 8th as I have been changing about for the last four days, so I expect my letters will follow on. Will write later, fondest love Leslie.

XXX

Back with the Battalion

19th April 1915

My dearest Phine

I am writing you to let you know I am off back to the Batt,[7] tomorrow, so by the time you receive this letter I shall be back again. I need not have gone for some time yet, but I felt I could not bear the waiting about down here at the Base. I have not had a letter from you since that one of the 8th, I suppose it is because I keep moving from place to place. So, write to my old address, when you receive this, as you know how long it seems, when you are eagerly waiting for a letter.

We are having awfully fine weather here, I think it will be terribly hot up in the firing line in a week or two.

There seems to be an awful strong opinion among the men that the War will be over by the end of June, I don't know why, but many of the Officers think so too and are making bets with one another about it. I hope it does and then, I want to get back, and come to tea again on Sunday afternoons.

I was thinking, it is nearly nine months since I saw you last. It seems ages, I shall hardly know you again when I see you but still, that would be impossible.

Well dearest, I think this is all this time, I am feeling pretty fit again, the only thing wrong with me is I feel so awfully tired, but I think I was always like that – laziness, I suppose your Mam would call it.

Well I will close now, with best respects to your Mam and Dad, hoping they are still in the best of health, also your sisters and brother with fondest and dearest love to my own darling Phine, from yours lovingly Leslie.

XXXXXXX

P.S. Don't forget dear, I want a nice long letter, with all the news to read when you get this to make up for the long wait, Leslie. XXX.

28th April 1915

My dearest Leslie

I received your card this morning dated 25th and am sorry to hear you have not received my letters. I have sent them just the same. I am sorry to hear you are not coming home; Mam had another card from Mick. Still I expect you will get my letters now because you are back in the firing line.

Dear Leslie, we have got a nice little farmyard now, we have got chickens.

Dear Leslie, don't you stop writing, write and let me know how you are. I have only had a letter and a card in a fortnight. I had another dream about you last night I dreamt that you were home, wounded in the arm. I wish it was true, not a dream. Dear Leslie, Payne is still in London. I see him down here the other day, he said he does not want to go back. I think it is a shame that they never sent you home. I think you have done your share.

Dear Leslie, Mam and Dad send you their very best wishes and hope to see you soon, so I will close now dear with fondest and dearest love

To my own darling, from your ever loving Phine.

XXXXXX

28th April 1915

My dearest Phine

I received your letter of the 24th yesterday. I was so pleased to hear from you after such a long wait. I am awfully sorry to have kept you waiting so long for a letter, I expect it will seem ages to you before you receive this one, but we have been so awfully busy these last few days, working day and night.

I have not heard from home since the 30th of March. I have written several times, but I suppose their letters are being sent to the Hospital, or the base, although I wrote and told them I am back with the Batt.

I am awfully sorry to hear about poor Mick, it must be awful the way they are treating them. What a blessing to everybody when peace is proclaimed. I hope it is soon.

I was rather unfortunate falling sick when I did for whilst I was away they made the promotion up, and if I had been there I should have been made a full Sergeant. Still I do not regret it, I am still alive and well, and then of course when I am a Sergeant I shall be too proud to write and speak to you, didn't you say so?

We are having beautiful weather out here, so different from the rain and snow we had through the winter. I never thought we should see the sun again, until we reached dear old England.

Well Phine dearest, this is all I have to say for the present, give my best respects to Mam and Dad, hoping they are still in the best of health, so once again au revoir, with dearest and fondest love to my own dear Phine, from your ever loving Leslie.

XXXXXX

2nd May 1915

My dearest Phine

I received your letters of the 28th last night, I was pleased to hear from you again. I have not had any of your other letters forwarded on yet so probably they have gone astray, or will be returned to you.

I am awfully sorry I had to keep you waiting for any news, but you see dear, whilst I was shifting from one place to another I could not get any letters censored[8] as it was useless writing any.

I am glad to hear you are keeping chickens, I shall know where to get me some eggs now when I am invalided home with that wounded arm you dreamt about. Barmy dreaming such a thing, and then wishing it was true that's a nice thing I must say, how hardhearted you must be, you don't think of poor me, and what I might have to suffer. Still I understand what you mean dear, and I don't suppose it will be for long.

We are having very fine weather out here, it is getting quite hot. How is it in Brentwood? I am always wishing I was still stationed there, I am sure it was the best years soldering I ever did and I suppose this is the worst.

So Payne is in London, he is very lucky, I don't suppose he was out here more than a month, still good luck to him, I can quite understand him not wanting to come again.

Well Phine dear, this is about all I can think of now. I have been thinking for about ten minutes and nothing will come to my mind. As your Mam says I must be barmy, I feel such a fool when it comes to letter writing. You must wait till I come home and then I will tell you everything, talk for hours till you are tired of listening.

So once more au revoir, with best respects and wishes to your Mam and Dad, hoping they are enjoying the best of health, also yourself with fondest love to my own darling Phine, from your ever loving Leslie.

7ᵗʰ May 1915

My darling Phine

I have received two of your letters which you wrote me whilst I was at the Convalescent Camp. I was glad to hear from one of them, that your Dad had obtained his job for good now. I hope he likes it alright.

Don't get worried if you do not hear from me for a day or two yet, as we are going to be very busy for a day or two.

I was very pleased your Mam had heard from Mick again, and that he is quite well.

I have not any more time to write now, as the post is just off, so I will say au revoir, with best wishes to your Mam and Dad, hoping they are quite well, with fondest and dearest love and kisses to my own dearest Phine, from your ever loving Leslie.

XXX

8ᵗʰ May 1915

My dearest Phine

I wrote you yesterday and was in such a hurry to catch the post that I did not tell you what I wanted to most.

When I came from Hospital to the Base, I was able to do a little job for the Officer in charge. He belonged to the Essex Yeomanry. A day or two ago he sent me a letter thanking me for the trouble, and enclosing a little present, a note for 20 francs.

I am sending half to you now. I want you to give it to your Mam, so that when she is sending Mick another parcel to get him some cigarettes or something. I know what it is to be without an English cigarette, or to go short of food, so I hope it will come in useful and that you will not be offended with me for sending it.

You can get the notes changed at any post office. A franc is worth 10 pence but in England they give you 9.5 D for them. There is also an English P.O.[9] which are difficult to change out here so I am sending it as well.

Hoping all are quite well at home, with fondest and dearest love to my own darling Phine, from your ever loving Leslie.

P.S. I hope your Mam will not be offended with me, if she is telling her, I don't care.

13th May 1915

My dearest Leslie

I received your letter yesterday and one on Monday. I was pleased to hear from you, also to hear you are still alright. Sorry I did not write before because Mam has not been so well, she is getting better now, thank God.

Dear Leslie, Mam said indeed she is not offended as she could not be offended with you whatever you done. She thinks it is very kind of you indeed, so does Dad, to think of Mick like that. When Mam gets up she is going to send him out a parcel.

Dear Leslie, we have had some more bombs on Southend. They dropped sixty bombs.[10] Dear Leslie, Mam had a letter from your Mother in the week and she said she is coming down to see Mam when she is stronger, Mabel as well. I wish you were coming with them, still I expect you will one day.

Dear Leslie, I will close now with very best of love and kisses to my own darling Leslie, from your ever loving Phine.

xxxxxx

P.S. Dear Leslie, I was just thinking whether I would send you any kisses. You have not sent any in two letters, you want your nose pulled.

XXXXXXXX

14th May 1915

My dearest Phine

I received your letter of the 5th quite safe. Sorry I have not written before, but we have had our mail delayed for two or three days, and we could only send postcards. I only received your letter yesterday.

I was surprised to hear you had another sister,[11] I hope she is well. I expect you have your hands full now for a bit, being housemaid and nursemaid.

I heard from home a day or two ago and Mother told me about the wrongly addressed letter she received, I think there is somebody a bit more barmy than I am.

Please excuse very short letter as I have no time to write more. Hoping your Mam and Dad are quite well. With fondest and dearest love to my darling Phine, from your loving Leslie.

XXXXXX

21ˢᵗ May 1915

My dearest Leslie

I received your cards and was so pleased to hear from you. I have not heard from you for over a week. I expect you have been busy again, by the papers you have. Dear Leslie, I wish the war was over, it seems like years not months. I will be glad when it is all over.

Dear Leslie, sorry I did not write before as I have been busy because I have everything to do now Mam is not better yet. She has a card from Mick in the week.

Dear Leslie, I will make this a short letter, so I will close now. Mam and Dad send you their very best respects and hope for your safe return, with best of love and kisses to my own darling, from your ever loving Phine.

XXXXX

22ⁿᵈ May 1915

My dearest Phine

I received your letter of the 13ᵗʰ and was glad to hear your Mam is getting better again. I hope she will soon be quite well.

You were talking of the Bombs they dropped on Southend, that reminds me, I am attached to the grenade Company for a day or two to learn about them.[12]

I have had a bit of luck and been promoted to Sergeant, so the time has come when I shall be too proud to speak to you now. Still I don't feel at all proud, so I think I will write, because I would rather be a private and have you, then a Sergeant without you.

Mother told me she was coming to see your Mam soon, as you say I wished I was coming, but still a day will soon come when I shall be down to see you, and not so very long now.

Mother has been telling me about how you are all helping poor Mick, so I should think he will be a lot more comfortable and happy now.[13] How is Pat, have you heard from him at all lately?

I suppose by the time you receive this letter, Whit Monday will have passed. Another holiday to make up for when we all get back. We are having splendid holiday weather, almost too hot to move.

Well Phine dearest, this is all I have to say in this letter, so once again au revoir, with best wishes to your Mam and Dad and hoping your Mam will soon be quite well again. With fondest and dearest love to my own darling Phine, from your ever loving Leslie.

XXXXXXXXXX

P.S. Here are some to make up, for you said I missed in my last two letters.

25ᵗʰ May 1915

My dearest Leslie

I received your card this morning dated 21ˢᵗ. I was pleased to hear you are still well, thank God, I was anxious when I did not hear. I hope you will forgive me not writing so often but I have been so busy and it takes me such a long time to write a letter. Poor Mam is still very ill, she has got to have her breast lanced. I hope she will be soon better, there is such a lot to do.

Dear Leslie, I am delighted to hear you are Sgt now, I suppose you won't speak, Mam said, swank. Won't your Mother be pleased? You will be Sgt Major before you come back, I hope so.

Dear Leslie, I suppose you are having rather a busy time now the weather is nice. I wish to goodness it was all over, it seems to last longer for wishing.

Mam had a card from Mick on Saturday. Still the same. She said to thank you again for sending that money. She thinks it so kind of you she said we will have a nice feast when you all come back. Dear Leslie, I don't think there is any more news just now, hoping to have a nice letter soon. I will close with very best of love and kisses

To my own darling Leslie, from your ever loving Phine.

XXXXXXXXX

The drums are calling

30th May 1915

My dearest Phine

I received your letters, one that you wrote on the 21st and the other on the 25th. I received them together last night. I was wondering what was the matter, not hearing from you so long, I suppose the first letter was delayed.

I am awfully sorry to hear your Mam is so bad, I sincerely hope she is much better by the time you receive this.

I am sorry if you think I am late in answering your letters but we seem to be so busy nowadays, hardly time to send a card even. You can see by the papers that we keep pushing on. We are having all our drummers who were wounded back again this week and they are going to form a corps of drums. I have been asked if I will go back again just where we are sat here, I have said I would I cannot resist the call of the drum.

All our drummers went home except one, you remember Tich the little drum Corporal? He is still here, he is a Sergeant now, his stripes reach to his elbow up to his should-knot, and he swanks awful.

From the news we get out here, I don't think this old war can last much longer now. Everything seems so favourable for us, and the French are doing wonders. So I don't think it will be long before we arrive home for that big feast dearest, so you had better think about what we are going to have. Glad to hear Mick is still alright. My word, won't he just set in at that party? I know I should if I was in his place.

That reminds me, they give us stewed plums and rice after dinner now, rather good living that, on active service, don't you think? I don't suppose your Dad lived like that in Africa, eh? I reckon they are fattening us up, for when we come home, although we don't want much feeding.

Well I must close now dear as we are off to the canal for a swim, a daily occurrence when we are in billets, and I think we need it, so once again au revoir. Hoping to hear your Mam is quite better next time you write and with best wishes to your Dad, hoping to hear from you soon, with fondest and dearest love to my darling Phine, from your ever loving Leslie.

XXXXXXX

Leslie was requested to join the Corps of Drums in his Battalion in France, as he had experience as a drummer from when he first joined the Grenadiers in 1908. While Leslie was with the Corps of Drums he was required to serve in the trenches and other Battalion duties as and when.

4th June 1915

My dearest Leslie

I received your letter and card yesterday. I was so pleased to hear from you, also to hear you are quite well. Dear Leslie, your Mother and Mabel came down Sunday and she gave baby such a nice present. It was very kind of her. Mam was so pleased. I wished you were here as well but it is no use wishing, I suppose you will be here as soon as you can.

Dear Leslie, I hope you will forgive me not writing before but I had not much news to tell you.

Mam is getting better, but she still has to go to the doctors every morning.

I am pleased you are Sgt. Mam said swank. She had another card from Mick on Saturday and he said he got the money Mam sent, that is a good job. She also had a letter from Pat, he is quite well.

Dear Leslie, Mam and Dad send you their very best respects and hope for your safe return. So I will close dear with very best of love and kisses to my own darling Leslie, from your ever loving Phine.

XXXXXXXXXXXXXXXXXXXX

6th June 1915

My dearest Phine

Just a line to let you know I am still in the best of health. I have not heard from you lately but I suppose you are very busy just at present with your Mam being so bad. How is she? I sincerely hope she is much better.

We are having some awfully hot weather out here now, almost too hot to move about. Still it is better than the awful winter we had.

Do you know if Miss Bullem has heard from Charlie Gransden at all since that letter was put in the paper? Because we have heard out here that he is in Germany, and is quite well. I suppose she knew he was made Sergeant before he was reported missing. If you know whether she has heard will you let me know please as we are rather interested to know about an old chum.

I saw in the papers that the Zeppelins have been over Brentwood. Did they do much damage? I hope not. I was glad to see that no one was injured by them.

Well Phine dearest, this is about all this time so once again au revoir. I am just off to Sunday tea, a bit different to when I used to come over to the quarters, still roll on. With best of all good wishes to your Mam and Dad and fondest love to my own darling Phine, from your ever loving Leslie.

XXXXXXXXX

Charlie Gransden was another sad loss for Leslie and the regiment. Charlie Gransden was never seen again since the First Battle of Ypres. Lance Corporal Charles Edward Gransden 15470 died on 29th October age 21. His name is one of many inscribed on the Menin Gate memorial in Belgium to those with unknown graves who died in the Ypres Salient.

16th June 1915

My dearest Phine

I received your letter of the 7th. I am so pleased to hear from you as I had not heard from you for over a fortnight, and your last letter took eight days to come. Still I must not be impatient, your Mam is so bad. I am glad to hear she is up and I hope she will soon be quite well again.

I have just heard from Mother and she told me she and Mabel come to see your Mam last Sunday.

She told me they brought your little baby sister a pelisse, whatever that may be, something to eat I suppose. Anyhow I hope she liked it.

I was glad to hear Mick was alright, and Pat as well, I hope he gets through it alright.

I am rather lucky joining the drums, we have to do a bit of work with the Transport, and produce whilst the Batt are in the trenches so you see I miss all the bullets and fighting now, just a shell or two come over now and again but they never do any harm, as we are well in the rear. I am not sorry either as I have had quite enough of it for a time.

Well Phine dear, this is all this time, but if you do not have time to write a letter just drop a postcard, so that I may know that you are alright.

With best respects and wishes to your Mam and Dad and hoping your Mam will soon be well again, and fondest and dearest love to my darling Phine, from your ever loving Leslie.

XXXXXXXX

26th June 1915

My dearest Phine

I received your letter yesterday. I was pleased to hear from you again, but I was so sorry to hear your Mam is still so bad. I sincerely hope it will not be long before she is well again.

Mother wrote and told me you had all the work to do. I wished I was at home and able to help you. Do you remember that Sunday when we started to clean up together? I don't think we should do much at that rate, do you?

We have been having some awful hot weather out here but the last three days it has simply pounded down with rain, and they call this country "Sunny France". Give me old England. It does seem years, as you say, those nine months, still I suppose the end will soon be here now. They have started to allow the men leave again, so with a bit of luck I expect to come over for 7 days, that's if the Drum Major will spare us. I expect he will, as he is looking forward for a leave himself.

I am feeling much better now, since I have not gone into the trenches. I have never felt better in my life. Everybody tells me I am growing fat, but I think they are only pulling my leg.

Well Phine dearest, I will close this short letter now, hoping to hear from you soon, with all best wishes to your Mam and Dad and dearest and fondest love to my own darling Phine, from your ever loving Leslie.

XXXXXXXX

Please excuse paper, as this is the only piece I have till Mother sends me more.

My dearest Leslie

Just a line, hoping you are quite well. I am so sorry to keep you waiting without a letter but you know I have been busy, but I have sent one every week or so. You ought to have one, but never mind dear Leslie, I think just as much in fact more of you, but it takes me such a long time to write a letter. I wish you were home so as I would not have to write. Roll on, it seems years but it will be all the nicer when you do come home won't it? I wish it was tomorrow, dear Leslie. Mam is much better now, that is a good job. I am sitting in the front room writing this and watching the girls going by with their young men. Don't I wish I was with you but it won't be long I hope. I am getting old now, soon be sixteen. I have got my hair up as Mam said I look so big with it down. I am to have my photo taken with it up and send you on. I do hope you are well. How glad I am you are not in the firing line. I hope you will never go back again.

Mam thanks you for your kind wishes and hopes to see you soon. Dad sends his best and respects. I will now close, dear Leslie, with very best of love and kisses, all my love to my own darling Leslie, from your ever loving Phine.

XXXXXXXX

Leslie was granted his first seven-day leave back to England since his embarcation to the war in Europe in October 1914.

2ⁿᵈ July 1915

My dearest Phine

I have had a bit of luck. I have been granted leave of 7 days, so I will be down to see you tomorrow just after 4 o clock. I arrived home today about 4 o'clock and I did not have an opportunity of letting you know, so au revoir till tomorrow, with best of love and kisses to my darling Phine, from Leslie.

XXXXX

Leslie returns back to France.

10ᵗʰ July 1915

Dear Mr and Mrs Hazeltine

I am very sorry I did not keep my promise and come and bid you farewell. I fully intended to do so on Wednesday, but as I expect you know, I had such an awful cold in my face, I was so mad with the pain that I could not come, so you must please excuse me.

Glad to say I have arrived back safe, and did not get submarined on our way over. Things are just the same as ever, everyone here seems to think we shall all be home by Christmas. I hope so it does seem a bit rotten having to come back here again.

I was awfully glad you allowed Phine to come to London for those two or three days. I think it was very good of you, whilst you were so unwell, and wanted her as much. I sincerely hope you will soon be quite well again.

Again hoping you will forgive me for not coming and my best wishes to you both.

Yours very sincerely,

Leslie

10th July 1915

My dearest Phine

Just a line to let you know I arrived here quite safe. I hope you got back alright Thursday night, and that Bruce looked after you. I hope you kept him in his place because I know what he is with the young ladies.

It seemed a very short time to be with you, still I was very glad to come home and see you all. Let us hope it will not be long before we're all home for good.

I must say it seems a bit strange coming back to the hard bed on the floor; it makes me think that leave was only a dream. I cannot quite realise it yet.

Well dearest, I have no news, just a line to let you know I am alright, so I will close, with fondest and dearest love to my own darling Phine, from yours ever loving Leslie

XXX

My dear Leslie

I received your card this morning and was so pleased to hear you are quite well. Dear Dad has gone up the Motor Transport[14] and he is going to London, so I expect we will soon be there as well. Mam said we will go as soon as she is done going to the Doctors. Dad is going next Monday.

Dear Leslie, I feel as miserable as anything since you went back. Mam said she wished she did not send that card so that I could have stayed till Thursday morning because she did not finish all her shirts. Dear Leslie, I will make this a short letter now because I am busy ironing. Mam and Dad send you their best respects and hope to see you again soon. So I will close now dear with best of love and kisses to my darling Leslie, from your ever loving Phine.

XXXXXXXX

17th July 1915

My dearest Phine
I was pleased to hear from you so soon. I received both letters.
We have been having quite an enjoyable time out here the last day or two. On Friday we had our Battalion sports day and they were quite as good as any we had in England. Only the band was not heard, so the drummers had to play sections. The Prince of Wales was present and he told us we played exceedingly well. I tell you we are "quite hot".

Then on Friday our C.O.[15] gave the Sergeants a dinner as he was leaving us to be made a General. It was very good of him. We had a fine time, and finished up with a good concert. I could not sing, so they made me play, I mean bang the piano. I gave them a few of the old dances and of course that set them off. Unfortunately, we had no lady partners, but we made the best of it. It seems hard to realise that there is a war on. Still I know there is one, they are just firing overhead at a German aeroplane – they nearly hit it. So I should tell your Dad not to come over here in one.

I am sorry to hear Mam is still attending the Doctors. I do hope she will soon be quite well again.

I am awfully sorry I have not wrote you before but what with concerts etc., and changing billets, I have hardly had a minute to spare, so you must please excuse me. I have just managed to get over the leave by now, and am settled down. Roll on the next one.

I had another stroke of luck when I got back, I had my rank of acting full sergeant confirmed by the C.O., so I am landed now.

Well I must close now my dearest, else I shall miss the post and what will make this letter another day late, so au revoir, with very best wishes to your Mam and Dad and all my love and kisses to my own darling Phine, from yours ever loving Leslie.
XXXXXX

19th July 1915

My dearest Leslie
Just a line hoping you are quite well. I have sent two or three letters since you went back, but I don't suppose you would have received them. Dear Leslie, I thought being as I never heard from you this week you were sent back to the firing line. I hope you have not gone back there. Dear Leslie, I hope you were back again for good, when you went I feel as miserable as anything.

Mam has had a card from Mick. He has received one of Mam's parcels and Dad's sister sent him one and he has received that but he still writes for more. Dear Leslie, I don't think there is any more news now, so I will close now dear, with very best of love and kisses to my own darling Leslie, from your ever loving Phine.
XXXXXX

20ᵗʰ July 1915

My dearest Leslie

I received your card on Wednesday and a letter on Thursday afternoon both dated the 24ᵗʰ so they took five days to come. Dear Leslie, I had the toothache yesterday morning and it nearly drove me mad. It was a bit better in the afternoon.

Dear Leslie, Mam is ever so much better now, she has finished attending the Doctors.

Dear Leslie, Mam has not heard from Mick for a long while now. Mam still keeps sending him parcels every week.

Dear Leslie, I don't think there is any more news now. Mam and Dad send you their best respects and hope for your safe return. So I will close now with very best of love and kisses to my own darling Leslie, from your ever loving Phine.

XXXXXXXX

20ᵗʰ July 1915

My darling Phine

I received your letter of the (16ᵗʰ Friday) but I am awfully sorry to hear you are still suffering from toothache.

I think it would be best to have them out, as your Mam suggests. I am sure it is the worst pain anybody could have.

I have not had it again since I came off leave, I must have handed it over to you before I came. I do hope it will soon be better.

So you are not going to leave Warley after all. I suppose your Dad is rather disappointed that he cannot go on the Motor Transport. I quite expected to see him flying over here on an aeroplane one of these days.

I have quite settled down now after my leave, it seems as if it was just a dream, it is here. You remember little Jack as you called him? He went on leave two days after I came and wishes to be remembered to you.

Well dear, I think this is all I have to say this time, so once again au revoir. With my best respects and wishes to your Mam and Dad and my best and dearest love to my dear sweetheart Phine, from your ever loving Leslie.

XXXXXXX

22nd July 1915

My dearest Leslie

I received your letter this morning I was so pleased to hear from you and to hear you have been made full Sgt. Dear Leslie, I think you have fine times out there, going to sports and concerts, that's more than I have here. I think I will have to come out there as a Nurse to join you I think.

Dear Leslie, one of Mrs Chadwick's twins have died and the other one is not expected to live. Don't you think it is sad? They died with whooping cough.

Dear Leslie, I don't think there is any more news now. Mam and Dad send their best respects and hope for your safe return so I will close with very best of love and kisses to my own darling Leslie, from your ever loving Phine.

XXXXXXXX

My dearest Phine

I have just received your letter of the 19th. You say you have sent two or three letters, I have received them all, the one that has just come is the fourth since I came back. I have answered each one, so probably my letters have been delayed. This makes my fourth one.

I am still on the same job with the drums. That reminds me, in future when you send my letters, do not put on the Brigade or Division etc., just put my Rank and name then:- "Drums"

1st Batt Grenadiers Guards

British Exped Force

Don't forget, will you? As it is rather important now.

Glad to hear Mick is still alright I suppose he is getting fed inwardly. Let us hope the end will soon come if it is only for his sake. I am sure everybody is getting tired of the war by now.

How is your toothache, is it any better yet? I was very sorry to hear you had it so bad. I also hope your Mam is better now, and finished attending the Doctor.

I have just heard from Mother and she asked me what I thought of the night when it rained so, and they all came home in borrowed coats. I thought it was rather amusing, did you? She says she wonders whether you enjoyed yourself. I should say by the way you slept till three o'clock the next afternoon, and then wanted to know if I was up, that you did not do so badly.

Well my dear, I will close, but cheer up, because I do not like to hear you have been miserable since I have been back, we shall all be home for good soon. So once again au revoir, with best wishes to your Mam and Dad and best of love and kisses to my darling Phine, from your ever loving Leslie.

XXXXXXXXXXXXX

26th July 1915

My dearest Leslie

I received your card this morning and a letter on Friday. I was so pleased to hear you are quite well. Dear Leslie, I received the brooch[16] on Saturday and it looks very nice, I am very pleased with it. Mam likes it very much, she thinks it is great novelty.

Dear Leslie, Mam has got Mona ill now, so I have not had much time to write. There is always one of us ill since I have been in this house. Mrs Height told Mam the other day that nearly every lady who has been in this house has been the same.

Dear Leslie, I don't think there is any more news now so I will close now with very best of love and kisses to my dearest Leslie, and from your ever loving Phine.

XXXXXXXX

30th July 1915

My dearest Phine

I received your letter of the 26th quite safe. I was sorry to hear Mona is ill. It does seem as if there is always one of you ill in that house, I hope it is not going to be your time next. What with your toothache and your Mam being bad, and now Mona, you must have quite a houseful. Is your Mam better yet, you do not say if she is?

I am glad to hear you received the brooch, and that you are pleased with it.

We are hearing yarns out here that we are having a longer rest whilst we wait for the Irish Guards at Warley to come out and join us, them and the Welsh guards, with our 3rd and 4th Batt are supposed to come out and make with the rest of us out here, a Guards Division.[17]

We are still going strong with are corps of drums. We have to play at Officers mess some nights whilst we are in the billets, so you can tell we are not any old nagtime band. I think the men are very proud of their band, and I can assure you I am very proud to be in it, out of the way of the bullets.

Well Phine dear, this will have to be another of my short letters, or I shall not catch the next post. Hoping to hear in your next letter that everyone at home are quite well. With my best respects and wishes to your Mam and Dad and best and fondest love and kisses to my own darling Phine, from your ever loving Leslie.

XXXXXXX

P.S. Do you remember that kisses my Aunt asked you to give me? I never received them, so do not forget, you are in my debt.

2nd August 1915

My dearest Leslie

I received your letter on Saturday and a letter this morning. I was so pleased to hear from you also to hear you are still quite well.

Dear Leslie, I am sorry to keep you waiting for a letter but I have not been well. I have had a sick headache. I was in bed all day Saturday, but I am better now, so is Mam and Mona. Dear Leslie, I sent over too many letters last week with the other address on them so I don't expect you will get them.

Dear Leslie, fancy asking me did I enjoy myself the few days I was at your Mother's. I only wished I could have stayed longer if you were there.

Dear Leslie, I don't think there is any more news now. Mam and Dad send you their best respects and hope for your safe return. So I will close now, with very best of love and kisses to my own darling Leslie, from your ever loving Phine.

XXXXXXXX

6th August 1915

My dearest Phine

I received your letter of the 31st. I should hardly think they would stop the parcel from Mick. I always understood they opened the parcel in front of the men, and if they were alright let them have them. Surely, they would have told him if they did not let him have it.

Don't you think he would have asked for a parcel in his card if he had not been receiving any, probably he forgot to mention it? I expect he had the contents and forgot about them when he wrote to you after.

We have been having some awful wet weather today, it has not stopped raining since I wrote you last and it is awfully chilly. I believe the winter has set in.

We had another concert here the other night, it was very good, and we finished up with the piano and a few flutes playing some of the old dances. It brought back the old times again.

I must close this very short letter now dearest, it is nearly seven and we are off for a long march this morning, so I will close.

With best of wishes and my respects to your Mam and Dad and fondest and dearest love to my own darling Phine, from your ever loving Leslie.

XXXXXX

10th August 1915

My dearest Leslie

I received your letter yesterday afternoon and a card this morning dated the 8th. That letter only took only one day to come, that was quick, it always takes two or three days. Dear Leslie, I was so pleased to hear from you, also to hear you are still quite well.

Dear Leslie, there was two of the Irish Guards buried today. They went on a route march, one dropped down dead and the other one died just after they came back. He was only 19.

Dear Leslie, I wish you were home it does make you feel wild when you see girls going by here with the soldiers. We have got the Bedfords here now so we see plenty of soldiers.

Dear Leslie, I don't think there is any more news now. Mam and Dad send their best respects and hope to see you soon. So I will close now dear, with very best of love and kisses to my own darling Leslie, from your ever loving Phine.

XXXXXX

13th August 1915

My dearest Leslie

I received your letter this morning and was so pleased to hear from you, also to hear you are quite well.

Dear Leslie, I have not had the toothache for over a week now.

Dear Leslie, it says in today's paper the war will be over by October. I hope it will, don't you Leslie? I went out this evening, that is only the fourth time since you went back, and I saw hundreds of soldiers of the Irish Guards.

Dear Leslie, I will close now with very best love and kisses to my own darling Leslie, from your ever loving Phine.

XXXX

15th August 1915

My dearest Phine

I was pleased to receive your letter of the 10th and to know you are quite well. The reason you get the letters quick is because we are so far down the line nearer the coast. I expect it makes a lot of difference.

I see in the papers they have visited England again with the Airships, did they come anywhere round your way again? It never says in the papers, and it always makes me wonder, one never knows what might happen.

We are still having fine weather out here; it gets a bit chilly at night, and makes one think of the coming winter. I hope it will not be as severe as last winter. There is no doubt we shall be out here for the winter and probably the one after that. We are settled down for another six months out here at last.

You know all this half page about the weather is just swank, something to fill the letter up with… It's a funny thing when one can't think anything they always mention the weather. You must think me an awful idiot at letter writing, but as soon as I start writing I forget all I was going to write. I can write just about as much as I can talk. You see I have filled nearly another page telling you I cannot write letters. (More swank.) It is not my fault; I meant to have a sleep this afternoon.

Only the Drummers thought a little bit of glee singing would be better, so of course sleep being out of the question I thought I had better answer your letter.

Well Phine my dear, I cannot think of any more to write just now, so I will close with the very best wishes and my respects to your Mam and Dad, and fondest and dearest love to my own darling Phine, from your ever loving Leslie.

XXXXXXX

17th August 1915

My dearest Phine

I received your letter of Friday the 13th. I was very glad to hear you had got rid of that awful toothache. I do hope you will not have it again.

I am hoping that you will receive this letter on the 19th. I believe that is your birthday, is it not? If I am you must excuse me, as I do not know one day from another out here.

I had a walk through the village last night, but I could not see anything that was any good as a present, and they charge the English always twice as much, so I must ask you to wait until I come back home.

Well Phine my darling, I must close. With best wishes and respects to your Mam and Dad and very many happy and pleasant returns of your birthday, with fondest and dearest love and many kisses to my own darling Phine, from your ever loving Leslie.

XXXXXXXXXX

20th August 1915

My dearest Leslie

I received your letter and birthday card yesterday and a field service card this morning. I was so pleased to hear from you, also so pleased to hear you are still quite well. Dear Leslie, thank you very much for the two cards, they are very nice. I think more of those than if you sent me a present and the two pieces of flowers.

Mam is going have them framed for me, so I think they will look very nice, don't you Leslie?

Dear Leslie, I had nice big box of Rowntree's Whipped Cream Walnuts from Mademoiselle for my birthday and your Mam sent me a nice handbag, and Mabel a birthday card.

Dear Leslie, do you remember this time last year when you were in our house? I wish you were home this year, still never mind it can't be helped. I hope you will be home this time next year, don't you?

Dear Leslie, I am sending you some of my birthday present. I couldn't eat them without sending you any. Dear Leslie, I had sent you a packet of Players this time. When you come home I see you were smoking them so I thought you like them best. Dear Leslie, I don't think there is any more news now so I will close now. Mam and Dad send you their best respects and hope for your safe return. So I will close with very best of love and kisses to my own darling Leslie, from your ever loving Phine.

XXXXXXX

P.S. Dear Leslie, excuse me not writing because I have been busy.

XXXX

26th August 1915

My dearest Phine

I received your letter of the 22nd and the cigarettes as well, thank you very much dear, they came just at the right moment. I had not a single one left and just was thinking how to get some when your letter came. I was awfully pleased, as the allowance we have now is so very short. I am sorry to say I have not received the chocolates or the packet of Players yet, perhaps they have gone astray. If so, it is the first time any of your letters have done so. I cannot understand it, were they packed securely? Perhaps they have been smashed in the post. Still never mind dear, thank you very much for sending them, I may receive them yet.

I think you ought to have gone up to London, the day out would have done you the world of good, you do not go out enough. No wonder you have toothache, that is why you were looking so pale when I was on leave. You only wrote the other day and said you had only been out four times since I came back. I know what it is, you are afraid of the Zeppelins coming over. Have you heard from Mick lately, I expect he is still hanging on for the end of the war? I often think of him, and how awful it must be, being confined all that time. Still roll on and the good times we shall have when we reach old England over again.

Well dearest, I must say au revoir once again, with my best wishes and respects to your Mam and Dad and all my fondest and dearest love and kisses to my own darling Phine, from your ever loving Leslie.

XXXXXXX

31st August 1915

My dearest Leslie

I received your card this morning and was so pleased to hear from you, also to hear you are still quite well. Dear Leslie, I am sorry I did not write before because I have been busy.

Dear Leslie, Mam had a card from Mick and he never said he received Mam's parcel. It said in the paper that you must not send the prisoners any tin stuff, so Mam said that is why he has not received her parcels, don't you.

Dear Leslie, I don't think there is any more news so I will close with very best of love kisses to my own darling Leslie, from your ever loving Phine.

XXXXXX

3rd September 1915

My dearest Leslie

Just a line hoping you are in the best of health as it leaves me at present.

Dear Leslie, Mam is going to let me have a day's outing this Sunday week. She is going to write and ask your Mother can I go up there. I wish you were there as well, it seems as though I have not seen you for years. I hope this war will soon be over, some people say here that it will last years and I hope not, don't you Leslie?

Dear Leslie, I am going to tell you something I know you will laugh. The other night we stop up till past eleven and I was upstairs and came down for something and fell down the stairs. It made Mam jump, she thought I was killed. I only hurt my back a bit. That was last week and it still hurts me.

Dear Leslie, I don't think there is any more news now. Mam and Dad send you their best respects and hope for your safe return.

So I will close now dear with very best of love and kisses to my own darling Leslie, from your ever loving Phine.

XXXXXX

6th September 1915

My dearest Phine
I have received your letter of the 3rd. I was awfully sorry to hear your back still hurts you, I hope it is nothing serious. I did not laugh; it might have injured you for life. I hope your back will soon be better, hoping you enjoy yourself when you go to London, I do wish I was there as well. With fondest dearest love and kisses from Les.
XXXXXXX

A Zeppelin is a cigar shaped rigid airship which varies in length from 120 meters upwards. It was first designed by its German inventor Count Ferdinand von Zeppelin in the late 1800's by being the first rigid airship. It was used for commercial transport and manufactured by several different manufactures in the early 1900's. Prior to WW1 the German Navy and Army saw the potential of using the airship design to carry out bombing raids on land and oversea. This gave birth to the first airship bombing raids in British history, these first took place in January 1915 over Great Yarmouth, King's Lynn and then eventually happening in London. These menacing airships were phrased by the British as being "Zeppelins" after their inventor. The Zeppelins struck terrible fear and destruction to the civilian population as they continued bombing several times throughout the war killing and injuring many innocent civilians including women and children.

Air raids over London, Zeppelins above.

My dearest Leslie

I received your letter Thursday and was so pleased to hear from you, also to hear you are still quite well.

Dear Leslie, I am sorry I did not write before because I have been busy all this week. You will be pleased to hear that I am going to work up the Army pay office where Dad works, only for a short time. I am filling in separation forms but we have hundreds to do yet.

Dear Leslie, I hope you will excuse me not writing before because I don't get much time not now, I am working overtime at present. I have to be there at 9 o'clock in the morning until 7 o'clock at night.

Dear Leslie, that last letter you sent it was four days coming.

Dear Leslie, have you heard of that big air raid on London and other places?

Mrs Hunn, the lady who lives next door to us, she stopped up to see them the other night and she could hear it but not see it.

Dear Leslie, I don't think there is any more news now, so I will close now. Mam and Dad send you their best respects, and dearest and fondest love to my own darling Leslie, from your ever loving Phine.

XXXX

13th September 1915

My dearest Leslie

I received your card this afternoon and was pleased to hear from you, also to hear you are still quite well.

Dear Leslie, we had another air raid last night but no people killed or any damage done.

Dear Leslie, they have got two big aircraft guns on Shenfield Common.

Dear Leslie, I don't think there is any more news now, so I will close. Mam and Dad send their best respects and hope for your safe return. I will close now dear Leslie with very best of love and kisses to my own darling Leslie, from your ever loving Phine.

XXXX

15th September 1915

My dearest Phine

I received your letter this morning, and was glad to hear you are still well. Do you remember this day a year ago, when our Battalion left London for the Front? Fancy a whole year and I have only seen you once whilst I had the seven day leave. I hope it shall not be out of England this time next year. I hope you like your new situation, although it seems a long time from nine in the morning until seven at night. I suppose I shall have to be satisfied with fewer letters now you are so busy. Still roll on when there are no separation forms to be filled in, then the war will be over.

I heard about the air raid, we are able to get the English papers the same day as they're published out here, where we are stationed at present. They seem to have done an awful amount of damage. The fellows who are on leave come back and tell us all about it, it seems that the last raid they made, they went right over Mother's house. I always worry and wait for your next letter when they make a raid.

Well Phine dear, I have no news. I am just as well as ever, and still resting away from the firing line. So once again au revoir, with my kind regards and the best of wishes to your Mam and Dad, hoping they are still enjoying the best of health, and fondest love to my own darling Phine, from your ever loving Leslie.

XXXXX

P.S. I noticed that you had my initials right on the envelope of your last letter, I meant to tell you, as there are two of our initials are reversed, the same as you used to put them.

XXXXXX

15th September 1915

My dearest Leslie

I have received your letter yesterday and was so pleased to hear you also are still quite well.

Dear Leslie, my back is better now. I suppose you have heard about the air raid they had in London the other day. We were frightened about your Mother if they dropped any bombs near her. They dropped some on Liverpool St. and in the centre of the city.

Dear Leslie, Mam is going to try and take Mona and the baby to Southend on Sunday to see if it does their whooping cough any good, they have got it awful. Mam said it is the old house, it is damp as it can be.

Dear Leslie, I don't think there is any more news now so I will close now. Mam and Dad send their best respects and hope for your safe return, and dearest and fondest love to my own darling Leslie, from your ever loving Phine.

XXXXX

18th September 1915

My dearest Leslie

I received your letter this morning and was very pleased to hear from you, also to hear you are still quite well. Dear Leslie, I hope they will send you home for a little while for the winter, don't you? Mam said if the first lot come home who went out just after the war started, her brother Pat will come with them, so would Mick if he was not a prisoner, poor fellow.

Dear Leslie, I dreamt about you last night. I dreamt you were home for good. When I woke up this morning I said to Mam I wish it was true. Dear Leslie, I don't like being up the Army Pay Office, there are too many men paid in the room where we are. Some of the girls like it, but I don't like it. One night last week one of the Army pay corp fellows asked to see me home, but I said no thank you, my Father will see me home; I am glad it is only for three or four weeks.

Dear Leslie, I don't think there is any more news now so I will close. Mam and Dad send you their best respects and hope for your safe return, and fondest and dearest love to my own darling Leslie, from your ever loving Phine.

XXXXXXX

21ˢᵗ September 1915

My dearest Leslie

I received your card yesterday dated 18ᵗʰ and was very pleased to hear from you, also to hear you are still quite well.

Dear Leslie, Dad found a nice brooch the other day, it is only brass and it's got Grenadiers Guard on the bottom of it, and it has got G.G. in the middle, it looks like a button on it, Dad found it.

Dear Leslie, they have got three aircraft guns and a search light on Shenfield Common. We see plenty of aeroplanes about here now, as I was coming home the other day I see three and one not long ago.

Dear Leslie, I wonder will they send you home for a little while for the winter? They ought to because you were out there last winter.

Dear Leslie, I don't think there is any more news now, so I will close. Mam and Dad send you their best respects and hope for your safe return, and fondest and dearest love to my own darling Leslie, from your ever loving Phine.

XXXXX

26ᵗʰ September 1915

My darling Leslie

Just a line to let you know I am still quite well. Dear Leslie, I have not heard from you for 10 days. I hope there is nothing the matter with you or I expect you are busy now.

Dear Leslie, Mick wrote for a pair of boots and Mam has just sent them. Dear Leslie, I have written ever so many letters but have not had any answer. Dear Leslie, I don't think there is any news now so I will close. Mam and Dad send their best respects and hope for your safe return, and fondest and dearest love to my own dearest Leslie, from your ever loving Phine.

XXXXXXXX

1ˢᵗ October 1915

My dearest Leslie

I received your card yesterday dated 26ᵗʰ. It was the first one for over a week. I thought you were killed. I was thinking all sorts of things. Mam wrote and asked your Mother if she had heard from you.

Dear Leslie, I was going up to see your Mother this weekend but she wrote back and said she was going to see Mabel, so I am going next week. Mam had a letter from your Mother this morning and she wants me to stop a few days, Mam said I can stop the week.

Dear Leslie, I was delighted when I had that card yesterday. I was as pleased as if anybody had given me five pounds. I kept saying to Mam before it came I would give anybody five pounds for a card. I was watching for every post.

Dear Leslie, I don't think there is any more news now so I will close. Mam and Dad send you their best respects and hope for your safe return, and fondest and dearest love to my own dearest Leslie, from your ever loving Phine.

XXXXXXXXXXXXXXXXXXXXXXXXXX.

4th October 1915

My dearest Leslie

I received your letter and money on Saturday and was so pleased to hear from you, also to hear you are still quite well. Mam was so pleased with the money she got, 7/6. It just come in time. Mam always sends Mick a parcel on Saturday. Dear Leslie, Mona is better from her whooping cough but the baby is just the same. Dear Leslie, I don't think there is any more news now so I will close. Mam and Dad send you their best respects and hope for your safe return, and fondest and dearest to my own darling Leslie, from your ever loving Phine.

XXXXXXXX

6th October 1915

My dearest Phine

I have received your letter of the 1st, also the previous ones you have sent. I am awfully sorry to have you waiting for any news, but we have not been able to send any letters, except when we get a green envelope, and they are very rare. You will see by the papers that we are having a very busy time but am glad to say I am still in the best of health, and have got rid of the abscess in my face.

Rather an expensive price to give for an old postcard, £5 don't you think so? I wished I could have been near at the time. I would have given you a packet of them for £5 or even 5 pence.

You have made me start wishing again, when you tell me you are going to stop at Mother's for a week. Roll on when I can get there as well, you will be out there for another warm time then. I'd like to be able to ruffle your mane for you again, I'd give anybody 5 pounds to be able to do it. I hope you enjoy yourself when you stay there.

We are having rather an unpleasant time just at present. The weather is very cold and awfully wet. Just lately we have had several nights out all the night hanging about for 13 or 14 hours on sentry waiting to guide the Battalion about to their respective places. I was out last night with SGT Tomblin (Little Jock) and to liven things up a bit he kept singing to me "Nobody Knows and Nobody Cares". It sounded quite pathetic in the deserted village with all the houses blown down and the shells dropping not far away.

It is just a year ago, today since we landed in Belgium and entrained to Bruges, fancy I never thought we should be out here in twelve months' time and starting on a second year of it, oh well! Never mind, roll on.

Well my darling I must close now, I will write you again as soon as I get the opportunity, with my best wish and kind regards to your Mam and Dad, hoping they are still enjoying the best of health, and fondest and dearest love and kisses to my own darling Phine, from your ever loving Leslie.

XXXXXXX

P.S. Please excuse paper and my awful scribble.

Green envelopes

Green envelopes were introduced in March 1915 and were designed to reduce the time taken in having the letters censored. Troops could then send letters regarding private matters back home to their loved ones and family.

There was a section on the outside of the envelope for the soldier to sign and honour that he had not put any information regarding military matters. A percentage of them were censored. The envelopes were only given out sparingly each week, so the troops had to make the most of them.

7th October 1915

My dearest Leslie

I received your card yesterday and was very pleased to hear from you, also to hear you are still quite well.

Dear Leslie, I hope your toothache is better. I have had it two nights, it does not pain me much in the day time. Dear Leslie, Mam met Sgt Payne when she was out. Mam said he looked as old as a man of 30 or more, he is going out the Front next week, so he told Mam.

Dear Leslie, I have finished work at the Army Pay Office last Saturday.

Mam and the babies and I am going to see your Mother on Sunday, but your Mother wants me to stop a few days as Dad said I might as well stop the week. Mabel is going to show me all the damage the Zeppelins have done. Dear Leslie, I don't think there is any more news so I will close. Mam and Dad send you their best respects and hope for your safe return, and fondest and dearest love to my darling Leslie, from your ever loving Phine.

XXXXXXXXXXX

11th October 1915

My dearest Leslie

Just a line hoping you are in the best of health as it leaves me at present. Dear Leslie, Mabel and I went in the Tower this morning, it was very nice, it was the first time I have been in there. Dear Leslie, it looks very lonely without you, I wish you were here, still never mind I expect you will be here someday, let's hope. Dear Leslie, I am going to have my photo taken while I am here so I will send you one.

Dear Leslie, I don't think there is any more now so I will close with fondest and dearest love to my own darling, from Phine

XXXXXXXX

13th October 1915

My dearest Phine

I received your letters of the 4th and 7th and today I received your letter of the 11th. I am sorry to hear you have had toothache again, I hope it will soon be better.

I hope you have an enjoyable time whilst you are in London, and please do not forget to send me the photo you have promised me. I should very much like to have another one of you, the other one is getting slightly soiled, and it is about two years since you had it took I think.

We are still very busy, still on the go, I expect there will be plenty of news in the papers in a day or two.

So you have finished working at the Army Pay Office, I am glad in a way, it was rather long hours don't you think?

What time do you arrive in the morning whilst you are staying in London this time about 6 o'clock in the afternoon, or is it a bit later this time? I should like to be there with you, still I suppose the time will soon come now, I think we are nearing the end.

Tell my Mother I have not heard from her lately, and that I am quite well and in the best of health.

Well I will close now dearest, with fondest and dearest love to my own darling, from your ever loving Leslie

XXXXXXX

Leslie's Battalion took part in the Hohenzollern redoubt near Auchy-Les-Mines which was part of the Battle of Loos

14th October 1915

My dearest Leslie

I received your card dated 9th on Tuesday. I was very pleased to hear from you, also to hear you are still quite well. Dear Leslie, a Zeppelin came over here last night. I was frightened to death, I was shaking from head to foot. It is the first time I have seen one. Dear Leslie, I am enjoying myself very much. I went to see the damage they done this morning, they have broken a lot of windows.

Dear Leslie, I wish you were here, it feels very lonely. I don't think there is any more news now so I will close with very best of love and kisses to my own darling Leslie, from your ever loving Phine.

XXXXXXXX

13th October Zeppelin raid over London
The raid was described as the 'Theatre Land raid' as bombs were dropped in the evening of 13th October on the Lyceum Theatre in Westminster, causing damage and wounding and killing many people. The five German Zeppelins also dropped bombs on Holborn. The total killed was 71 and 128 injured. This raid took place only 2.5 miles from where Leslie's mother and father were living and at the same time as Phine was staying over.

18th October 1915

My dearest Leslie
I received your card this morning dated the 16th and was very pleased to hear from you, also to hear you are still quite well., while I was at your Mother's. I had a letter from you when I came home on Saturday night. I did enjoy myself. I went all over the place, I was sorry to come back. Dear Leslie, I don't think there is any more news now, so I will close. Mam and Dad send you their best respects and hope for your safe return. With fondest and dearest love to my own darling Leslie, from your ever loving Phine.

XXXXXXXX

23rd October 1915

My dearest Leslie
I received your two cards dated the 17th and 19th and was very pleased to hear you are still quite well also to hear from you. Dear Leslie, I have had my photo taken but they have not come yet, the man is very busy.

Dear Leslie, we have got to have two men staying with us but only to sleep dear[18]. I have not heard from you since I have been back, only those two cards. Dear Leslie, I don't think there is any more news now so I will close, with fondest love to my own darling Leslie, from Phine.

XXXXXXXXX

24th October 1915

My dearest Phine

I am awfully sorry I have not been able to write you before but we are still so busy, time is so precious just at present. I expect now the winter is coming on we shall have plenty of time hanging on our hands.

I am glad you had an enjoyable time whilst you was in London. Mother told me of the scene you had at the railway station, how you kept losing Mabel and the dashing about to find her. Quite an exciting time altogether.

I should like to have been at home to see the Zeppelin. I have never seen one yet. Plenty of aeroplanes and fights in the air, but never a Zepp. I expect it gave you a slight idea of what the war is like.

Well I will write you again dearest, when I have time to spare. Will close now, with the best of good wishes to your Mam and Dad, and fondest and dearest love to my own darling Phine, from your ever loving Leslie.

XXXXXXX

26th October 1915

My dearest Leslie

I received your two cards this morning and was very pleased to hear from you, also to hear you are still quite well.

Dear Leslie, my photo will be done this week so I will send one as soon as I get them.

Dear Leslie, I have not had a letter for a fortnight, I expect you are busy.

Dear Leslie, we have got three men staying with us now.

Dear Leslie they don't half make me feel miserable. Every time I see them, I wish it was you. My dear Leslie, I don't think there is any more news now so I will close. Mam and Dad send you their best respects and hope for your safe return, with fondest and dearest love to my own darling Leslie, from your ever loving Phine.

XXXXXXXXXXX

31st October 1915

My dearest Phine

I received your last letter of the 23rd. I was glad to hear you are still quite well.

We are back now for a few weeks' rest, and we are glad of it too, it is getting awfully cold out here and we are having plenty of rain lately.

Well nothing exciting is happening out here just as yourself, there is no news to tell you, I expect we shall be settling down for the winter in a week or two.

We are billeted in a very nice place, the lady of the house looks after us like a Mother, she has invited us to supper tonight, we are having a rabbit pie. A decent meal for once in a way.

I am looking forward for the photo, when they are finished. I am in charge of the Drummers once again, as the Drum Major is on leave in England for 7 days. I am beginning to wish I was him having 3 separate leaves already. Still the next leave I want is when I come home for good.

We were supposed to have been inspected by the King last Friday only unfortunately he fell off his horse and injured himself. It was good for us in a way as it was pouring down with rain.

I see Sgt Payne has come out again, he has re-joined my Company, but I have not had a chance of having a good talk with him yet, to see if Warley has altered at all, since I was there last.

Well I cannot think of any more to write now dearest, so I will close with the best of wishes to your Mam and Dad and hopes that the news from Mick is still good, and with best and fondest love to my own darling Phine, from your ever loving Leslie.

XXXXXXX

My dearest Leslie
I received your letter last night dated 28th. I was very pleased to hear from you also still quite well.

Dear Leslie, my photo is not done yet because the man is very busy. We heard that the King fell off his horse last night in the papers.

Dear Leslie, I wish this blessed war was over. It seems as if it is getting worse instead of better. Dear Leslie, I am sorry I did not write before, but I don't get much time now because these men make such a lot of work. I will be glad when they are gone, one of them is a Copl and the others are privates.

Dear Leslie, I wonder when you will get leave. I don't suppose you will get another one, not for a long time. Dear Leslie, Mam has not heard from Pat for a long while now. Dear Leslie, I don't think there is any more news now. Mam and Dad send you their best respects and hope for your safe return, so I will close, with very best of love and kisses to my own darling Leslie, from your ever loving Phine.

XXXXXXXX

6th November 1915

My dearest Phine
I received your letter of the 1st and I am pleased to hear you are quite well. We are beginning to get busy again, and move from our resting billets at the beginning of next week, so perhaps it might be a few days before I will be able to write you again.

We had a concert here last night and the night before given by the band, it was splendid, I am glad I went, it seemed years and years since I heard them play last.

We are having awful unusual weather now, it is perishing at night and every morning a thick frost, I expect it will start snowing any day now.

Well I am expecting another leave but I do not suppose it will take me until the new year has started. Still I am not worrying about it, I had to wait too long for the last. Well dearest, I will conclude this short letter in order to catch the mail. With best wishes and my respects to your Mam and Dad and fondest and dearest love to my own darling Phine, from your ever loving Leslie.

XXXXXX

12th November 1915

My dearest Leslie

I received your letter yesterday and was very pleased to hear from you, also to hear you are still quite well. Dear Leslie, Mam had a letter from your Mother and she said that the two ladies upstairs have got the whooping cough.

My dear Leslie, Colonel Brook asked Dad would I go and help the servant to do the work until the cook comes back, she is getting married tomorrow, I am only going today, Friday, until next Tuesday.

Dear Leslie, I don't think there is any more news now. Mam and Dad send you their best respects and hope for your safe return, so I will close, with fondest and dearest love to my own darling Leslie, from your ever loving Phine.

XXXXXXXXX

14th November 1915

My dearest Leslie

Just a line hoping you are quite well as it leaves me at present.

Dear Leslie, did you receive the photo and postcard I sent to you in the week? I have not heard from you for nearly a week.

Dear Leslie, Mam had a card from Mick this morning and he said that the boots and cardigan they fitted him fine, he said that he is working in a clay pit.[19] Dear Leslie, I don't think there is any more news now. Mam and Dad send you their best respects and hope for your safe return, so I will close, with very best of love and kisses to my own darling Leslie, from your ever loving Phine.

XXXXXX

16th November 1915

My dearest Phine

I received your letter of the 9th also the card, I think it is very nice, thank you very much.

I am sorry I have not written before, but we have been on the move quite a lot just lately. It is getting awfully cold out here, still we do not have to go in the trenches, so I cannot grumble.

Enclosed you will find 10fs for some cigarettes for Mick, when your Mam sends this Xmas parcel. I am very sorry to hear that you have had no news from Pat, I hope he is quite well.

I am waiting to hear from home. I have not heard for about three weeks or more. Mail has been held up for three days, so perhaps that is the reason.

Well I must not stop to write more now, so I will conclude, with my very best wishes to your Mam and Dad, hoping they are quite well, and fondest and dearest love and many kisses to my own darling Phine, from your ever loving Leslie.

XXX

19th November 1915

My dearest Phine

I have received your two letters of the 12th and the 14th and was very glad to hear from you. You asked me in your last letter if I received your photo and also the card you sent. Yes, my dear, I did. Did you not receive my two letters in answer? I answered by return of post to each of them. When I had your photo, I answered immediately it was very good indeed, I am awfully pleased with it and have nearly worn it out with looking at it.

Perhaps my letters have been delayed. Well dearest, how did you like being out of service for a few days, you are having quite a variety of different situations.

I have been very busy today making a currant pudding for dinner. It was a fair success anyhow everybody ate it, although tonight they are all complaining of pains in the stomach. They say it was my fault for not putting a pinch of salt in the flour, of course I said I was cook, and it did not require it. I don't know if I was right or not.

It is getting very cold out here, but no snow yet awhile, they tell me you are having plenty in England.

Well I will close my short letter as it is so late, so au revoir, with the best of wishes to your Mam and Dad and fondest and dearest love and many kisses to my darling Phine, from your ever loving Leslie.

XXXXXXXXXXXXXXXXXXXXXXXX

23rd November 1915

My dearest Leslie

Just a line hoping you are still quite well as it leaves me at present.

Dear Leslie, I sent two cards like that what I sent you. I expect it got delayed.

Mam had a letter from your Mother about a week ago. Dear Leslie, I have just received your letter as I was writing this letter. I was very pleased to hear from you. Dear Leslie, one of our men what we have got here he Swank awful. He went away on Friday for four days, he has just come back. I wish he had never come back, he makes an awful noise when he goes up the stairs. Dear Leslie, I don't think there is any more news now. Mam and Dad send their best respects and hope for your safe return, so I will close, with fondest and dearest love to my own darling Leslie, from your ever loving Phine.

XXXXX

26th November 1915

My dearest Leslie

I have just received your four cards. I was very pleased to hear from you and also to hear you are still quite well. Dear Leslie, I wish you were coming home for

Christmas, I hope you will be spared to come home for the new year. Dear Leslie, have you received the cigarettes I sent you?

Mick wrote home for a Christmas pudding so Mam is sending him one on Monday. It takes six weeks to get there. Dear Leslie, I don't think there is any more news now, so I will close, with fondest and dearest love to my own darling Leslie, from your ever loving Phine.

XXXXXXXXXXXXXXXXXXX

My dearest Leslie

I received your two letters 8th and 16th and also three cards this week. I was very pleased to hear from you, also to hear from you are in the best of health.

Dear Leslie, the card which I had yesterday I only had Les on it, so I expected that is because you never had a letter. I see on the others where you have received letters you have put with fondest love Les. I will pay you out when you come home if God spares you. I don't suppose you have heard any more about coming home on leave.

Dear Leslie, I told you in my last letter that I was over at Colonel Brooks, I did not like it. I would never go to service, it is too hard. Dear Leslie, Mam thanks you very much for the money, she thinks it was very kind of you.

Dear Leslie, I don't think there is any more news now, so I will close, with fondest and dearest love to my own darling Leslie, from your ever loving Phine.

XXXXXX

2nd December 1915

My dearest Phine

I have received your letters quite safe, I am awfully sorry I have not written before, but I never seem to get a chance as we change our billets every two days now, and we never seem to be settled.

I expect you are wondering what is the matter. I sent that card in a hurry with just Les on it, so when you wrote and told me I sent four cards at once to make up for it.

We are having awful cold weather. I shall not be sorry when it is all over, I am just about getting fed up at the best, still I suppose it will wear off.

I received the cigarettes, quite safe, thank you very much.

Well I am very busy dearest, so I will write you again when I have a chance, so once again au revoir, with best wishes to your Mam and Dad, and fondest and dearest love to my own darling Phine, from your ever loving Leslie.

XXXXXXX

P.S. Excuse my awful scribble, but I am in such a hurry to get this letter off and the house in this billeting is maddening. Everybody seems to have gone mad.

5th December 1915

My dearest Leslie
I received your card and letter dated the 1st and 2nd I was very pleased you are still quite well, Dear Leslie I am sorry to hear you are so miserable never mind you must cheer up, I will be very glad when this blessed war is over it is enough to give anybody the pip. Dear Leslie Mam heard this morning that the Guards were coming home for the winter it was Mr Rudd who told her, I hope it is true. Dear Leslie you didn't half frighten me when I read the letter saying that all the people in the house had gone mad what did you mean. Dear Leslie I have heard two or three people say that the Grenadier Guards have gone to Serbia is it true. Dear Leslie I don't think there is any more news now Mam and Dad sends you their best respects and hopes to see you soon so I will close with fondest and dearest love to my own darling Leslie
From your loving Phine

XXXXXXXXXXXXXXXXXX

8th December 1915

My dearest Phine
I received your letter of the 4th and was pleased to hear from you, and to know you are quite well. I am sorry to hear your Mam has been unwell, I hope she is better by now and quite well again.

I hope you will forgive me for not writing before this, but we hardly seem to have time, we are always on the move. The weather is simply awful, not very cold, but wind and rain and mud up to our knees. The day before yesterday we were billeted in an old barn. We were at practice[20] at the time, when a big gust of wind blew the roof off. We all managed to dodge out safe and sound, except two horses, but though they were buried under the bricks and beams, they were not hurt at all. I think it was one of the closest shaves we have had out here. Only one chap cut his hand, the remainder of us treated it as a great joke.

I have not heard any more about leave, but am just waiting till the time comes, I expect it will be after Xmas. Still the time will come, I am longing to see you again soon. Well I will close now dearest, with best wishes to your Mam and Dad, and fondest and dearest love to my own darling Phine, from your ever loving Leslie.

XXXXXXXXXXXXXXXXXX

10th December 1915

My dearest Phine
I received your letter of the 5th, and was pleased to hear from you. Glad to say I got over my fit of depression, I am quite happy again now, only fed up out here now and again.

No dearest it is only a yarn about us coming home for the winter, quite a lot were saying so out here, but it is untrue. Good heavens, do people think that the Guards cannot stick the winter out here? We did it last winter and what we have done once we can do again. There certainly was a rumour about us going to Serbia, but there is nothing in it, and I am sure we do not want to go there. What amused me about your letter was that you asked me if the Grenadiers had gone to Serbia, and yet I am writing to you from France and you are writing me here and asking if we are gone. Still I suppose one must make allowances for anybody Irish.

Well I have no news, it is just the same day after day, so once again au revoir, with the best of wishes to your Mam and Dad and fondest and dearest love and kisses to my own darling Phine, from your ever loving Leslie.

XXX

15th December 1915

My dearest Leslie
I received your letter last night dated the 10th and was pleased to hear from you, also to hear you are quite well.

Dear Leslie, Mam has not heard from Mick for about 5 or 6 weeks.

Dear Leslie, when I wrote and told you that I heard that the Guards had gone to Serbia I did not think that they would send you been as you were in the Drums.

Dear Leslie, I will be very pleased to see you again if God spares you.

Dear Leslie, I think there is not any more news now. Mam and Dad send you their best respects and hope to see you soon, so I will close, with fondest and dearest love to my darling Leslie, from your ever loving Phine.

XXXXX

16th December 1915

My dearest Phine
Glad to say I am still in the best of health. We are having a fairly easy time now, four days in the trenches and then four days in billets. It is rather wet, we have rain nearly every day, so you can imagine how muddy it is in the roads and in the trenches.[21]

I am pleased to say I receive all your letters now, it is unfortunate that all the others have gone astray, still never mind now.

I expect when you get this letter you will be counting the days to Xmas, I am sorry I cannot be there with you, but as I have told them at home, I must leave it till Easter. I expect we shall be nearly finished out here by then, and then for a good old time.

I thank you for your offer of anything I want, but we get all we require. We have plenty of gifts of vests, mittens, every day nearly. All I should like is a few cigarettes now and again, just a few in your letters, because they charge so much for a parcel to come. Only have them in the packet, because they get damaged otherwise please.

We are fairly safe where we are, we lose a man now and again unfortunately, with stray shots but there is no hard fighting. I expect it will start again when the winter has passed, and then I hope to help drive them back.

I see my name was mentioned in the "Weekly Dispatch" of the 13th as being wounded. That refers to when I was wounded in October last year, so if you saw it don't think I have been hit again.

Well Phine dear, I will close now to catch the post. Hoping to hear from you again very soon. Give my best regards to your Mam and Dad and wishes for a bright and Merry Xmas.

My thoughts are with you all at home in England so au revoir, with best and fondest love to my own darling Phine

From Leslie   XXXXX

17th December 1915

My dearest Phine

I received your letter of the 13th and was pleased to hear you are quite well.

You know you were asking me whether the yarn about Serbia was true, well I have just heard that we are going there next January. Whether it is true or not I cannot say, but still I am inclined to think it is and of course that will mean no leave. Still never mind, I suppose this war will end some day or other, and I am sure I shall live through it all, just to come back and be able to tease you.

I am sorry to hear your Mam has not heard from Mick lately, I hope all is well with him, perhaps his letters have been delayed with the Xmas rush on. I suppose they are all writing home for Xmas.

Well it takes us to be in the trenches on Xmas day, so just give us all an Xmas thought, and think of us when you are eating the Xmas pudding. I suppose we shall eventually have a Xmas altogether, perhaps next year.

Well I will close for now dearest, hoping your Mam and Dad are still in the best of health and fondest and dearest love to my own darling Phine, from your ever loving Leslie.

XXXXXXX

21st December 1915

My dearest Leslie

I received your letter last evening and card today. I was very pleased to hear from you, also to hear you feel better now but I am so sorry that you are likely to go to Serbia, I do hope it is not true. I have made up my mind for such a good time when you come home on leave and so has Mam. I have not sent you anything for Xmas, I was waiting until you came home, but still Leslie dear you may not go now, perhaps you will get leave this month, I wish you could try to. I am so disappointed, so is Mam as she said she did not feel well last time and she is gagging to give you a good teasing, but I feel sure you will come over now. Dear Leslie, thank you very much for the card, the words were very nice indeed. Dear Leslie, I don't think there is any more news now.

Mam and Dad send you their very best respects and hope to see you soon, so I will close with fondest and dearest love to my own darling, from your ever loving Phine. XXXXXXXXX.

P.S. Dear Leslie, hope we will see you soon.
From Phine
XXXXX

26th December 1915

My dearest Leslie

I received your card and was very pleased to hear from you, also to hear you are still quite well. Dear Leslie, Mam had a card from Mick saying he has not received any parcels since Mam sent the boots, she has sent three since then. Dear Leslie, have you heard if you're coming home, I hope you are. Is it true that you are going to Serbia? Dear Leslie, we have got another man staying with us now and he can play the piano. Dear Leslie, I don't think there is any more news now. Mam and Dad send their best respects and hope to see you soon, so I will close with fondest and dearest love to my darling love, from your ever loving Phine.

XXXXX

27th December 1915

My dearest Phine

I received your letter yesterday also the cards, and the one from your Mother, thank you very much. Glad to say we had a better Xmas day than I thought we should. We had a good dinner and in the evening, we had a bit of a concert till 11:30 pm, in fact under the circumstances we had a jolly fine time.

I liked your cards, they were very nicely worded. I am sorry I could not get a better one to send you, still it cannot be helped.

We have not heard any more about the going to Serbia business, so I hope it is not true. Still do not worry yourself dearest about my leave. I must sit tight and await my turn, it won't be long now. When I do come there will be another one to do the teasing your Mam and you, where do I come in, I can manage you easy.

Well Phine dear, I will close now. I want to catch the post, and also write a sympathetic letter to my brother Bruce. He has just written me a touching letter how his first love affair tragically ended. The young lady had given him up for an old friend back from the Front, and she would not give him the Brooch he bought back but sent him a photo of herself wearing it. And now he calls her an "old Jew". Very ungentlemanly, don't you think so? He consoles himself by playing football now. Well I will close now dearest, with fondest and dearest with very best wishes to your Mam and Dad and fondest and dearest love to my own Phine, from your ever true Soldier Boy, Leslie.

XXX

29th December 1915

My own dear Phine

I received your letter of the 26th, also your card and was glad to know you are still quite well.

Please make allowances for my card, it is the only one in the shop, and the only shop in town, and by the looks of the town I should think it was the only one in France (like it anyhow).

You ask me if we are going to Serbia, well I cannot say dearest, but there certainly is a big move coming off, and I think we are going elsewhere out of France, I am afraid.

Still, according to the rumours we shall have another leave first, but we do not depend on it, I don't want you to expect me, and then be disappointed. So, try and forget about it. Trust in God and we shall all be home for good in time. Although we may have to spend another Xmas away from home, I am thinking of you always that's what keeps me cheerful all the time.

Well I will let you know if anything happens dear, so now I will close once again, wishing you a bright and happy year to come, and fondest and dearest love to my own beloved Phine, from your ever true Leslie.

XXXXXXXX

My dearest Leslie

I received your letter last night and was very pleased to hear from you, also to hear you are quite well. Dear Leslie, I am very sorry I did not write before but I have been very busy this last week or two.

Dear Leslie, Mam has not heard from Mick for about a month. It was in the paper that four of Mick's Regiment have escaped from Germany. They were in the same camp as Mick is, so Mam is going to try and find out where he lives if she can. Dear Leslie, I don't think there is any more news now. Mam and Dad send you their best respects and hope for your safe return, so I will close with fondest and dearest love to my own darling Leslie, from your ever loving Phine.

XXXXXXXXXXX

29th December 1915

My dearest Leslie

I received your three cards dated 23rd 24th 25th and was very pleased to hear from you, also to hear you are still quite well. Dear Leslie, I have sent two letters before Christmas and one after. Have you heard any more about going to Serbia? I do hope you don't go and I hope we will see you soon. Dear Leslie, the Gloucesters, who we have got with us, said that they expect to go to the Front next month. I said to the fellow we got here that he ought to go out there and take your place and let you come home. I think you have done your bit, it seems a shame the poor fellow's out there while there is fellows at home sitting by the fire.

Dear Leslie, one of our chicks is very spiteful, he will not let Madgie or Mona go out in the yard. Prince[22] and the chick had a fight, when Mam see them she smacked the window and broke it. Dad did laugh when she done it. Dear Leslie, I don't think there is any more news now. Mam and Dad send their best respects and hope to see you soon, so I will close with fondest and dearest love to my own darling, from you ever loving Phine.

XXXXXXX

P.S. Dear Leslie, Mam and Dad and I expect to see you next week or the week after, please God.

XXX

31st December 1915

My dearest Leslie

I received your letter this morning and was very pleased to hear from you, also to hear you are still quite well. Dear Leslie, Mam had some bad news. She had a letter from Mick this morning and he told Mam that he was wounded through the right ear and out through the left side of his nose. Mam is upset, she has been crying all day long. Dear Leslie, I hope I will see you soon. I will tease you all the time you are here. I do hope that going to Serbia is not true. Dear Leslie, I don't think there is any more news now. Mam and Dad send their best respects and hope to see you soon, so I will close with fondest and dearest love to my own darling Leslie, from your ever loving Phine.

XXXXXXX

P.S. Dear Leslie, when do you expect to come on leave? XXX

Notes 1915

1. On the night of 19th and 20th January 1915 two German Zeppelin air ships flying from Hamburg were on their way to bomb Humberside. The strong winds managed to blow them off course which diverted the airships over Great Yarmouth and Kings Lynn where the Germans dropped their bombs. The bombing caused the deaths of four civilians and 16 others were injured.
2. Leslie's Battalion was relieved from the trenches in the Fleurbaix area and billeted in the village of Rue-du-Bois near La Bassée France.
3. The Battalion moved to the main Estaires–La Bassée road area, France.
4. Enteric fever – a form of typhoid.
5. Batt – Battalion.
6. Phine's father's working full time at the Army Pay Office at Warley Barracks.
7. Leslie's Battalion were having spells in and out of the trenches and were billeted in the town of Estaires, France.
8. Leslie's letters were censored by his Battalion company officers.
9. P.O. – postal order.
10. On 10th May 1915 Zeppelin L238 dropped bombs on Southend, killing one person and causing two casualties.
11. Phine's new sister Enna was born on 1st May 1915.
12. The new Mills grenade was issued to bombing parties in the company in May 1915, which resulted in new training on how to use these bombs.
13. Leslie's mother sent regular parcels to Mick in the prisoner of war camp, socks, shirts, food and money was collected and sent to him.
14. Motor Transport – A.S.C. Army Service Corps, their core purpose was transport and supplies. To enable this to happen they used horse and motorised transport, including railways and waterways. They were at the centre of many logistics, including supplies of food and ammunition to the Front.
15. C.O. – Commanding Officer.
16. Leslie sent a metal Grenadier Guards sweetheart brooch. This had the Grenadier Guards flaming grenade symbol on it, the same style as his brass cap badge.
17. The New Guards Division was formed. This contained all the separate Guards Battalions all in one division – Irish, Scots, Welsh Coldstream and Grenadier Guards.
18. As the war went on, more and more soldiers were stationed at Warley Barracks. This led to the need for more accommodation. It was decided that people's homes in Brentwood would be inspected and a survey made for billets, if requirements were met following the survey the occupants were to have at least two soldiers billeted with them.
19. Prisoners of war in Germany were put to work at destinations near or in the prison camps. These could have been mines/clay pits or farms depending on the location of the camp.
20. At practice – Leslie was practising playing musical instruments with his musicians.
21. Leslie and the Battalion were in the area of Rue-du-Bacquerot, Laventie.
22. Prince was the name of the Hazeltine's dog.

New year, new hope 1916

1916
Drums 1ˢᵗ Grenadier GRDS
2ⁿᵈ January 1916

My dearest Phine

I received your letter of the 29th. I was very pleased to hear from you. I am sorry to say I shall not be home again on leave as early as you expect. I have found that there are quite a lot of men who have not had a leave yet, anyhow I expect to be home about the beginning of March. It can't be possible before then. Still it is not so long to wait.

I was quite amused when you wrote about the chicken and Prince fighting. It must have been quite funny and then your Mam breaking the window. I think you will have to fatten that chick up for dinner, he is rather too ferocious.

We are having a rest of six days at the present time and tomorrow we are having our Xmas day, and celebrating it with a concert and a big dinner. From what I can see it will be quite a pleasant affair with the band there, etc.

Well I will conclude this short letter, hoping to see you again, very soon now, and also hoping your Mam and Dad are in the best of health. With fondest and dearest love to my darling Phine, from your ever loving Leslie.
XXXXXXXXX

2ⁿᵈ January 1916

My dearest Leslie

I received your letter and was very pleased to hear you are still quite well. Dear Leslie, I am sending Mick's letter on, what do you think of it? The men billeted here are going to Southend on Friday to guard the east coast because we have had another great air raid. Dear Leslie, I don't think there is any more now. Mam and Dad send you their respects and hope to see you soon, so I close with fondest and dearest love and lots of kisses to my own darling Leslie, from your ever loving Phine.
XXXXXXX

My dearest Leslie

I received your letter and card dated 29ᵗʰ Dec and was very pleased to hear from you, also to hear you are quite well. I was very pleased with the card, it was very nice. Dad is going to make a fretwork frame for the three of them. Dear Leslie, your Mother sent me six nice handmade handkerchiefs.

Dear Leslie,

I hope we will see you soon. I am looking forward for you coming home. I was surprised when I got the letter last time. I hope I will see you soon. Dear Leslie, Mam had another letter from Mick. I don't think there is any more news now. Mam and Dad send you their best respects and hope to see you, so I will close with fondest and dearest love and lots of kisses to my darling Leslie, from your ever loving Phine.

XXXXXX

4th January 1916

My dearest Phine

I received your letter dated the 29th, and was glad to hear from you again. I did not receive the two cards you mentioned, I received one, the other one must have got lost in the post. Well Phine dearest, this is only a short letter, and I think the last, till I come on leave. I expect to be home next week, I think I start about Monday or Tuesday night, and reach London the day following. I will write you immediately when I reach home, and come to Warley the next day.

So, to give me the good hiding you have promised me for some time, so au revoir for the present. With best wishes to your Mam and Dad, and fondest and dearest love to my own darling Phine, from your ever loving Leslie.

XXXXXX

5th January 1916

My dearest Leslie

Just a line hoping you are quite well as it leaves myself at present. Dear Leslie, I have sent you two lots of cigarettes and you have not said you had them. We have got two more men billeted with us in place of those others. Dear Leslie, I don't think there is any more news now so I will close with fondest and dearest love and lots of kisses to my own darling Leslie, from your ever loving Phine.

XXXXXXXXXXX

P.S. Excuse this short letter.

7th January 1916

My own dearest Leslie

I received your letter and was very pleased to hear from you, also to hear you are still quite well. Dear Leslie, I am sorry you are not coming home this month. Mam was looking forward for you coming home as well. Dear Leslie, I have got a cig case for your birthday. Mam said will I keep it until you come home. Mam thought it might get delayed, if you like I will send it. Dear Leslie, Mam had a letter from Bruce this morning and he is coming down this afternoon for a few hours and your Mother. Dear Leslie, I don't think there is any more news now. Mam and Dad send you their best respects and hope to see you soon, so I will close with fondest and dearest love and lots of kisses to my own darling Leslie, from your ever loving Phine.

7th January 1916

My dearest Phine

I received your letter of the 31st and was pleased to hear you are well. I was very sorry indeed to hear poor Mick had been wounded, and so badly.

Does he mean he was hit before he was captured, or just recently? By the way I read your letter it seems as if it had just happened I am very sorry, and sincerely hope it will not affect him in any way.

We are going back down country for another long rest next week, and I suppose it will be there, that I shall get my leave again. They have started the old hands again, and I am not very far from the top. By the end of February, I expect. I will close now with the best of wishes to your Mam and Dad and fondest and dearest love to my own darling Phine, from your ever loving Leslie.

XXXXX

10th January 1916

My dearest Leslie

I received your letter dated the 7th and was very pleased to hear from you, also to hear you are still quite well. Dear Leslie, when I wrote and told you that Mick was wounded I meant he was wounded and then taken prisoner. Dear Leslie, we have got the Irish Guards here you know, on Friday some of the men were throwing one of the bombs never exploded, until the men got near it, it killed two men instantly, four seriously wounded, one died in hospital and twelve slightly wounded. The three fellows are going to be buried tomorrow. Mam said you don't have to go out to the Front to get killed. Dear Leslie, your Mother and Bruce came down on Saturday tea time, Mam wanted some stout and Bruce came with me. Dear Leslie, Bruce is getting like you every day. He did make me feel miserable when he first came in because I wished it was you. Dear Leslie, I wish you was coming home for good I want you to come home and yet I don't because it makes me miserable when you go back. Dear Leslie, I don't think there is any more news now. Mam and Dad send you their best respects and hope to see you soon, so I will close with fondest and dearest love and lots of kisses to my own darling Leslie, from your ever loving Phine.

XXXXXXXXXX

13th January 1916

My dearest Phine

I received your letter of the 4th, also one tonight dated the 10th. I was glad to hear you are still well. I am returning Mick's letters, they are very interesting, I should think his wound has healed alright, still it must have been very painful and an awkward place to have it.

I must apologise for not writing before, but we are having quite a lot of changing about at present, and next week we go back for another long rest.

We are also busy at present, getting an orchestra together among the drummers. Quite hot too, we have violins, cornets, clarinets and flutes and play several of the old dances, including the "Incognito Waltz", the old favourite at the Warley dances. Only we have come to a stop now, we have no more music.

I see Mick's letter he is asking for some flute pasts of marches. I could send you a few if you think they would be of any use to him. Write and let me know.

Whilst writing this letter I have just received one that you wrote on the 7th, it has been delayed for a week. I think it would be best if you kept the cigarette case till I come home on leave thank you very much. I am glad I received this letter, because I was going to "Strafe" you for not writing me a letter on my birthday, so I'm glad to see you did remember.

Well I will close now dearest, with best wishes to your Mam and Dad, and fondest and dearest love to my own darling Phine, from your ever loving Leslie.

XXXXXXXXXXXXXXXXX

14th January 1916

My own dearest Leslie

Just a line hoping you are quite well as it leaves myself at present. Dear Leslie, I am very sorry I did not send you a birthday card. I never thought of your birthday until Saturday night when your Mother and Bruce went back. Mam went to the Essex Christmas tree and in the afternoon, took all the children. Dear Leslie, we have got one of the billeting men's wife here, she has been here for nearly a fortnight now. Dear Leslie, I will be very pleased when it is your turn to come home. It seems as though it is years since I see you last. Dear Leslie, I don't think there is any more news now. Mam and Dad send you their best respects and hope to see you soon, so I will close with fondest and dearest love and lots of kisses to my own darling Leslie, from your ever loving Phine.

XXXXXX

16th January 1916

My dearest Leslie

I received your card yesterday dated 13th and was very pleased to hear from you also to hear you are still quite well. Dear Leslie, I hope you are not offended me not sending you a birthday card, you did not forget to send me one. I am very sorry, still never mind I think just as much.

Dear Leslie, I don't think there is any more news now. Mam and Dad send you their best respects and hope to see you soon, so I will close with fondest and dearest love to my own darling Leslie, from your ever loving Phine.

XXXXXXXX

18ᵗʰ January 1916

My dearest Leslie

I received your letter yesterday dated the 13ᵗʰ of Jan. I was very pleased to hear from you, also to hear you are still quite well. Dear Leslie what did you mean that you would strafe me for not writing, one of the billeting men said it means damn you, I said you would not say that, mam said perhaps it was something in French.

Dear Leslie, would you mind sending the marches for Mick if you please, Dad said he will copy them out and send them back to you.

Dear Leslie, I don't think there is any news now. I am just going to help Mam do the washing. Mam and Dad, send you their best respects and hope to see you soon, so I will close with fondest and dearest love, from your ever loving Phine.
XXXXXXXXXXX

Drums, 1ˢᵗ Gren GDS
19ᵗʰ January 1916

My dearest Phine

I received your letters dated the 14ᵗʰ and 16ᵗʰ and was pleased to hear from you. Don't think I am offended because you did not send a birthday card, I quite understand. Just wait till I come home again, I will get my own back.

I have just written a letter to my brother Bruce telling him off for going to Warley. I could not see what there was to interest him there, also for escorting my young lady about when she goes out shopping. I suppose I shall get a saucy letter in reply.

Well things are still quiet out here, no news to tell, so I will close, hoping your Mam and Dad are quite well, with my best respects to them, and fondest love to my own darling Phine, from yours ever loving Leslie.
XXXXXXXXXXXXXXXXXXXXXXX

21ˢᵗ January 1916

My dearest Leslie

Just a line hoping you are still quite well as is myself at present.

Dear Leslie, I have just received your card as I had just started this letter dated 13ᵗʰ. Dear Leslie, we had a lot of Darby's men come in today, some of them have joined the Essex, there is some more coming in to join the 4ᵗʰ Gloucester's who are billeted with us.

Dear Leslie, Mam had another letter from Mick this morning. Mick wrote asking Mam to ask me to write to him, he said I was old enough to write letters.

Dear Leslie, it will not be long now before I see you now. Mam has not heard from Pat a long while now. Dear Leslie, I don't think there is any more news now. Mam and Dad send you their best respects and hopes to see you soon, so I will close with fondest and dearest love and lots of kisses to my own darling Leslie, from your ever loving Phine.
XXXXXXX

22nd January 1916

My dearest Leslie

I received your letter dated the 19th of Jan tonight. I was very pleased to hear from you, also to hear you are still quite well. Dear Leslie, have you received the cigarettes I sent you in my letter dated the 16th? Dear Leslie, you wrote your last letter on the day I was 16 and 4 months. Mam had a letter from Mick and it was dated the 6th of Jan. He said he had not received the parcel Mam sent him for Christmas, but perhaps he has got it by now. I hope he has, poor fellow. I think it must be awful out there. I am going to write to him now when I have finished this letter. Dear Leslie, I don't think there is any more news now. Mam and Dad both send you their best regards, so I will close with fondest and dearest love to my own darling Leslie, from your ever loving Phine.

XXXXX

25th January 1916

My dearest Phine

I received your letter dated the 18th also one today dated the 21st, and am glad to hear you are quite well.

I am sorry you thought I meant damn you when I wrote the word "STRAFE". It is a German word, what the Germans shout across to us in the trenches, and it only means "Perish you". Nearly all the men out here say it. It is like a slang word. Tell that chap who told you it meant damn, that he is only a "Brod" and he will soon know the meaning of "Strafe" when he comes out here. You know dearest I would not say such a thing to you.

I received your card, it is very nice indeed. Tell your Dad I will pick out some "Marches" and send them on tomorrow. I was glad to hear Mick is still well.

I am sorry to hear you have not heard from Pat, I hope he is alright and quite well.

Well it is getting near the end of the roll for leave now, they send 5 a night now, and there are about 50 more men to go, after that they start the top of the roll again, and I am not far down, so it will not be so very long now. Unless of course it happens to get stopped like they did this time last year, I don't think it will though.

Well Phine dear, this is all this time. Give my best respects to your Mam and Dad, hoping they are still in the best of health, and fondest and dearest love and kisses to my own darling Phine, from your ever loving Leslie.

XXXXXXXXX

29th January 1916

My dearest Leslie

I received your letter dated the 25th. I was very pleased to hear you are still quite well. Dear Leslie, have you received the cigarettes I sent you last week and two cards? Dear Leslie, it won't be long now before you will be home, I expect about another three weeks.

Dear Leslie, I don't think there is any more news now. Mam and Dad send you their best respects and hope to see you soon, so I will close with fondest and dearest love to my own darling Leslie, from your ever loving Phine.

XXXXXXXXXXXXXXXXXXXXXXXXXXXXXXXXXXXXXXXXXXXXX
XXXXXXXXXXXXXXXXXXXXXXXX

7th February 1916

My dearest Phine
I am awfully sorry to disappoint you, but the leave has been stopped.
I hear it has been stopped for a week only, but I do not know for certain. I will write again tonight and explain, as the post is just going now. So, au revoir with fondest love to my dearest Phine, from Leslie.
XXXXX

8th February

My dearest Phine
I suppose you have received my letter of yesterday, saying the leave has been cancelled. I hope you are not disappointed, it is hard times but cannot be helped.

The reason it has been stopped is because as soon as the men who are on leave are back, we are going to a different part in the line,[1] and shall have a very long march, of course as soon as we reach there and settle down, they will start the leave again. I heard it rumoured when we start again, but I will not say as I don't want to disappoint you again. So, I shall just wait till I reach England before I write and let you know. At all events, it will not be so very long to wait, and it is something to look forward to.

I was pleased to read Mick's letter, it was very interesting, especially the last part about the three chaps who want your address, a very nice photo indeed!

I am rather glad they are prisoners, although I should not say so.

Well which one are you going to have? I suggest the steward on the steamer, you see he is always away at sea, and it would give the other fellow a chance. You know the one I mean, he is out here, a big idle good for nothing, but he loves you very dearly, and he always will. I should write and tell Mick, it is too late or I shall be doing something desperate.

Well I heard about the big air raid, I was glad to hear they did not visit your part of the world, although they did a lot of damage. Roll on the end of this war I think it is about time they finished.

Did your dad receive the music I sent, will it do alright? I hope it will.

Well Phine dearest, my candle is burning very low so I must close, give my best respects and wishes to your Mam and Dad, hoping they are both in the best of health, and fondest and dearest love to my own darling Phine, from your ever loving Leslie.

XXX

P.S. Hoping to see you very soon now. Les.

XXXXXXXXXXXXXXXX

14th February 1916

My dearest Phine

I have received your letter dated the 7th, and was pleased to hear you are quite well dear.

You mentioned in your letter that you had sent me two lots of cigarettes but I am sorry to say I did not receive them. Did you send them in a letter, if so I have not received your letters? I can't think what is the cause, it is not the first time either. I don't mind not receiving the cigarettes, but I always look forward to your letters. I think it would be best not to send any more cigarettes, as they only get stolen.

Well dearest we start on a long march tomorrow to "somewhere else in France" so it may be a day or two before I shall write you again, but I will write at the first opportunity.

Well dearest, I will close now, I am hoping to see you very soon now, so best wishes to your Mam and Dad, and fondest and dearest love and lots of kisses to my own dearest Phine, from your ever loving Leslie.

XXX

17th February 1916

My dearest Leslie

I received your letter this afternoon and was very pleased to hear from you, also to hear you are still quite well as it leaves myself at present. Dear Leslie, I am sorry to hear your never received the cigarettes, I think it is a shame don't you? I am longing to see you now, expect you will be home about next week don't you? Dear Leslie, we have got two nice quiet men billeted here. They sit indoors at night and wear fancy clothes, they look very nice. Dear Leslie, I don't think there is any more news now, so I will close. Mam and Dad send you their best respects and hope to see you soon, with fondest and dearest love to my own darling Leslie, from your ever loving Phine.

22nd February 1916

My own dearest Leslie

Just a line hoping you are quite well as it leaves myself at present. Dear Leslie, I expect you will be coming home soon because Mrs Rudd told Mam yesterday that Sgt Holden came home last Friday and got married on Saturday. He lives up Warley. I know him by sight. Dear Leslie, the Gloucesters have gone away from here and we are getting the Scottish Rifles here, we are having two of them to stay. Dear Leslie,

I am awfully sorry I did not write before but I have been very busy with the shirts last week. Dear Leslie, I don't think there is any more news now. Mam and Dad send you their best respects and hope to see you soon, so I will close with fondest and dearest love and lots of kisses to my own darling Leslie, from your ever loving Phine.

XXXXXX

23rd February 1916

My dearest Phine

I received your letters of the 11th, 15th, and 17th and am pleased to hear you are still quite well. I am sorry to have not wrote before, but we have been so busy shifting about, you will see by the date of this letter, that we are quite near England.

We are having awful cold weather, quite near the sea,[2] and it rains and snows nearly all day long. So, make matters worse we are under canvas.

Well Phine dearest, I have no news, except to tell you the leave starts again next Sunday night. So, roll on not so long to wait now, so I will close now, with best wishes to your Mam and Dad and fondest and dearest love, from your ever loving Leslie.

XXXX

28th February 1916

My dearest Phine

I have just received your letter of the 22nd. It has been delayed owing to us changing about so just latterly. I am glad to hear you are quite well.

I expect to be coming home very shortly, I was coming home again on the 26th when they cancelled it again for the whole army. I think it was because it was too rough to cross the channel. It is expected to start again in a few days. It is awfully annoying to keep on disappointing you, still I keep on hoping and it will be all the sweeter when it does come.

I am feeling a little queer this evening, as I had to be inoculated again this afternoon. From how it feels now I think it will be a bit worse than before. Still I am excused for two days so I shall have a good rest.

As I have a bit of a headache, you must let me make it as an excuse for a short letter, so I will close now dearest.

With best wishes and my respects to your Mam and Dad and fondest and dearest love and lots and lots of kisses to my own darling Phine, from your ever loving Leslie.

XXXXXX

29ᵗʰ February 1916

My dearest Leslie

Just a line hoping you are quite well as it leaves myself at present. Dear Leslie, Dad has been moved into the huts what they have built for the Army Pay Corp. He has to sleep up there. We have had awful lot of snow, it has been snowing all this week. I wish you were coming home this week, I would give you a good hiding. I would snowball you, we have got plenty of snow in our yard, it comes over the tops of our shoes. Dear Leslie, I don't think there is any more news now. Mam and Dad send you their best respects and hope to see you soon, so I will close with fondest and dearest love to my own darling Leslie, from your ever loving Phine.
XXXXXX

6ᵗʰ March 1916

My own dearest Leslie

I received your card dated 4ᵗʰ and was very pleased to hear from you, also to hear you are still quite well. Dear Leslie, I don't suppose you will come home now because there was three hundred of the Irish Guards went out yesterday to the Front. Mam and I went up to Dad and had our tea there. As we went in the gate there was two Irish Guards passing by and one said to Mam, I should put her in the Guards – he meant me. He stopped and spoke to Mam and he said he had been wounded and was at a Hospital, then Mam told him that you were there, he asked what your name was and he said he knew you. Dear Leslie, Mam had a letter from Mick this morning. Dear Leslie, I don't think there is any more news now. Mam and Dad send you their best respects and hope to see you soon, so I will close with fondest and dearest love and lots of kisses to my own darling Leslie, from your ever loving Phine.
XXXXXXXXXXXXXXXXXXXXX

11ᵗʰ March 1916

My dearest Leslie

I received your letter yesterday dated and was very pleased to hear from you, also to hear you are still quite well as it leaves myself at present. Dear Leslie, I expect they are keeping the troops back from going on leave for this big battle but they won't tell you. But it is better late than never. Dear Leslie, it seems that something is telling me that you won't come home. Mam had another letter from Mick this morning and his photo, it is nothing like him. Mam would not have known him if he had not put on the back of the postcard where he was. Dear Leslie, I don't think there is any more news now. Mam and Dad send you their best respects and hope to see you soon, so I will close with fondest and dearest love and lots of kisses to my own darling Leslie, from your ever loving Phine.
XXXXXXXXXXXXXXXXXXXXXXXXXXXXXXXXXXXXXXXXXXXX

P.S. Dear Leslie I don't suppose you will come home now because the German Navy are out.

15th March 1916

My dearest Leslie

I received your card this morning dated the 12th and was very pleased to hear from you also to hear you are quite well. Dear Leslie, I have not had a letter for about a fortnight. I expect you have been busy and I don't suppose you will come home, it does not seem like it. The Scottish Rifles what we have in Brentwood and the Royal Scots, they are going to go to the coast next week. There is many tales going about here that the Germans are going to try and land, so I expect this is why they are keeping the troops back from coming on leave.

Dear Leslie, it is better waiting than have something happen to you on the sea, like the old tale better late than never. Dear Leslie, I don't think there is any more news now so I will close. Mam and Dad send you their best respects and hope to see you soon, so I will close with fondest and dearest love and lots of kisses to my own darling Leslie, from your ever loving Phine.

XXXXXXXXXXXX

17th March 1916

My dearest Phine

I suppose you are thinking awful things about me, for not writing you before, I am very sorry indeed, but I have not had a minute to spare. We have been changing about from place to place, every other day. I received your last 3 letters of the 29th, 6th and the 11th quite safe and am pleased to know you are quite well.

We have had a terrible lot of snow out here, more than eighteen inches deep. We were in tents at the time, and it was awfully cold.[3]

It has left me with a fine cold in the head, I have been quite queer for the last week, but feeling a bit better now.

I am rather glad the leave has been stopped whilst this weather is on, I'd much rather have it whilst it is warm. Besides I don't like being snowballed either.

You need not bother about any old German Navy being out, that is not what it is stopped for, it is as you say a big Battle coming off. Still, I shall be home very soon now, any day I might come.

"Young Titch" as you call him, has just come off a month's leave, for extending from the 12 to 21 years. He said he had a fine time, although it was rather cold. I would like to have been him.

Well Phine dearest, I have been writing this letter in snatchers and now I am wanted again, off somewhere else I suppose always on the move, we are so busy. So, I will close now, with best wishes and respects to your Mam and Dad, hoping they are quite well, and fondest and dearest love and kisses to my own darling Phine, from your ever loving and devoted Leslie.

XXXX

18th March 1916

My dearest darling Leslie

I received your card yesterday dated the 13th and was very pleased to hear from you, also to hear you are still quite well. Dear Leslie, I wrote a letter to Mick but I have not had any answer yet. I would send you Mick's photo but it might get lost in the post. Mam said she would not like to lose it because there are English, Irish, Scotch, French, Russian's and foul German sentries, so it will be something to keep when the blessed old war is over. I wish it was over tomorrow, it seems as though it is never going to end. The Irish Guards are giving a Saint Patrick's ball on Friday the 24th. I should like to go but I would not go without you. I should feel miserable all the time I was there. I should be thinking of you out in the trenches. They had their sports yesterday, they were very good. All the fellows of the Irish Guards were dressed up in fancy dress. I went up with Mam and the ladies. Dear Leslie, have you heard any more about coming home? They are keeping you a long time.

Dear Leslie, I don't think there is any more news now. Mam and Dad send you their best respects and hope to see you soon, so I will close with fondest and dearest love to my own darling Leslie, from your ever loving Phine.

XXXXXXXXXX

Back to the trenches
Leslie had been on leave to England and was now back in France.

No. 4 company 1st Grenadier Guards
1st April 1916

My dearest Phine

I had just sat down to write this when I received your letter. I did not get back till half past three yesterday morning (Friday). We had to stay at Boulogne till the next day, after staying all day at Folkestone, so you can guess we were awfully tired when we did arrive back home.

You see by the address that I am in No. 4 Coy, now, I have left the Drums. The Adjutant told me I should have to go back as it is getting near for me to be made Quarter-Master Sgt of one of the companies. So, I shall have to visit the trenches again now, still I shall be alright. I know God will watch over me, and my love for him and you darling, will help me through alright. I must wait now till I get promoted, and then I shall be alright again, no trenches then. Any how I feel I am doing my bit better than when I was with the Drums.

It makes me feel safe and strong to think that I am working for a girl at home like you. Don't worry I shall be alright, only roll on the end of it.

We have had splendid weather here, since I have been back, only I wished the same as you that I had not come on leave. It is so hard to leave all the loved ones at home.

Well I will close now darling, so au revoir, with best wishes to your Mam and Dad and fondest and dearest love and lots of kisses to my own dearest Phine, from your ever lovingly Leslie.

XXX

7th April 1916

My own dearest Leslie

I received your letter dated the 1st and was very pleased to hear from you, also to hear you are still quite well as it leaves myself at present. Dear Leslie, I am very sorry to hear you have left the Drums, still the summer is coming now, it won't be so bad as the winter in the trenches will it? I am quite proud to hear you are getting promoted. Dear Leslie, I am pleased to know that I am making you feel safe and strong. Mam said she is going to send you a bill in every month for my keep because you said you were working for a girl like me at home. We have had splendid weather, since you went back it has been quite hot. Dear Leslie, Mam had a letter from Mick this morning and he said the weather is very hot out there and is still working in the pit from six in the morning until six at night.

We have got two more men, they are horse men. Dear Leslie, I stopped until Sunday up at your Mother's because Mr Charmers treated us all to the theatre we went to see all scotch, it was very good. Dear Leslie, I don't think there is any more news now. Mam and Dad send you their best respects, so I will close with fondest and dearest love to my own darling Leslie, from your ever loving Phine.

XXXXXXXXXXXXXXXXXXXXXXX

P.S. Dear Leslie I am using pencil. Freddy said would you mind getting him one of your badges if you can because he is saving them. XXX

9th April 1916

My dearest Phine

I have received your letter of the 3rd and was so pleased to hear from you.

I heard about the Zepp raid and was wondering if they visited Brentwood. I always worry when they visit the East coast, it is as bad as if you were in the trenches and I always look forward to your next letter. I was very glad to hear they had bought one of them down.

We are just going back after a spell in the trenches. We were in a particular warm quarter and had several casualties, but am glad to say I am alright. My word, how I used to sit and think where and what I was doing at the same time a week or two ago. It came a bit hard going into the trenches off leave, but I have got settled down now, and just long more than ever for the end of this rotten old war, and coming back to my dear Phine.

I had a long chat in Sgt. Payne's dugout the night before last, he is properly fed up poor chap. I would not be surprised if he does not return to England soon, he is not in the best of health. He was telling me he was engaged to be married this March if he had not come out again. Do you know his girl? He said she lives in the Ongar road, I did not know before now.

Well Phine dearest, I must cut this letter short. I thought I should have more time, it's half past nine now, and we are off to catch the train back to billets in a quarter of an hour. It sounds strange doesn't it, a train to the trenches. It is about a mile behind the line, we only use it at night and it runs ever so silent.

Well Phine, I must close now, with all best wishes and respects to your Mam and Dad and fondest love and kisses to my own darling Phine, from your ever loving Leslie.

XXX

10ᵗʰ April 1916

My dearest Leslie

Just a line hoping you are quite well as it leaves myself at present. Dear Leslie, we had the Zepps over here again last Sunday, but they never dropped any bombs. There is an aircraft gun and a searchlight up on Shenfield Common. Mam is frightened out of life last night, about two o clock she woke us all up and brought us down stairs. She said she heard them. Freddy went out to see if he could see it, he said it was a train, they make a sound like a Zepp. Dear Leslie, do you know Miss Thorne who got the bad eyes? She is about 19, she is getting married to an Irish Guard on the third of May.

Dear Leslie, I don't think there is any more news now. Mam and Dad send you their best respects and hope to see you again soon, so I will close with fondest and dearest love to my own darling Leslie, from your ever loving Phine (God bless you).

XXXXXXXXXXXXXXXXXXXXXXXXXXXXXXXXXXXXXXXXXXX
XX

11ᵗʰ April 1916

My dearest Leslie

I received your letter dated the 9ᵗʰ and was very pleased to hear from you, also to hear you are still quite well as it leaves me at present. Dear Leslie, ever since you went back something seems to tell me that something is going to happen to you. I don't know what I should do if it did. I said to Mam I would be an old maid.

Dear Leslie, I wish this blessed old war was over. I am getting the hump of it and I am home here so I don't know what you must feel like out there. Dear Leslie, I don't think there is any more news now. Mam and Dad send you their best respects and hope to see you again soon, so I will close with fondest and dearest love and lots of kisses to my own dearest Leslie, from your ever loving Phine.

XXXXXXXXX

14ᵗʰ April 1916

My dearest Leslie

I received your card this morning dated the 11ᵗʰ and was very pleased to hear from you, also to hear you are still quite well as it leaves myself at present. Dear Leslie, I am going to have my teeth out at last because I have been mad with toothache ever since I came back from your Mother's. I am going to have my two front teeth stopped and four back ones out. I thought I should have gone mad with it yesterday, two or three times since I have been back. Dear Leslie, we have got a Sgt billeted here now, he belongs to the South Nott's Hussars and he is Irish, he comes from Dublin.

Dear Leslie, I don't think there is any more news now. Mam and Dad send you their best respects and hope to see you again soon, so I will close with fondest and dearest love and lots of kisses to my own darling Leslie, from your ever loving Phine.

XXX

God bless you.

16th April 1916

My own darling Phine

I received your two letters dated the 10th and 11th and am glad to hear you are quite well.

I say, what a cheerful letter your last letter was saying you cannot help thinking something is going to happen to me. What makes you think that? That night I received your letter I had been out of the trenches for 5 hours guarding the Company into a new position and then when we arrived there we had a terrible shelling, I thought the last day had come. I was properly fed up and then I received your letter, I was pleased then, but when I read it I thought how cheering. It made me feel quite down on my luck. You must get rid of that idea, that something will happen to me. I shall be alright, I quite expect to see the end of this war quite safe and sound, with God's help.

We had a pretty wet time in the trenches this time, but we had a very quiet time, I kept on wishing I was still on leave though, and building castles for the future, when this rotten war is over.

Well I must close this short letter. I am just going to Mount guard for 24 hours. I will write again soon.

With best wishes to your Mam and Dad and fondest and dearest love to my own darling Phine, from your ever-loving Leslie.

XXX

16th April 1916

My own dearest Leslie

I received your letter yesterday dated the 11th and was very pleased to hear from you, also to hear you are still quite well. Dear Leslie, Mam and I went out yesterday and we met one of the Grenadier Guards, he lives up Woodman rd. I think his name is Holden. I have seen him two or three times. Dear Leslie, Easter will soon be here, a week today is Easter Sunday. Mabel will be 19 on Thursday the 20th. Mam is sending her a H. S. shoe horn and button hook and I am sending her one of those French cards like you sent me. We can get them here now. Dear Leslie, I don't think there is any more news now. Mam and Dad send you their best respects and hope to see you again soon, so I will close with fondest and dearest love to my own darling Leslie, from your ever loving Phine.

XXXXXXXX

(God watch over you and protect you)

XXXXX

16th April 1916

My dearest Leslie

I received your card on Monday and a letter on Wednesday. Pleased to hear you are still quite well. Mam was so pleased to hear from you, she said she was sorry she sent that card for me to come home because she thought your Father might want me to stop there and she thought you were gone. Mam said she will write as soon as she gets time.

Dear Leslie, Dad went and passed for the Motor Transport and Major Brook would not let him go because he works under the Government, so he will still be in Warley. Dear Leslie, we are having awful wet weather here, it is raining nearly every day. I have had the toothache nearly every day since I have been back. Mam said I will have to have them out because nothing won't cure them. Dear Leslie, I don't think there is any more news now. Mam and Dad send you their best respects and hope for your safe return, so I will close now, with very best of love and kisses to my own darling Leslie, from your ever loving Phine.

XXXXXXXX

The case containing all the letters and postcards.

A postcard from a letter on 1st August 1914

Leslie in his uniform from a letter on 24th September 1914

New year card for 1915 mentioned in the letter dated 27th December 1914

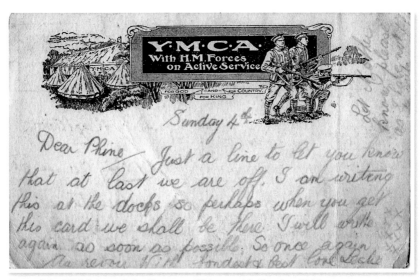

One of the Y.M.C.A. cards Leslie sent to Phine on 4th October 1914

NOTHING is to be written on this except the
date and signature of the sender. Sentences not
required may be erased. If anything else is added
the post card will be destroyed.

I am quite well.

I have been admitted into hospital
{ sick } and am going on well.
{ wounded } and hope to be discharged soon.

I am being sent down to the base.

I have received your { letter. on 25ᵈ
{ telegram.
{ parcel.

Letter follows at first opportunity.

I have received no letter from you
{ lately.
{ for a long time.

Signature }
only. }   Les

Date 24ᵗʰ Dec 1914

[Postage must be prepaid on any letter or post card
addressed to the sender of this card.]

(24386) Wt.W3497-393 1,000m. 9/14 M.R.Co.,Ltd.

Field service postcards from 1914

Grenadier Guard Sweet Heart Brooch like the one Phine
would have received from Leslie. She talks about this in her
letter on 26th July 1915

20th August 1915 – Phine's birthday cards from Leslie

The first photo of Phine sent to Leslie, on November 14th 1915. She is also wearing her brooch

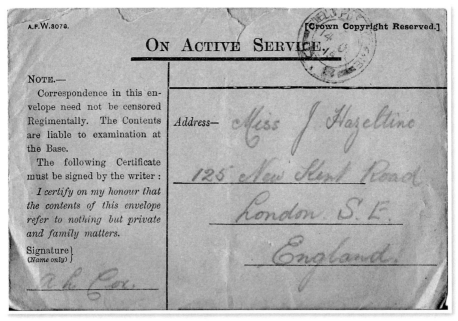

This is one of Leslie's letters to Phine in the green envelopes, introduced during March 1915.

27th December 1915

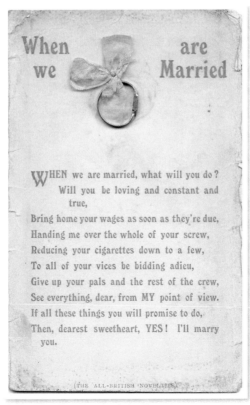

A card sent to Leslie 22nd April 1916

said in the last (4) letter (the cheerful one I mean) that you would never have another young man if anything happened to me.

Don't write a letter slating me for what I have just wrote, but I could not help smiling ~~for you were telling me~~ about the fortune teacup I made me think how true that chap's reading of the tea-cups turned out.

Well I suppose I must close now, give my best wishes to your Mam & Dad hoping they are

My dearest Phine
I received your letter dated the 14th, and was so sorry to hear you had been suffering so from toothache. I hope by the time you receive this letter that you have been and had them seen to. I am sure it will be the best plan, instead of having such a maddening pain every day alike. By the way, ask your

The original letter Leslie sent to Phine, asking her to marry him in his shy way.

the ring but (3) the somebody was too shy to ask. Well you never knew how true it was, I did mean to ask your Mam & Dad's consent, but whether it was shyness or not I cannot say. I argued with myself that it was hardly fair to ask, whilst I am in danger out here and again I thought perhaps you were too young yet to know your own mind. I often wonder if you will ever find somebody you will like better, or I did untill you

Mam, if the (2) cost of the dentist will be in my next month's bill.

Don't laugh will you when you read this, but of course I know you will, and so will your Mam. You remember the night we were strolling on Liverpool Street platform, when Bruce went back, you were telling me about the chap who told you your fortune in the tea-cup. You said he told you somebody wanted to become engaged to you and that he could see

Miss J. Hazeltine
No 17 King Edward Road
Brentwood
Sat. 22/4/16.   Essex

My Own Dearest Leslie
                    I received your two
letters yesterday dated the 16th and 18th and I was
more than pleased to hear from you also to
hear you are still quite well, I am sorry
that I made you feel so miserable when I said
about something might happen but I only felt a
bit upset you going back in the horrid old
trenches, but I have lost that feeling now, thank
god, I know he will spare you so you must not
think no more about it will you. well hear
Leslie about your letter, mam and Dad did not
laugh, she said she felt sorry for you as Dad
was just the same, and a funny thing, she said
that Dad wrote to her just as you have to me,
as he was shy in asking 'mam' mother, but
Dear Leslie it is all wright mam and Dad
said you can have their consent and mam
said it lays between me and you now, if we think

The original letter Phine sent to Leslie saying yes to his shy
proposal of marriage.

---

enough of one another, well I am sure I do
and I feel certain you do, as I feel in my mind
that you are, even now I dont think that
you would like anyone better than me, and
for goodness sake dont think that of me, because
I am certain I could never like anyone at all;
never mind better. So whatever your wish is, mine
is the same, I really thought you knew that
I could not think more of you than I do, so
you wont have that feeling any more, well,
Dear Leslie mam said that I am not too young
to be engaged but of cause too young to be
married, that is different and of cause I know
my own mind I am not such a child as you
think, I know wheather I love you or not. well
Leslie I do but I could not tell mam that when
she asked me if I like you, I said yes but I
did not tell her what I have told you, well
Leslie primise me you wont think that of
any more because I do love you I never no one
else, mam and Dad sends you there very best
respects and prays for your safe return and
myself I hope to see you very soon God will watch
over you so I will close now Dear Leslie with very
    best of love and kisses with my love to my own
        darling Leslie from yours always loving
P.S. I hope this letter will cheer you   X X Phine.

The drawing of the ring which Phine sent to Leslie mentioned in her letter dated 23rd May 1916

The card Phine sent with her letter to Leslie dated 22nd April 1916

With Fondest Love from *Brentwood*

Two eyes are watching so eagerly,
Eyes that are loving and true
Waiting and longing and hoping
Hoping they'll soon see you.

29th August 1916

VERY URGENT

One Million Nice Girls
are wanting

HUSBANDS

Now's your Chance,
I'd make you a dear little

WIFE

Having some Cash of my own

I would go halves with You.

Am a bit shy, but you can write to me at

BRENTWOOD

29th August 1916

A card sent from Phine on 25th January 1917

Leslie sitting down, with an old pal, stood behind
him. Sent with a letter dated 8th July 1917

24th July 1917

Replica military medal like the one Leslie
would have received mentioned in the letter
of 26th October 1917

The photo of Phine looking grand mentioned in the letter dated 22nd November 1917

Phine in her munitionette uniform mentioned in the 2nd June 1918 letter. She is also wearing her sweet heart brooch

A selection of some of the letters

Leslie and Phine on their wedding day – 21st September 1918

Leslie and Phine with her three sisters on their wedding day

Phine with Yvonne her first daughter in the 1920s

Leslie in his world war two uniform with Yvonne on her wedding day to my grandfather William Harold Pearmain in May 1940.

Phine in the late 1960s with her pet budgie on her shoulder.

Proposal from the trenches

18ᵗʰ April 1916

My dearest Phine

I received your letter dated the 14ᵗʰ and was so sorry to hear you had been suffering so from toothache. I hope by the time you receive this letter that you have been and had them seen to. I am sure it will be the best plan, instead of having such a maddening pain every day alike. By the way, ask your Mam if the cost of the dentist will be in my next month's bill.

Don't laugh will you when you read this, but of course I know you will, and so will your Mam. You remember the night we were strolling on Liverpool Street platform, when Bruce went back, you were telling me about the chap who told you your fortune in the tea cup? You said he told you somebody wanted to become engaged to you and he could see the ring, but the somebody was too shy to ask. Well you never knew who it was. I did mean to ask your Mam and Dad's consent, but whether it was shyness or not I cannot say. I argued with myself that it was hardly if all to ask, whilst I am in danger out here and again I thought perhaps you were too young yet to know your own mind. I often wonder if you will ever find somebody you will like better, or I did until you said in the last letter (the cheerful one I mean) that you would never have another young man if anything happened to me.

Don't write a letter strafing me for what I have just wrote, but I could not help smiling when you were telling me about the fortune tea cup, it made me think how true that chaps reading of the tea cups turned out.

Well I suppose I must close now, give my best wishes to your Mam and Dad hoping they are well. From your ever loving Leslie.

XXX

20ᵗʰ April 1916

My own dearest Phine

I received your letter dated the 16ᵗʰ and pleased to hear you are quite well. I hope you have had your teeth attended to, and are now free from toothache.

I was surprised when you wrote and said how near Easter is. I can hardly realise it will be Good Friday tomorrow. I am glad you mentioned Mabel's birthday, I had clean forgot. I dropped her a post card this morning. Still better late than never. I am always the same, I can never remember anybody's birthday, only my own. I've had too many of them now, so I think I shall start to forget them.

We are all being treated on Saturday to the pictures by our Captain, it is quite a swell affair, all the pictures of the day and singing, etc. One would hardly believe it but it is so. Unfortunately, about a fortnight ago, during one of the tunes, old Fritz started to shell the town, and one came through the roof of the picture palace.

Nobody was injured, however, although some of the troops wanted their money back, having to come out before time.

Well I cannot think of any more to write about (I always was a rotten letter writer) so I will close with the best of wishes and my respects to your Mam and Dad, and fondest and dearest love to my own darling Phine. From your ever loving Leslie.

XXX

22ⁿᵈ April 1916

My own dearest Leslie

I received your two letters yesterday dated the 16ᵗʰ and 18ᵗʰ and I was more than pleased to hear from you, also to hear you are still quite well. I am sorry that I made you feel so miserable when I said about something might happen, but I only felt a bit upset you going back in the horrid old trenches, but I have lost that feeling now, thank God. I know he will spare you so you must not think no more about it, will you. Well dear Leslie, about your letter, Mam and Dad did not laugh. She said she felt sorry for you as Dad was just the same, and a funny thing, she said that Dad wrote to her just as you have to me, as he was shy in asking Mam's Mother, but dear Leslie it is alright. Mam and Dad said you can have their consent and Mam said it lays between me and you now, if we think enough of one another. Well I am sure I do and I feel certain you do, as I feel in my mind that you are. Even now I don't think that you would like anyone better than me, and for goodness sake don't think that of me because I am certain I could never like anyone at all, never mind better. So whatever your wish is, mine is the same. I really thought you knew that I could not think more of you than I do, so you won't have that feeling any more will you?

Dear Leslie, Mam said that I am not too young to be engaged but of course too young to be married, that is different and of course I know my own mind. I am not such a child as you think. I know whether I love you or not. Well Leslie, I do, but I could not tell Mam that when she asked me if I like you. I said yes but I did not tell her what I have told you. Well Leslie, promise me you won't think that anymore because I do love you, I never loved no one else. Mam and Dad send you their very best respects and pray for your safe return and myself I hope to see you very soon. God will watch over you. So I will close now, dear Leslie, with very best love and kisses all my love to my own darling Leslie, from yours always loving Phine.

XXXXXXXXXX

P.S. Hope this letter will cheer you up.

27ᵗʰ April 1916

My dearest Phine

I have just received your letter, and I am so sorry I cannot answer your letter fully.

I have just time to scribble a few lines, and now it is a case of trotting to the other side of the town to get a chum of mine to post it.

We are off to the trenches tonight for 16 days, and I don't suppose I shall have a chance of writing till we come out again. Anyhow, I am just as pleased as the proverbial dog with two tails, now I have received your letter. You must thank your Mam and Dad for me for their consent, until I can write them myself.

Well dearest, excuse this scribble and short letter I will write again at the very first opportunity.

With best wishes to your Mam and Dad, and all my dearest love and kisses to my own darling Phine, from your ever loving Leslie.

XXXXXXXXX

1st May 1916

My dearest Leslie
My own darling Leslie.
Just a line hoping you are quite well as it leaves myself at present.
Dear Leslie, I am sorry I did not write, because I had been busy. I have had only one card all this week. Mam said she expects it will be terrible for the letters to come over now. Dear Leslie, we had the Zepps over here the other night. We could see it quite near, we were up half the night. I was not quite so afraid as I was before when I see that one in London. Dear Leslie, I don't think there is any more news now. Mam and Dad send you their best respects and hope to see you again soon. So, I will close with fondest and dearest love to my darling Leslie, from your ever loving Phine.
God bless you.
XXXXXXXXXXXX

6th May 1916

My dearest Phine
I have received your letter dated Monday the 1st and am pleased to hear you are well, I hope that means your poor face is better, you did not say if it was or not.

I am sorry I have not written you before not even a card, but as I explained in my other letter dearest, we are up here for 16 days and I cannot post a letter even if I write one. I've managed to get my last letter off and also this one, as we are the reserve line, but we go up to the Front tonight, so I cannot write again for another five or six days, so you will understand, won't you?

I was surprised to hear the Zepps have been over again, but then we have not had a paper for over a week. An Officer told us though that there was some serious trouble in Dublin and that a lot of shooting had been going on. I was sorry to hear that, especially at such a time as this when the Country is at war.[4]

I have been quite queer the last few days and had to see the Doctor, but am pleased to say I am quite well again now.

Well Phine dearest, I must make this a short letter, as I have quite a lot of work to do, so once again au revoir, with best wishes and my respects to your Mam and Dad and fondest and dearest love to my own fondest and dearest Phine, from your ever loving Leslie.

XXXX XXXXXXX

5th May 1916

My dearest Leslie

I received your letter yesterday dated the 26th. I was very pleased to hear from you also to hear you are still quite well as it leaves myself at present. Dear Leslie, I wish this blessed war was over. Fancy going in the trenches for 16 days. I think you have done your bit, they ought to give you a rest, but I suppose they think that you have had a rest because you were back in the Drums. Dear Leslie, we had got two more men of the 21st Nott's Sherwood Rangers Yeomanry coming in on Saturday. That will be four we will have. I wish that the Sgt that we have got here was you. He is a nice fellow, he is only twenty-eight. He got married last July. Dear Leslie, I don't think there is any more news now. Mam and Dad send you their best respects, so I will close with fondest and dearest love and lots and lots of kisses to my own darling Leslie, from your ever loving Phine.
XXXXXX

11th May 1916

My own dearest Leslie

I received your letter yesterday dated the 6th. I was very pleased to hear from you. I was very sorry to hear you have not been well. I suppose it is being in those blessed trenches working hard all day long for 16 days and don't get no sleep, that will make you feel bad. I wish this war was over so we will all be together again. Mam says it seems to her that the war has always been on and always will. Dear Leslie, it was Dad's birthday yesterday the 10th, he was 42, he is getting on.

Dear Leslie, I don't think there is any more news now. Mam and Dad send you their best respects. So, I will close with fondest and dearest love and kisses to my own darling Leslie, from your ever loving Phine.
XXXXXXXXXXXXXXXXXXXX
P.S. God bless you and hope you are feeling better. Phine.
XXXXX

12th May 1916

My own dearest Phine

I have received your letters dated the 5th and the 8th and am glad to hear you are quite well. I am so pleased to hear you are free from toothache. I hope you will not feel it again.

We have just come out of the trenches today, and finished our 16 days. We had a very warm time whilst we were there, but now we are going down the line for a month's rest, to a place on the coast not very far from old England.

I am writing my Mother with this post, asking her to get the ring, so she will let you know when she will get it.

Well dearest, you must excuse this short letter, it is so late and I am awfully tired coming from the trenches so I will close.

With my best respects and wishes to your Mam and Dad and fondest and dearest love to my own darling Phine, from your ever loving Leslie.

XXX XXXXXXXXX

P.S. Dear Phine, I thought perhaps you would be interested to hear this. You remember CPL Fox? The very tall fellow at the dances (he is a Sergeant)? He was wounded at Neuve Chapelle and re-joined us today with a draft. He has joined my Company. Another of the old ones.

15th May 1916

My own dearest Leslie

I received your card this morning dated the 11th. I was very pleased to hear from you, also to hear you are still quite well as it leaves myself at present. Dear Leslie, we set one of our chickens. Dad put ten eggs under her but we only got five chicks and one of those died today because it was born with funny feet. Dear Leslie, Mam had a card from Mick this morning. He asked Mam to send him a cup because he said the one he is using he made out of a piece of cloth. Dear Leslie, I hope you are better. I think they ought to give you a rest. I will be glad when this war is over. Dear Leslie, I don't think there is any more news now. Mam and Dad send you their best respects, so I will close with fondest and dearest love and lots of kisses to my own darling Leslie, from your ever loving Phine.

XXXXXXX

God bless you. X

Excuse scribble as I am in a hurry. X

19th May 1916

My own dearest Phine

I received your two letters dated the 11th and 15th, and am glad to hear you are still quite well. No more toothache I hope. I am glad to say I am feeling quite well again now, I suppose it is the fine weather and the rest we are having. A month's rest will do me the world of good and put me right again, though I thought I was in for a bad time. I quite expected I should have to go to Hospital, I was in such pain. Still I am quite fit again now.

I was interested to hear about the chicks. You will have quite a poultry farm soon. I suppose the cockerel is still alive and pecking at everybody.

Glad to hear Mick is still alright, I bet he will be awfully pleased when this war is over and it won't be very long now. I think it will be over before I get another leave anyhow, and that is only about 4 or 5 months. Well Phine dearest, I have no more to say this time, so I will close with my best wishes and respects to your Mam and Dad, hoping they are enjoying the best of health, and fondest and dearest love and lots of kisses to my own darling Phine, from yours always loving and true Leslie.

XXX

20th May 1916

My own dearest Leslie

Just a line hoping you are quite well as it leaves myself at present. Dear Leslie, we have had rain for three days and three nights and it is too hot to move. I am writing this letter in the garden because it is too hot indoors, still we wanted some rain for the gardens. Dad has put nearly all the potatoes in his garden because we can't get any, we have not had any for a long while now so Dad has put plenty in.

We have killed three of our old hens last Thursday. Now we have got two old hens, eleven young hens a year old and ten chicks seven or eight weeks old, but we only get two or three eggs a day.

Dear Leslie, I don't think there is any more news now. Mam and Dad send you their best respects and hope to see you soon, so I will close with fondest and dearest love and lots of kisses to my own darling Leslie, from your ever loving and true Phine.

XXXXXX

23rd May 1916

My own dearest Leslie

I received your card and letter. I was very pleased to hear from you, also to hear you are still quite well as leaves myself at present.

Dear Leslie, about the ring, Mam and I and the two babies went up to your Mother's on Saturday. We went up early because the shops shut at one. Dear Leslie, we went over to M. Plante[5] but he never had one to fit me, they were all too small. There was one I like and so did your Mother like it so, M. Plante is going to make me one like it. Your Mother said it was very uncommon, it has got three rings and then two white Diamonds and one blue Sapphire across the ring. Dear Leslie, I am very sorry I did not write before but I have been very busy. We have got four men now; they make a lot of work because they are horse men.

Dear Leslie, I don't think there is any more news now. Mam and Dad send you their best respects and hope to see you soon, so do I. I wish the blessed war was over, I don't think it can last much longer, do you Leslie? I should think you are getting fed up with it now. I should if I was out there. I am getting fed up at home here. Dear Leslie, I don't think there is any more news now, you have got all the news, so I will close with fondest and dearest love and lots of kisses to my own darling Leslie, from your ever loving Phine.

XXXXXXXXXXXX

P.S. Dear Leslie I am very sorry I did not write before, Phine.

XXXXX

29th May 1916

My own dearest Leslie

Just a line hoping you are quite well as it leaves myself at present.

Dear Leslie, Dad's brother came down on Saturday. He said when the Franco German war was on there was a fountain somewhere in France, it stopped running and three months to that very day the war was over, and he said about three weeks ago, the very same fountain has stopped running, so let's hope that in three months the war will be over.

Dear Leslie, your Mother came down on Sunday evening with the ring. It is very nice indeed, thank you very much for it. I wished you were home to have got it, still it can't be helped. Dear Leslie, I don't think there is any more news now. Mam and Dad send you their best respects and hope to see you soon, so I will close with fondest and dearest love and lots of kisses to my own darling Leslie, from your ever loving and true Phine.

XXXXXXXXXX

P.S. God bless you and spare you to come home.

XXXXX

30th May 1916

My own dearest Leslie

I have just received your letter dated the 27th. I was very pleased to hear from you, also to hear you are getting better.

Dear Leslie, I think they ought to send you home for a while for a rest. I don't suppose you would get much rest if you came home. I will be glad when you come home for good, then I will give you a good hiding and will not let you have a bit of peace. Dear Leslie, you know we had four chickens? Well Dad set one about two months ago but we only got four chicks out of nine, we did have six but she killed two when they were two days old, now we have got the other three sitting so we will have quite a farmyard soon.

Dear Leslie, I don't think there is any more news now. Mam and Dad send you their best respects and hope to see you again soon. So I will close with fondest and dearest love and lots of kisses to my own darling Leslie, from your ever loving and true Phine.

XXXXXXXXXXXXXXXXXX

P.S. God bless you and bring you back safe soon.

XXXXXXXXX

1st June 1916

My own dearest Phine

Just a few hasty lines in answer to your letter of the 27th. I was glad to hear you are quite well. We are very busy just now changing to another district, and I am also in – waiting this week so you can guess what time I have to spare. I am writing this in a hurry, and it is nearly midnight. You say you have not heard from my Mother, it is strange, I have not heard from her for over a fortnight now, and I also asked her to send me some things out. I hope nothing is wrong at home.

Well dearest Phine, I will write you more fully as soon as possible, with best wishes to your Mam and Dad and fondest and dearest love to my own darling Phine, from your ever loving and true Leslie.

XXXXXXXXXX

P.S. Please excuse paper.

XXX

3rd June 1916

My own dearest Leslie

Just a line hoping you are quite well as it leaves myself at present.

Dear Leslie, we are losing our men this week and I am pleased to see the back of them. Dear Leslie, I am very pleased with the ring, it is very nice, it is uncommon. Dear Leslie, I will make this a short letter as I have not had one from you this week, yet so I have not much to say. Mam and Dad send you their best respects, so I will close with fondest and dearest love and lots of kisses to my own darling Leslie, from your ever loving Phine.

XXXXXXXXX

God bless you.

11th June 1916

My own dearest Leslie

I received your letter dated 2nd and was very pleased to hear from you, also to hear you are quite well. Dear Leslie, we have had the old cockerel killed at last. He is a big bird, he weighs 7lbs 11 half ounces, but Mam could not eat him, so we had to sell him. One of the men we got here killed him, he is gone now. Mam went as white as death. Dear Leslie, as I was writing this letter I have just received your letter dated the 7th. Dear Leslie, we got twenty-seven chicks now and there's another lot of chicks to come off yet. Dear Leslie, I don't suppose the war will be over yet because the men we got have had to give their coats to have a pocket put inside their coats for these gas masks, so they will soon be off to the Front. Dear Leslie, I don't think there is any more news now. Mam and Dad send you their best respects and hope to see you soon, so I will close with fondest and dearest love and tons of kisses to my own dearest Leslie, from your ever loving true Phine.

XXXXXX

(God bless you)

13th June 1916

My own dearest Leslie

Just a line hoping you are quite well as it leaves myself at present. Dear Leslie, we had my Dad's two sisters and there little girl from London yesterday only for the day they had to go back because one goes to work, but the other one her husband is out at the Front in the Buffs. He is 36, he was only up two months when they sent him out, while there is young fellows home here been up 18 months. I think it is a sham, don't you? And you have been out there two years in Oct, but let's hope the war will be over before October comes.

Dear Leslie, I don't think there is any more news now. Mam and Dad send you their best respects and hope to see you soon, so I will close with fondest and dearest love and lots of kisses to my own darling Leslie, from your ever loving Phine.

XXXXX

God, bless you and bringing you back and safe XXX

P.S. Dear Leslie, I have just received your letter dated the 10th. Dear Leslie, I am sorry to hear about poor old Payne. Dear Leslie, I don't think there is any more now so I will close with fondest and dearest love to my own dearest Leslie, from your ever loving and true Phine.

XXXXXXX

My own dearest Phine

I received your letter of the 17th and was pleased to hear from you. I am sorry I have not wrote before, but of course being in the trenches till now I could not write before. We go in again tomorrow for about 5 days.[6]

Thank you very much dearest for asking if there is anything I want, but I have all I require, all I want is the war to end soon, so I may come back to you for good and of course your letters with all the news in. If I do want anything, I will let you know.

I have been suffering for the last few days with my left knee. I think it is a displaced cartilage, it swells up a lot when I march a long way. It does not pain much only when marching, but the Doctor cannot do anything if I went to him. Of course, if it gets worse I shall have to go to the base and have it operated on, but there is no fear of that yet.

We are having awful hot weather just now, it is too hot to move about, but of course we have had a thunder storm occasionally, just to wet us through. I do wish the war would end or at least let us make a move. It is so monotonous these long trenches. We dare not move about in daytime, in case we get shelled, we can only work at night so we have a long day of about 16 hours, sleeping and thinking of home and what they are doing there.

It is awfully tiring but still it will end someday, and very soon, I hope now.

Well you will think I am getting fed-up, by the tone of this letter, but I am quite alright and happy, how could I be otherwise when I have such a loving girl as you in my thought day and night.

Well I must close now, so once again au revoir, with best wishes and respects to your Mam and Dad, and fondest and dearest love to my own darling Phine, from your ever loving and true Leslie.

XXXXXXXX

24th June 1916

My own dearest Leslie

Just a line hoping you are quite well as it leaves myself at present. Dear Leslie, the Army Pay Corp had a dance last night. Mam went to it, she can't walk today she is so tired. It was from half past seven until 3 o'clock, it was four when she got home. Mam wanted me to go, but I would not. I would have gone if you were there, I would not want asking twice.

Dear Leslie, we have got 35 chickens now all together. Dear Leslie, I don't think there is any more news now so I will close with fondest and dearest love to my own darling Leslie, from your ever loving and true Phine.

XXXXXXXXXXXXXXXXXXXXXX

1st July 1916

My own dearest Leslie

I received your letter yesterday dated the 23rd. I was very pleased to hear from you, but I am very sorry to hear you are suffering so much pain with your knee. Dear Leslie, do me a favour and go sick with your knee then you will come home. I think you have been out there quite long enough. I should love you to come home. Dear Leslie, it will only get worse if you don't have it seen to, perhaps if you leave it for a week or two and then have it operated on it might make you lame for the rest of your life. Dear Leslie, do try and get home if you can so you can have a bit of rest.

Dear Leslie, I don't think there is any more news now. Mam and Dad send you their best respects and hope to see you soon, so I will close with fondest and dearest love and lots of kisses to my own darling Leslie, from your ever loving and true Phine.

XXXXX

God watch over you and bring you back safe.

8th July 1916

My own dearest Leslie

I received your card yesterday. I was very pleased to hear from you, also to hear you are still quite well as it leaves myself at present.

Dear Leslie, I forgot to tell you in my last letter that it was Mam's birthday last Sunday. She was 36, she is getting on. Dear Leslie, have you heard if Payne is getting better, poor fellow? I shouldn't care for him to be my young man, I should be afraid of him. Dear Leslie, I don't think there is any more news now. Mam and Dad send you their best respects and hope to see you soon, so I will close with fondest and dearest love to my darling Leslie, from your ever loving and true Phine.

XXXXXXXXX

11ᵗʰ July 1916

My own dearest Leslie

I received your letter and card and was very pleased to hear from you, also to hear you are still quite well. Dear Leslie, I am pleased to hear that your knee is getting better. Dear Leslie, do you think that the war will end this month? Mam said she don't suppose it will be over for another year. I am getting fed up with it, it makes me worse when I see the girls passing by with their young men. I think they ought to be out there as well as you.

Dear Leslie, I don't think there is any more news now. Mam and Dad send you their best respects and hope to see you soon, so I will close with fondest and dearest love to my own darling Leslie, from your ever loving and true Phine.

XXXXXXXXX

P.S. Dear Leslie, you did not quite finish your last letter, you never put any kisses.

XXXXX

12ᵗʰ July 1916

My own darling Phine

Just a line in answer to your letter of the 8ᵗʰ which I received yesterday.

Wish your Mam many happy returns for me, if it is not too late, and tell her I shall be home to help her celebrate the next. Of course, that is if she is going to have any more. You generally stop there, don't you? Or start getting younger.

No I have not heard any more about poor Payne, I hope he is getting better, I feel very sorry for him. Of course, he may not be so bad as they say.

I see we are still advancing on all fronts. It is good. It is bringing the end a lot nearer. You have not mentioned Mick lately; I hope he is still alright.

What do you think of the new order about all wounded men wearing two inches of gold braid on their left sleeve?[7] It is a fairly good idea I think there will be an awful lot entitled to wear it.

Well this is only a short note. I will close with best wishes to your Mam and Dad, and fondest and dearest love to my own Phine, from your ever loving and true Leslie.

XXXXXXXX

15ᵗʰ July 1916

My own dearest Leslie

Just a line hoping you are quite well as it leaves myself at present. Dear Leslie, Mam has had three cards from Mick this week. Saying he has not received any of her parcels for about five weeks, so Mam don't know whether to send any more or not. Dear Leslie, I dreamt last night that you were wounded in both your legs. Dear Leslie, I don't think there is any more news now. Mam and Dad send you their best respects and hope to see you soon, so I will close with fondest and dearest love to my own darling Leslie, from your loving and true Phine.

XXXXXXXX

18th July 1916

My own darling Phine

I was very pleased to hear from you, I received both your letters dated the 11th and the 15th.

I must apologise for not finishing my letter, I thought I did, still that can wait now till I come home. I don't think it is going to be so long now. We have made a good start driving the Bosch back everywhere.[8] There is certainly some hard work to be done yet, but still we have made a start, and that is the main thing. Before then it seemed as if the war was on for ever.

I am sorry to hear Mick has not been receiving his parcels, perhaps it is a way of spiting our prisoners, on account of the "big push". It would be just their way of having their own back.

I hope he will receive them. I should not think they would dare stop them like that. Perhaps it would be best not send any more, until your Mam hears again whether he has received them or not.

I see you are having those dreams and fancies again, thinking I have been wounded or that something has happened to me. Don't worry dearest I shall be alright. Trust in God.

I must keep safe to return to you. It will not be long now. You ask my Mother, she knows, she knew from the beginning I should be away for two years and then come back.

Well dearest, I will close now, so once again au revoir, with best wishes to your Mam and Dad and fondest and dearest love to my own darling Phine, from your ever loving and true Leslie.

XXXXXXXXXXX

22nd July 1916

My own dearest Leslie

I received your letter and cards, I was very pleased to hear from you, also to hear you are still quite well as it leaves myself at present.

Dear Leslie, your last letter you sent was eight days coming and your cards you sent I had the one you sent on the 16th and two days after I had the one sent on the 14th.

Dear Leslie, it looks as though you will have your other leave before the war is over. Dear Leslie, I don't suppose you have come across any badges for Freddy yet. Dear Leslie, will you wear the gold braid because you have been wounded, but perhaps it only means they're badly wounded. We had some wounded come in last Saturday and Sunday, they looked awful. As the last three came out they laid them on the ground while they settled the motor because they were badly wounded. One little fellow, he was no bigger than Freddy and as thin as anything, and he died on his way up to the Hospital. Poor little fellow, he did not look about 17. When I see him lying on the ground the tears come up my eyes and Mam cried as if he was her son, I don't know what I should have done if I had seen you when you was wounded.

Dear Leslie, I don't think there is any more news now, so I will close with fondest and dearest love to my own darling, from your ever loving and true Phine.

XXXXXXXXXXXXXXXXXXXXXXXXXXXXXXXXXXXXXXXX

P.S. Dear Leslie, Mam heard from Mick, he is quite well.

XXXX

God bless you and bring you back safe.

25ᵗʰ July 1916

My own dearest Leslie

I received your letter and card today both dated the 18ᵗʰ. I was very pleased to hear from you, also to hear you are still quite well as it leaves myself at present. Dear Leslie, Mam said was any of those fellows married or anyone we knew what you see killed? Dear Leslie, Mam had a letter from your Mother this morning, she said she is coming down next month. Dear Leslie, I don't think there is any more news now. Mam and Dad send you their best respects and hope to see you soon, so I will close with fondest and dearest love to my own darling Leslie, from your ever loving Phine.

XXXX

27ᵗʰ July 1916

My own dearest Leslie

Just a line hoping you are quite well as it leaves myself at present.

Dear Leslie, we are having awful weather here, it is raining and is cold as ice. Dear Leslie, several of the girls up the shop was weighed yesterday, so was I too. Guess what do you think I weigh? Eleven stone. Mam said I will be as big as she is before long.

Dear Leslie, I expect you will be home next week or the week after, I am longing to see you, it seems such a long time since I have seen you.

My dearest Leslie, I don't think there is any more news now at present. Mam and Dad send you their best respects and hope to see you soon, so I will close with fondest and dearest love and tons of kisses to my own darling Leslie, from your ever loving and true Phine.

XXXXXXXXXXX

28ᵗʰ July 1916

My own darling Phine

I have received your letters of the 22ⁿᵈ and the 25ᵗʰ and was glad to hear you are still quite well. I suppose you are beginning to worry why I have not written before. I am very sorry but we have been so very busy lately. We are hoping the next time we go in the trenches will be to take part in the "big push".

I had almost forgotten the badges for Fred, but I will try and get him some, they are rather difficult to get out here.

I cannot understand how the cards and letters have been so long coming. Of course, it depends a lot upon whether we are in the front line or in reserve. They take longer then you see they are two days before they get posted at our end.

I am glad to hear Mick is still well and alright, he must be awfully fed up though.

Those fellows I mentioned, I think two were married, but there were none that you or your Mam knew. We have had quite a number of casualties since then. I am just off to see my Platoon play a football match for the Battalion Championship, so wish us luck.

Well I will conclude now, with best wishes to your Mam and Dad and fondest and dearest love to my own darling Phine, from your ever loving and true Leslie.

XXXXXXX

31st July 1916

My own dearest Leslie

I received your card, I was so pleased to hear from you, also to hear you are still quite well. Dear Leslie, we have had the Zepps over here again. The war has been on two years on Friday, it seems to me as though it has been on twenty years. Dear Leslie, fancy I have only seen you twice in two years. Dear Leslie, it was Essex Day last Thursday. Mam got some flags and Madgie sold them. She only had twelve shillings worth and she got 17/6 half then she took 14 flags back so that was not bad. Dear Leslie, I don't think there is any more news now. Mam and Dad send you their best respects and hope to see you soon, so I will close with fondest and dearest love to my own darling Leslie, from your ever loving and true Phine.

XXXXXXX

10th August 1916

My own dearest Leslie

I received your letter this evening dated the 10th. I was very pleased to hear from you, also to hear you are still quite well as it leaves myself at present.

Dear Leslie, I received the note and thank you very much dear. Dear Leslie, I did not know what to get. Mam said I ought to get something to wear what will keep and so you can see me in it when you come home, please God, so I got a nice gold bracelet. Mam said I got a nice ring so I ought to have something nice to go with it.

But dear Leslie, I hope you don't mind, Mam gave me the extra money. It is a very nice one, I am sure you will like it. I wish you were here to see it.

Well dear Leslie, I am sorry you are going in the trenches. Mam and Dad send you their best respects and hope to see you soon, so I will close with fondest and dearest love and lots of kisses to my own dearest Leslie, from your ever loving and true Phine.

13th August 1916

My dearest Leslie

I received your two cards yesterday. I was very pleased to hear from you, also to hear you are still quite well as it leaves myself at present. Dear Leslie, your Mother and Bruce is coming up on Sunday. Dear Leslie, we have got Cpl of the Army Pay Corps coming to sleep here while the war is on and his name is Mr Cox. He is a married man.

Dear Leslie, I don't think there is any more news now. Mam and Dad send you their best respects and hope to see you soon, so I will close with fondest and dearest love to my darling Leslie, from your ever loving and true Phine.

XXXXXXXXXXXXXXXXXXXXXXXXXXXXXX

22nd August 1916

My own dearest Phine

I received your letter of the 15th and was glad to hear you are well. I am glad you received my letter safe.

Certainly, I do not mind your Mam giving you the extra money, but I wonder if she would object to me paying the extra money. If she would let me know how much it is, I should very much like to send it on.

Well you know if she has any objections, as I should very much like to give you the bracelet myself. I would have sent more, only I had no more cash just at the time. I am very glad you like it, and roll on when I can come home to see it. Ring before next birthday I hope, with God's help.

We are still trotting round country from place to place, we get plenty of changes nowadays. It is far better than the old routine of in and out of the trenches in the one place. I am sure from what we see and hear out here, that the war will not last much longer. I think it is a matter of months now. Poor old Fritz does not know which way to turn, he is being pressed in on all sides. The allies are doing splendid, don't you think so?

Well I am still as awful at letter writing as ever, so I shall have to pack up. Although I should be fairly good at it after two years corresponding out here.

Give my best respects and wishes to your Mam and Dad, hoping they are enjoying the best of health. With fondest and dearest love to my own darling Phine, from your ever loving and true Leslie.

22nd August 1916

My own dearest Leslie

I received your letter this evening dated the 17th. I was very pleased to hear from you, also to hear you are still quite well as it leaves myself at present. Dear Leslie, your Mother and Bruce did not come down because your Father got five days' holidays so they went to Berkshire to bring Mabel back and your Mam said she will come down another time. Dear Leslie, I had such a lovely blouse from your Mother and Father and Mabel. Dear Leslie, I don't think there is any more news now. Mam and Dad send you their best respects and hope to see you soon, so I will close with fondest and dearest to my own darling and true Phine.

God bless you and bring you back safe soon.

25th August 1916

My own dearest Leslie
Just a line hoping you are quite well as it leaves myself at present. Dear Leslie, we had the Zepps over here last night. I wish it was all over, they say it will last seven years.

Dear Leslie, Mam has not heard from Mick for about a fortnight now. Dear Leslie, I am longing for October to come. You said you would only be out there two years, it seems to me as though you have been out there for twenty-two years.

Dear Leslie, I will make this a short letter because I am going to write a letter to your Mother. Mam and Dad send you their best respects and hope to see you soon, so I will close with fondest and dearest love and lots of kisses to my own dearest sweet heart Leslie, from your ever loving and true Phine.

God watch over you and bring you back safe.

29th August 1916

My own dear Leslie
I received your letter this morning dated the 22nd. I was very pleased to hear from you, also to hear you are still quite well. I was wondering if anything was the matter. Dear Leslie, Mam said of course she don't mind you paying the extra money as it is your present. Dad said to Mam after she got it that it was not a present from you or Mam. But dear Leslie, I do hope you are not cross with me for running you in to all that money will you dear, never mind I will pay you back some day as you can see by my card. I will go shares with you. Well dear Leslie, what do you think of the good news Romania joining us? I think your words will come true now that it will soon be over.

Dear Leslie, I don't think there is any more news now. Mam and Dad send you their best respect and hope to see you very soon, with God's help, so I will close with fondest and dearest love and lots of kisses to my own darling Leslie, from your ever loving and true Phine.
XXXXXXXXXX

P.S. Dear Leslie, I forgot to tell you that Dad bought me a nice bicycle. Dear Leslie, the bracelet was £2/5/-
XXXX from Phine XXXXX

3rd September 1916

My own dear Leslie

Just a line hoping you are quite well as it leaves myself. Dear Leslie, we are waiting for the Zepps, it is half past two, we have got all the children sleeping downstairs sleeping on chairs. We have heard the bombs drop, they are quite near Brentwood. There is about 20 or 30 search lights, we are all sitting here waiting for the bombs to drop. Dad is up the Office. It would not be so bad if he was down here. Mam is frightened out of her life, it is as bad as been out the Front. Dear Leslie, I am falling asleep writing this letter. I don't think there is any more news now. Mam and Dad send you their best respects and hope to see you soon, so I will close with fondest and dearest love and lots of kisses to my own darling Leslie, from your ever loving true Phine.

XXXXXXXXXXXXXXXXXXX

Leslie's Battalion was in action at the third stage of the Battle of the Somme between 15th and 25th September, attacking the village of Lesboeufs.

17th September 1916

My own dearest Leslie

Just a line hoping you are quite well as it leaves myself at present. Dear Leslie, Mam was told the other day from a woman that her husband came home last week for good because he has been out there two years, and he said that all the men who have been out there two years are coming home, so I expect you will be coming if it's right.

Dear Leslie, we have got another fellow of the Army Pay Corp staying with us.

Dear Leslie, I am very sorry I did not write before because I have been busy. Dear Leslie, I don't think there is any more news now. Mam and Dad send you their best respects and hope to see you soon, so I will close with fondest and dearest love to my own darling Leslie, from your ever loving and true Phine.

XXXXXXXXXXXXXXX
XXXXXXXXXXX
XXXXXXXXXXXXXXXXXXXXXXX

27ᵗʰ September 1916

My own dearest Leslie

I received your letter dated the 16ᵗʰ. I was pleased to hear from you, also to hear you are still quite well as it leaves myself at present. Dear Leslie, I suppose you heard about the Zepps been brought down. One was brought down five miles from Brentwood in a safe place named Billericay[9]. Mam, Mona and I went there on Sunday. Mam bought a piece of it, it is about a foot long and some small pieces. We see it come down in the night before it lit all the street up. It was a lonely night, we jumped right with joy when it came down.

Dear Leslie, have you heard anything about the Sgts coming home out there? Dear Leslie, I don't think there is any more news now, so I will close with fondest and dearest love to my own darling sweetheart Leslie, from your ever loving and true Phine.

XXXXXXXXXXXXX

The Battalion was relieved from the battle after the taking of Lesboeufs and went in to the nearby village of Carnoy.

6ᵗʰ October 1916

My own darling Leslie

I received the letter this morning dated the 28ᵗʰ. I was very pleased to hear from you, also to hear you are still quite well as it leaves myself at present. Dear Leslie, when I got your card this morning I was as pleased as if it was five pounds. I was wondering if anything had happened to you because I was speaking to a fellow the other day who was on leave and he said that there was only about twelve Guards left. He said that they were walking on heaps of dead men.

Dear Leslie, I wonder if you will be lucky enough to come home. You have been out there two years this month, it seems to me like twenty-two. There are a lot of men home now who went out there in the beginning. If Mick was not a prisoner I expect he would be home. Dear Leslie, Mam had a card from him yesterday and asked her who I am engaged to, but we must not write and tell him.

Dear Leslie, that P. meant that we had got a piano at last. Dear Leslie, I hope you will soon be home to play it, with God's help.

Dear Leslie, I don't think there is any more news now. Mam and Dad send you their best respects and hope to see you very soon, so I will close with fondest and dearest love to my own darling Leslie, from your ever loving true Phine.

XXXXXXXXXXXXXXX

Dear Leslie, excuse the pencil.

7ᵗʰ October 1916

My own dearest Leslie

I received your card yesterday. I was very pleased to hear from you, also to hear you are still quite well. Dear Leslie, we have not heard from your Mother since she sent the blouse, that was only a few times I have written twice but have not had any answer yet. I expect she is busy.

Dear Leslie, we have bought a Zepp down. I stood on the other side of our road about half past two Sunday morning and see it come down.

Dear Leslie, I don't think there is any more news now. Mam and Dad send you their best respects and hope to see you soon, so I will close with fondest and dearest love to my own darling, from your ever loving Phine

XXXXXXXXXXXXXXXXXXXXXXXXXXXXXXXXXXXXXX

P.S. Dear Leslie, I hope you are not cross with me sending that card. I thought it would be a bit of fun.

12ᵗʰ October 1916

My own dearest Leslie

I received your letter and the money this morning dated the 29ᵗʰ. I was very pleased to hear from you, also to hear you are still quite well. Dear Leslie, I would like to buy you a ring for your birthday. Would you like just a plain one like a wedding ring? I would like you to wear it on your left hand and the second finger. Dear Leslie, you said in your last letter did I see anything of the Zepp come down. I see three come down, we danced with joy when we see it burning, it was a lovely sight. The last one which came down near London was only twenty miles, then the one before that was only six and the one which was about eighteen or nineteen miles from here. We never went to bed until half past three and half past four.

Dear Leslie, I don't think there is any more news now. Mam and Dad send you their best respects and hope to see you soon, so I will close with fondest and dearest love to my own darling sweetheart Leslie, from your ever loving and true Phine.

Dear Leslie, will you mark which one the board fits you¹⁰
XXXXX

Dear Leslie, I had this letter returned yesterday. XXXXXX
My own dearest Leslie
I received your letter this evening dated the 24ᵗʰ. I was very pleased to hear from you, also to here you are quite well, and I am very pleased to hear your knee is getting better. Dear Leslie, I was wondering what was the matter because I did not hear from you and I wonder if they will send you home, I think they ought too. Mam met Payne in the town the other day. He is married, he got seven days' leave, he has been in France. Dear Leslie, I don't think there is any more news now. Mam and Dad send you their best respects and hope to see you soon, so I will close with fondest and dearest love to my darling sweetheart Leslie, from your ever loving and true Phine.
XXXXXXXXXXXXXXX

Back to the field hospital

Leslie was suffering with a knee injury caused from long marches and conditions in the trenches. He had been admitted to hospital as he could hardly stand.

Ward A.8, 22nd General Hospital
24th October 1916

My dearest Phine

Just a line to let you know I am quite well and in the best of health.

I am settled in Hospital and have been confined to my bed for the last five days, but I hope to be up in a couple of days now. My knee is practically better so I expect to be off to the Base in a week or so.

We are in a nice place close to the sea,[11] and it is very comfortable. Quite a change after the excitement.

9th November 1916

My own dearest Leslie

I received your letter dated the 3rd. I was very pleased to hear from you, also to hear you are well in yourself. Dear Leslie, I am sorry to hear about your knee. I think they ought to send you home. I expect they will when you go down to the Base. I think you have done your share. Dear Leslie, I thought there was something the matter with you, been as I did not hear from you. Dear Leslie, I don't think there is any more news now. Mam and Dad send you their best respects and hope to see you soon, so I will close with fondest and dearest love to my own darling sweetheart Leslie, from your ever loving and true Phine.

XXXXXXX

P.S. Dear Leslie, excuse the short letter but I am in a hurry.

XXXXXXXXXXXX

God bless you and bring you back safe.

22nd November 1916

My own dearest Leslie

Just a line hoping you are quite well as it leaves myself at present. Dear Leslie, have you heard anything about coming home? I am very sorry to hear you are still weak. I don't suppose they will send you up to the trenches again. I think they ought to send you home for the winter, it is not much use in sending you up in the trenches with your knee, that will only make it worse. You ought to kick up about it, I would. You have been out there over two years now.

Dear Leslie, I don't think there is any more news now. Mam and Dad send you their best respects and hope to see you soon, so I will close with fondest and dearest love to my own darling sweetheart Leslie, from your ever loving and true Phine.

XXXXXXXXXXXXXXXXX

My own dearest Leslie

I received your letter dated 10th. I was very pleased to hear from you, also to hear your knee is getting better. I was wondering what was the matter. Dear Leslie, I received the money quite safe, thank you very much. I sent a cardboard with holes in. I wanted to fit it on because I want to buy you a nice ring for your birthday. Did you get it? I have one letter returned. I have written five or six letters since you have been in hospital. I think they ought to send you home. I think you have done your bit, you have been over there two years. I think it is a shame.

Dear Leslie, Mam met Payne up in the town about three weeks ago, with his wife. He is married now, he said he has been out in France all the time he is Sgt Major.

Dear Leslie, I don't get much time now. I am going to work, I have to be there at half past eight and have one till two for dinner, then I get from half past four to quarter past five for tea, and then I don't finish until half past seven. I serve in a shop at a printer.

Dear Leslie, I don't think there is any more news now. Mam and Dad send you their best respects and hope to see you soon, so I will close with fondest and dearest love to my own darling Leslie, from your ever loving and true Phine.

XXX

P.S. excuse me for the scribble.

No. 5 Convalescent Camp Depot, a.p.o.23. B.E.F.
25th November 1916

My own dearest Phine

I received your two letters dated the 22nd. Fancy I received your last letter in two days. I had one from home which took ten days to come.

I was relieved to hear you received the money alright. You say you sent a letter with a cardboard in. I have not received it. Probably it will be returned to you, unless they send it on to me.

My knee is still the same, it does not improve at all. I can walk alright, but it pains me all the time, but I don't think any more can be done for it.

I was surprised to hear you were out at work, the hours seem rather long. I hope you like it all right. It seems everybody in England works now. Mother wrote and told me she was going to work at Xmas in the Post Office.

There is no chance of coming home. I know I have been out over two years, but it makes no difference. You see they want all the men they can get, and it is especially hard for a Sgt to get home as they want them so much. I almost wish I was a Private, fellows with the same complaint as I have been sent home, but they will not send us, unless we are extremely bad.

Well I have no more to say now, so I will close give my best wishes to your Mam and Dad, hoping they are quite well, with fondest and dearest love and kisses to my own darling sweetheart Phine, from your ever loving and true Leslie.

XXXXXXXXXXXXXXXXXXXXXXXXXXXXXXXXXX

27th November 1916

My own dearest Leslie
I received your letter yesterday dated the 10th. I was very pleased to hear from you, also to hear you are still quite well. I am pleased to hear your knee is nearly better. Dear Leslie, I had another letter returned yesterday. We are having awfully cold weather here too, we had to have a fire up the shop it was so cold. Dear Leslie, do you think they will send you back up to the trenches? If they do, I think it is a shame. I should kick up and try and come home, it is about eight months since I saw you, it seems more like eight years.

Dear Leslie, I don't think there is any more news now. Mam and Dad send you their best respects and hope to see you soon, so I will close with fondest and dearest love and lots of kisses to my own sweetheart Leslie, from your ever loving and true Phine.
XXXXXX

4th December 1916

My own dearest Leslie
I received your two letters, dated the 25th and the 29th. I was very pleased to hear from you. I was sorry to hear your knee is not any better. Dear, I like my work very much, it is not hard, I only serve in the shop and do marking off, that is putting prices on things. We only sell stationery, leather goods and daily papers, so it is so nice work serving all day. We are rather busy now dressing the windows for Christmas. There are three girls besides me working in the shop. I don't get much time, by the time I get home at night it is nearly eight because we don't leave off until after seven, nearly all the other shops in Brentwood shut at six, that is another new order out.

Dear Leslie, it don't look as though the war will be over by 1916, does it?

I was saying to Mam the other day you will soon be twenty-four. Mam said what about you going on for eighteen, it only seems the other day since I left school. Dear Leslie, it was three years last month when we first knew you, it does not seem that time does it. Dear Leslie, I don't think there is any more news now. Mam and Dad send their best respects and hope to see you soon, so I will close with fondest and dearest love and lots of kisses to my own darling sweetheart Leslie, from your ever loving and true Phine.
XXXXXXXXXXXXXXXXXXXXX
Dear Leslie, excuse pencil because it is for quickness.

No. 5 Convalescent Depot, a.p.o s/23 B.E.F.
6th December 1916

My own dearest Phine

I received your letter dated the 4th, and was so pleased to receive such a nice letter. You will have to write me one like that always now. I was very interested to hear about your work. I like to hear what you are doing, it cheers me up so out here, so don't forget dearest more news in your letters. I cannot write more myself as you as we are under the restrictions of the censor.

As you say the time does fly, fancy three years since we know each other, I did not think it was so long as that, it only seems three months.

You said in your last letter that it was eight months since I was home and that it seemed like <u>eight years</u>, and now in this letter you say it seems only the other day that you were at school. <u>Irish</u> of course, absolutely, still your Mam being Irish, I suppose there is an excuse for you. Please don't show her this or it will mean more trouble for me when I come home. Having my nose pulled or something.

I think I shall be here till after Xmas, in fact I am almost certain. I hope I do, we have a fine Mess here and they are going to keep up Xmas in the old style. It will be far different to the last two I have spent out here. Still for all that I hope with God's help to spend the next one with you in England. It would be a lot better if it lasted another year, but I do not think there is any fear of that.

I felt quite shocked when you reminded me in your letter, that I should soon be twenty-four. It seems quite old, doesn't it? Still, I do not feel any older, I feel just the same as I did when I enlisted.

Well I think I will close now, and don't forget darling, all the news in your next letters, with best wishes to your Mam and Dad and fondest and dearest love to my own darling sweetheart Phine, from your ever loving true Leslie.

XXXXXXXXXXXXXXXXXXX

11th December 1916

My own dearest Leslie

I received your last letter yesterday dated the 6th. I was very pleased to hear from you, also to hear you are still quite well. Dear Leslie, you did not say in your last letter how your knee is getting on. I hope it is nearly better. Dear Leslie, I received a letter from you last Thursday dated 30th of Nov. Dear Leslie, your last letter only took four days to come. Did I tell you that Mam has met Payne in the town the other week and that he told Mam that he had a job somewhere in France and he is also Sgt Major. He got seven days leave and came home and got married. Mam see him one Saturday as he was going back to France on Sunday. Dear Leslie, Mam has not heard from Mick for several weeks. Dear Leslie, a fortnight today it's Christmas. I suppose it will be a quiet Christmas like it was last year.

Dear Leslie, I don't think there is any more news now. Mam and Dad send you their best respects and hope to see you soon, so I will close with fondest and dearest love and tons of kisses to my own darling sweetheart, from you ever loving and true Phine.

XXXX

No. 5 Convalescent Dept., <u>a.p.o S23 B.E.F</u>
15th December 1916

My own dearest Phine

I received your letter of the 11th yesterday, and was pleased to hear you are quite well. You asked me how my knee is, well it is a lot better, and all the swelling has left it, but it is still very weak, and pains me a little at times. I have to be very careful with it. I have got a job here today, offered me, which will keep me here at least three months, so I think with a long rest like that, away from the trenches, it should soon be well.

The job is pretty easy, all that worries me is the Batt might make enquires after me which they do, if anyone is away from the Batt too long, and of course that means going back at once. Still I do not think they will worry about me, after being out here so long. I hope not anyhow, because I can do with a rest. Of course, while I stop here, it delays my leave so long, but I think it's best to do without it for a while, rather than join the Batt and probably have my knee get worse.

It is hard luck because I so much want to come home and see you, as you say it seems years since I was home.

We had a whist-drive[12] in the mess here, last week, of course some of us had to act as lady partners and as Miss Cox I won the ladies' first prize. It is so difficult to get a Xmas present from me, and then when I got home I can get you something else.

Yes, you did tell me about Payne before, I expect he is on the same act as I am, with a three months' job in a convalescent camp.

I suppose as you say Xmas will be a quiet one at home, but from the preparations they are making here, I think we are going to have a very merry one.

I'm sorry to hear your Mam has not heard from Mick lately, I hope she will soon hear, and that he is alright.

Well I think this is all I have to say this time, so I will conclude with my best wishes and respects to your Mam and Dad, and fondest and dearest love and hundreds of kisses to my darling sweetheart Phine, from your ever loving and true Leslie.

XXX

No. 5 Convalescent Depot, a.p.o S/23 B.E.F
17ᵗʰ December 1916

My own darling Phine

I have just received your letter of the 12ᵗʰ Oct, which you had returned, it seemed strange receiving a letter two months old!

I received the ring-card and I have marked the size which fits my second finger. I presume you mean the one next to the little finger. I do not care much about wearing a ring, but I should be very pleased to have one from you to wear. It will remind me of you at home, but that is hardly necessary as I am thinking of you always, night and day. I awful wish this old war was over so that I could be with you. Still I suppose it is more or less a test to see what we are made off. What do you think of the French's answer to the German's peace offerings? Rather a nasty smack for them, advancing two miles and taking 9,000 prisoners. I expect we shall have another go at them soon. I have started on my job, it is very easy, and I am told it will last three months or probably four so my knee should be quite well by then.

Well I will conclude now dearest, as like you, I have got to get to work. It is only myself that calls it that, no one else does. Give my best wishes and respects to your Mam and Dad, sincere wishes for a happy Xmas and fondest and dearest love and hundreds of kisses to my darling sweetheart Phine, from your ever loving and true Leslie.

XXXXXXXXXXXXXXXXX

20ᵗʰ December 1916

My own darling Leslie

I received your letter this morning dated the 15ᵗʰ. I was very pleased to hear from you, also to hear your knee is getting better. Dear Leslie, Mam heard from Mick the day before yesterday. He says he is quite well and was looking out for his Christmas parcel, but all the prisoner's parcels got damaged in Holland so Mam don't know whether he will get it or not.

Dear Leslie, I am glad you are going to have a happy Christmas. Dear, of course I don't mind having the dressing case for a Christmas present, I will only be too pleased with it because you won it and it came from France.

Dear Leslie, I have left my job. I had to come home because Mam had an awful cold and we have had the Doctor and nurse to the baby. Mam could not manage without me, because she has the two Pay Corp. So, I told Mam I am not going out too work anymore. I did not care for it because the hours were long and it was awfully cold in the shop. I have got chapped hands, I have never had them before. Dear Leslie, I don't think there is any more news now. Mam and Dad send you their best respects and wish you a happy Christmas so I will close with fondest and dearest love and lots of kisses to my darling Leslie, from your ever loving and true Phine.

XXXXXXXXXXXXXXXXXX

Leslie was posted temporarily at the Guards base depot Le Havre and given light duties while his knee recovered.

1ˢᵗ Grenadier Guards, Guards Division, Base Depot, B,E.F
27ᵗʰ December 1916

My own darling Phine

Just a few lines to let you know I am alright. I arrived here at the Base just before Xmas, we had a pretty good day. We had a nice dinner, and in the evening a Pantomime called "Jack and the beanstalk". It was an excellent affair, run by the chaps of our Division.

I met Payne here last night, he is staying just near, and is acting Sgt Major on some job or other.

I do not know how long I shall be here, but probably a fortnight or so before I join the Batt. My knee is still about the same, it does not seem to improve.

I suppose I shall have to wait a day or two till I receive any of your letters, I have not had any sent on from the Convalescent Camp yet.

Well I will write again soon. I am on guard at present and rather busy, so au revoir, with best wishes to your Mam and Dad and fondest and dearest love to my own darling sweetheart, from your ever loving and true Leslie.

XXXXXXX

Notes 1916

1. In February, the Battalion was moved to Calais, France, and then moved on to Belgium.
2. The Division was billeted under canvas in the Calais area in France.
3. On 16th March Leslie's Battalion arrived at Ypres and went into the trenches.
4. The Easter Rising was an uprising of the Irish in Ireland.
5. H. H. Plante, Goldsmith, Silversmith and Jeweller, St James London S.W. by appointment of his Majesty the King.
6. The Battalion was in the Ypres area.
7. The wound stripe was authorised to be used from July 1916. It was worn on the left sleeve on the soldier's uniform and was made of gold braid and was 2" in length. A soldier who was wounded more than once would have multiple stripes for each time they were wounded.
8. 1st July was the start of the first phase of the Battle of the Somme offensive. Leslie refers to this in his letter.
9. On 24th September, Zeppelin L32 was shot down and crash landed near Billericay in Great Burstead, Essex.
10. Ring size board for measuring correct fitting of a ring to a person's finger.
11. 22nd General Hospital Camiers, Hauts-de-France region in France.
12. Whist drive – an old English card game.

Forget-me-not 1917

5th January 1917

My own dearest Leslie

I received your letter yesterday dated the 27th Dec. I was very pleased to hear from you, also to hear your knee is not worse. Dear, I am sorry to hear you are going back to the Batt, I suppose you will soon have your leave then. Bruce says he hopes you get it while he is staying in Brentwood because he will not be able to get a pass. Dear Leslie, I have sent four or five letters since you have been down at the base. Dear Leslie, Bruce stopped here until after twelve and when he got up to his billet he was locked out because one of the other fellows was in before Bruce and locked the door, so Bruce came back and slept here all night.

Dear Leslie, I don't think there is any more news now. Mam and Dad send you their best respects and hope to see you soon, so I will close with fondest and dearest love and tons of kisses to my own darling sweetheart Leslie, from your ever loving and true Phine.

XXXXXXXXXXXXXX

1st Batt Grenadier Guards
Guards Division Base Depot
Le Havre B.E.F
6th January 1917

My own darling Phine

I am sorry I have not written you before, but I have hardly a minute to spare here at the base. I am Sgt in waiting and I am on the go all day long. I had your letter of the 20th and Xmas card forwarded on. Thank you for the card, it is a nice one. I was sorry to hear the baby had been ill, I hope she is well again now. So you have finished working out now.

I received your letter of the 28th and Bruce's letter on the same day, about six days ago, I am sorry I did not answer before. Tell Bruce I will write him later, and I have not received the parcel he sent me at Xmas yet, but it will probably be sent on.

I could stop here a good while, if I wished, but I am off to the Batt as soon as possible about a weeks' time, so that I may get my leave. I am entitled to one now, and I should like to try and get home whilst Bruce is at Warley.

Well I am very busy darling, so I will make this a short letter. Give my respects and best wishes for a Happy New Year to your Mam and Dad, and fondest and dearest love and kisses to my own darling sweetheart Phine, from your ever loving and true Leslie.

XXX

7ᵗʰ January 1917

My dearest Leslie

I received your card this morning. I am sorry to hear you have joined the Battalion, still never mind, you might stand a better chance to come home for good. There are two soldiers home for good here in Brentwood because they have been out in France the whole time, so I think you ought to come home.

Dear Leslie, there is a young married woman started up at our works last Monday and she can tell fortunes by the tea cups. She told me mine, and she said I was going to have a pleasant surprise, and I am going to meet somebody very tall, but she did not know if it was a man or woman and I am going to be parted from a very near relation and I am going to have a letter, but it is a long way away.

My dear Leslie, I hope you will like this card. Dear, I wish you many happy returns of the day and hope you will be home for good for your next birthday. Mam and Dad wishes you the same. My dearest Leslie, I don't think there is any more news at present so I will close with fondest and dearest love and tons of kisses to my own darling sweetheart Leslie, from your ever loving and true Phine.
XXXXXXXXX

My own darling Leslie

I received the dressing case it is very nice indeed.

Bruce comes down nearly every night. Your Mother and Mabel are coming down on Sunday. Mam and Dad went up to see your Mother Thursday and she was in bed down in the kitchen with a cold.

Dear Leslie, I wonder what they sent for you from the Battalion. Your Mother expects you home any day, she told Mam that every knock on the door she thinks it is you.

Dear Leslie, I don't think there is any more news now. Mam and Dad send you their best respects and hope to see you soon, so I will close with fondest and dearest love and lots of kisses to my own darling sweetheart Leslie, from your ever loving and true Phine.
XXXXXXXXXXXXXXXXXXXXXXXXXXXXXXX

8ᵗʰ January 1917

My own dearest Leslie

Just a line wishing you many happy returns of the day and hoping you will be in England for your next birthday. Dear, I wonder if they will send you home this month while Bruce is staying in Brentwood. Your Mother told Mam that she expects you home any day. Mam and Dad went up to see your Mother Thursday before last and she was in bed down in the kitchen with a cold. Dear Leslie, I could not get the ring here so I had to send away for it and Mr Ringe said he will not be able to get it until Tuesday.

Dear Leslie, I don't think there is any more news now. Mam and Dad send you their best respects and wish you a happy return of the day, so I will close with fondest and dearest love and lots of kisses to my own dearest Leslie, from your ever loving and true Phine

XXXXXXXXXXXXXX

13th January 1917

My own dearest Leslie

I received your letter yesterday dated the 6th. I was very pleased to hear from you, also to hear you are still quite well as it leaves myself at present. Dear Leslie, I wonder how many days they will give you this time. Some of the men are getting ten days and a month. Dear, it is turned nine months since you were home, I like you to come home but when you are gone back I think I wished you had not come home.

Dear Leslie, you know I wrote and told you that your Mother was coming down Sunday before last, well she was not well so she said she would come down Sunday. Well that was last Sunday. Bruce came down in the afternoon and we waited tea till after five and she did not come. Mam can't make it out, we have not had a letter and Bruce has not had one, he wrote to her last night. Dear Leslie, I don't think there is any more news now. Mam and Dad send you their best respects and hope to see you soon, so I will close with fondest and dearest love and lots of kisses to my own darling sweetheart Leslie, from your ever loving and true Phine.

XXXXXXXXXXXXX

P.S. Dear Leslie, I have just got the ring, what shall I do? Send it out to you or wait till you come home, as it is so little it might get lost in the post? Write back and tell me, from Phine.

XXXXXXXXXXXXXXXXX.

14th January 1917

My own dearest Phine

I received your two letters dated the 5th and 8th, I am so sorry to keep you waiting for an answer but as I told you in my last letter I hardly have a minute to spare. I am so busy with being Sgt-in-waiting.

I am afraid I shall not get home whilst Bruce is in <u>England</u> Brentwood because whilst I stay at the base I cannot get a leave, and they will not let me go for a week or two yet. Still I am trying hard to get to the Batt so I may have my leave. Of course, being here, I am missing a very rough time in the trenches whilst this weather looks, it is mud up to the waist in the front line now.

You said in your last letter you have sent four or five letters to me at the Base, I have only had three which you sent on the 28th, 5th and 8th. There is one thing I notice, you always put No. 2 Coy and I am in No. 4. When you write again dear, underline the word Base Depot, then the letters will not go up the line. Well I must conclude now darling. I have a lot to do, I will write you again at the first opportunity, give my best wishes and respects to your Mam and Dad, and fondest and dearest love and kisses to my own darling Phine, from your ever loving and true

Leslie.

XXX

P.S. Remember me to Bruce, and I hope he is passing through alright.

P.S. Can you tell me dear what is the meaning of " Ben-my-Chree"? A Sgt of the Irish Guards told me it was Irish, but would not tell me what it means.

Les XXXXX

19ᵗʰ January 1917

My own dearest Leslie

Just a line hoping you are quite well as it leaves myself at present. Dear Leslie, you said you could stop down at the base if you like. I think I should, because they have had another Battle. Dear, your last letter I had was dated the six and I have not had one since. I suppose you are busy and I thought you might not have liked it because I did not send you a birthday card. I went out on Saturday afternoon with Mam to get the shopping and forgot all about it and it was too late to send it on Monday, still never mind dear. Dear Leslie, your Mam came down on Sunday for a few hours. She did not come before because it was snowing. We have had a lot of snow this winter. I suppose you have had a lot out there too. Dear Leslie, I don't think there is any more news now. Mam and Dad send you their best respects and hope to see you soon, so I will close with fondest and dearest love and lots of kisses to my own darling Leslie, from your ever loving and true Phine.

XXXXXXXXXXXXXXX

20th January 1917

My own dearest Phine

I received your letter dated the 13ᵗʰ and I have also received one dated the 2ⁿᵈ which had been up to the Batt and back. I think it was because you put No. 2 Coy on the envelope.

You ask me how long I shall have when I come back on leave, it will be 10 days when I can get it, but I shall not join the Batt for at least a week yet.

I have been a bit anxious over your letter, when you said my Mother did not come down and had not written either. I hope she is alright, but I am worrying and cold. That I feel too fed up to write a letter. We are having some awful weather out here, it snows every day.

It must be awful up in the trenches, we have a lot come in every day from Hospital who have come down with frostbite.

I am afraid I shall not manage to get home on leave while Bruce is at Brentwood, in fact it is doubtful if I shall join the Batt in time to go. It is rumoured they are stopping it at the beginning of February, and if I get to the Batt I should have to wait probably a fortnight before I get home.

I will close, with best wishes to your Mam and Dad and fondest and dearest love and kisses to my own darling sweetheart, from your ever loving and true Leslie.
XXXXXXXXXXXX

25th January 1917

My own dearest Leslie
I received your letter yesterday dated the 20th and also had one on Saturday. I was very pleased to hear from you, also to hear you are still quite well. Dear Leslie, you did not say in your last letter if your knee is getting better. Dear Leslie, you may be home now before Bruce goes back, he has got to stay another week. He ought to have gone back tomorrow, but he will not go back until tomorrow fortnight. Dear, I suppose you have heard about the explosion in Silvertown,[1] don't you think it is terrible? Hundreds of people that are wounded and burnt to death. Mam said it looks as though the end of the world is coming. Did I tell you that Mam is going out to work, she is working up the huts with Dad from six to eight every morning.

Dear Leslie, I don't think there is any more news now. Mam and Dad send you their best and hope to see you soon, so I will close with fondest and dearest love and lots of kisses to my own darling sweetheart Leslie, from your ever loving and true Phine.
XXXXXXXXXXXXXXXXXX

1st Battalion Guards
Guards division Base Depot
25th January 1917

My own darling Phine
I received your letter dated the 19th and I was glad to hear from you. I also received your card of the forget-me-not, it is very nice, but I don't think I shall ever forget, not if the war lasted fifty years. I only wish I was at home with you.

How funny of you to think that I was expecting a birthday card. I did not mind in the least. I had your letter, that was quite sufficient. I am kept so busy all day long, that I never have a minute to spare, and when I do I am so tired. Still never mind dearest, we shall soon all be home for good.

What an awful affair that explosion must have been, did you hear it at Brentwood? We heard out here that it was not far from Ilford.

Well I will close for now dear, so once again au revoir, with best wishes to your Mam and Dad, and fondest and dearest love to my darling sweetheart Phine, from your ever loving and true Leslie.
XXXXXXXXXXXXXXXXXXXXXXXXXXXXXXXXXXXXXXXX

30ᵗʰ January 1917

My own dearest Phine

I received your letter of the 19ᵗʰ and was very pleased to hear from you. It seems that the letters take a lot longer to come and go than they should, as they all come here first before they are ported.

We have been having some awful weather, it is something awful at night time and snowing at a quarter past five in the morning is more than a joke. I am afraid when I do come on leave I shall not leave my bed for the ten days I am there.

There have been no drafts going up the line yet, so I am still here, but hope to be off up in about ten days' time. I should like to come home again, I am feeling a bit homesick down here, there is no excitement here like in the trenches to take one's mind off home.

I heard from Mother yesterday. She said she had been down to see you at Brentwood. She tells me Mabel is crazy on dancing now, goes to one every Saturday night, in time too. How is Bruce? Remember me to him, I suppose he is still swanking with that dog-leg² on his arm. I wonder how long he is going to keep it, or whether he will be Sergeant soon. My word, if he does, there will be no holding him. He told me he thought he was coming out after Xmas, I suppose there is no signs yet.

Have you heard from Mick lately? When I think of them in Germany, I stop grumbling. Fancy all that time away from England, when most of us out here have been home once or twice.

Well I suppose I must conclude now, I am still very busy. So once again au revoir, give my best respects and wishes to your Mam and Dad, hoping they are still in the best of health, with fondest and dearest love and kisses to my own darling sweetheart, from your ever loving and true Leslie.

XXXXXXXXXXXXXX

30ᵗʰ January 1917

My own dearest Leslie

I received your letter on Sunday dated the 25ᵗʰ. I was very pleased to hear from you, also to hear you are still quite well. Dear Leslie, you said in your last letter that it was very cold out there. It is terrible cold here too, my hands are chapped so, that I don't know what to do with them. Dear Leslie, Mam has gone to a dance tonight. She wanted me to go but I did not want to, if you were home dear I would go; I suppose it will be long while before you will be able to go to a dance with your Phine. Dear Leslie, I will send the ring out next week because nobody is allowed to send parcels for a week. There is a lot parcels at Southampton for the Front. Dear Leslie, I don't think there is any more news now. Mam and Dad send you their best respects and hope to see you soon, so I will close with fondest and dearest love and lots of kisses to my own darling sweetheart Leslie, from your ever loving Phine.

Phine goes to the dances

10th February 1917

My own dearest Leslie

Just a line hoping you are quite well as it leaves myself at present. Dear Leslie, Bruce went back yesterday. My dear Leslie, I told you in my last letter that Mabel and Mam was going to Saint Patrick's Ball. Mam said she would like me to go, do you mind if I go? Mam went to London last Tuesday and got me a nice evening dress, it is pea green trimmed with gold beads. I wished you were home so you could go. Mam said if I go some of the Irish Guards might be after me in my green dress, still dear it is a long way off yet, the seventeenth of March. You might be home by then, I don't like going there without you. It would bring old times back to me, I would be thinking of you the whole evening.

Dear Leslie, did you know Dolly Weare? She used to go to all the Cpl Dances. She is tall and thin. She got married today to a Sgt of the Irish Guards. Dear Leslie, I don't think there is any more news now. Mam and Dad send you their best respects and hope to see you soon, so I will close with fondest and dearest love and tons of kisses to my own darling sweetheart Leslie, from your ever loving and true Phine.

XXXXXXXXXXX

P.S. Dear Leslie, poor old Bruce did look downhearted, he did not want to go back because while he was here his young lady wrote and broke it off with him.

XXXXX

11th February 1917

My own dearest Leslie

Just a line hoping you are quite well as it leaves myself at present. Dear Leslie, I have not had a letter since last Friday week. I was wondering if you had gone up to the Batt. Mam said perhaps the letters had been sunk because the Germans have sunk several of our ships this last fortnight, they sunk two in twenty-four hours last week, they are going to sink every Hospital ship terrible.[3] Dear Leslie, your Mother said that I better not send the ring because nobody is allowed to register a parcel which is going out to France. Dear Leslie, I don't think there is any more news now. Mam and Dad send you their best respects and hope to see you soon, so I will close with fondest and dearest love and tons of kisses to my own darling Leslie, from your ever loving and true Phine.

XXXXXXXXXXXX

12th February 1917

My own darling Phine

I have received your two letters dated the 30th and the 7th and was pleased to hear from you. I have been too busy to write before, and we have had such awful cold weather, it simply froze one to sit in a tent and write.

I was glad to hear you went up to Mother's. I wish I could have been there, still I suppose the day will soon come when I can stop home for good, roll on.

So, Mabel had you on dancing when you went up. Mother wrote and told me she was crazy on it. She must be if you were dancing in the kitchen all morning. I suppose you will go to the ball on St. Patrick's Day, I hope you have a good time, I should like to be there with you. Still no good wishing, I see that they have stopped the leave now for a time, I do not know what for or how long.

I am still waiting to go up the line, but they will not let me yet. I am glad in a way as my knee has been painful lately, and I am afraid I should only be up here a short time with it.

Well I must close now dearest, I have a lot to do, so once again au revoir, with best wishes to your Mam and Dad and fondest and dearest love and kisses to my own darling sweetheart, from your ever loving and true Leslie.

XXXXXXXXXX

P.S. I am obviously awaiting the ring; I hope it will arrive safe.

Les XXX

17th February 1917

My own dearest Leslie

I received your letter yesterday evening dated the 12th. I was very pleased to hear from you. I am sorry to hear your knee has been paining you. Dear Leslie, I think I told you in my last letter that we are not allowed to register a parcel to France, your Mother said it is safer to keep it until you come home. Did I tell you that I had your name put on the ring? Dear Leslie, Mam and I was wondering all sorts of things because I had not heard from you for a fortnight, so she went up to your Mother's yesterday after dinner to see if she had heard from you. While she was gone I had your letter. Dear Leslie, I don't think there is any more news now. Mam and Dad send you their best respects and hope to see you soon, so I will close with fondest and dearest love and lots of kisses to my own darling sweetheart Leslie, from your ever loving and true Phine.

XXXXXXXXXXXXXXXXXXXXXXXX

21st February 1917

My own dearest Leslie

Just a line hoping you are quite well as it leaves myself at present. Dear, I received your card, it is very pretty. Mam had a letter from Bruce on Wednesday evening. He said he is staying in an empty hall before he came on the course, at the schools he was in a hotel. Dear, your last letter you sent was five days coming, there must be something the matter with the post because Mam went up to your Mother's last Friday afternoon and your Mother said she sent a letter in the morning and Mam has not got it yet. Dear Leslie, Mam has not heard from Mick for several weeks. I suppose they have gone down in the ships.

Dear Leslie, don't you think you will get your leave now? Still never mind dear, I would rather you stop down at the Base then go up to the Batt with your knee.

Dear Leslie, I don't think there is any more news now. Mam and Dad send you their best respects and hope to see you soon, so I will close with fondest and dearest love and tons of kisses to my own darling sweetheart Leslie, from your ever loving and true Phine.

XXXXXXXXX

24th February 1917

My own darling Leslie

Just a line hoping you are quite well as it leaves myself at present. Dear Leslie, I went to a Sgt dance last night of the Irish Guards. It was very nice, but I did not enjoy it because every fellow I danced with I was wishing it was you and it bought old times back. I did not sit one dance out, what I did not have with the fellows I had with Mam, they have got some new dances now. Last night was the first time I ever done them. Mam has done them before, because she has been to the dances at the schools where Bruce was, one was the "Doris Walty", it is very pretty.

Dear Leslie, I wish you could get home so you and I go to the Saint Patrick's Ball. Mam bought me a pretty dress, it is all gold with a green slip so that you can see the gold through it.

Dear, I hope you did not mind me going to the dance. When I was dancing I thought to myself I wonder what poor old Les is doing now. Mam kept on saying we want Les here, specially when she was doing the "Military two-step", don't you remember when you used to do the "Boston two-step"?

Dear Leslie, I don't think there is any more news now. Mam and Dad send you their best respects, so I will close with fondest and dearest love and tons of kisses to my own darling sweetheart Leslie, from your ever loving and true Phine.

XXXXXX

25th February 1917

My dear Leslie

I received your letter dated the 23rd. I was very pleased to hear from you. Dear Leslie, I suppose you will be home next week or the week after. Mam has not heard from Mick for nearly four weeks, she is beginning to worry because she used to hear every week, sometimes twice.

Dear Leslie, we have got the Royal Scots and the Scottish Rifles, some of them are in Huts. Dear Leslie, I don't think there is any more news now. Mam and Dad send you their best respects and hope to see you soon, so I will close with fondest and dearest love to my own darling Leslie, from your ever loving Phine.

XXXXXXX

27th February 1917

My own darling Phine

I received your three letters, we have not had any mail for six days owing to the post being closed, and when I received them, I had them in reverse order. The one you posted on the 21st I had first, and yesterday I had one dated the 11th.

I did not write, as the letters were not crossing to England, so I thought I would wait till they did. I have been awfully busy, there is a draft here of 200 or more and I have a lot of work to do paying them and seeing to their clothing. I hardly have a minute to go to meals, so please forgive me for not writing you before. I know you must be thinking terrible things of me for not writing before, but it is not my fault.

I had a letter from Mother. She told me you had been to London with Bruce, and that you also went to the pantomime.

You asked me about the St Patrick's Ball, certainly go if you wish darling. I am sure I have no objections, except to being out here and not being able to come with you. But don't run off with an Irish Guard will you? And in that new green dress too.

You told me Bruce was downhearted when he went away because his girl had chucked him, but that is nothing, he has had about half a dozen since the war started and I expect he has another by now, so I have no sympathy for him.

Well I will close for now darling, as I have any amount of work to do, so au revoir, with best wishes to your Mam and Dad and fondest and dearest love to my own darling sweetheart Phine, from your ever loving and true Leslie.

XXXXXXXX

2nd March 1917

My own dearest Leslie

Just a line hoping you are quite well as it leaves myself at present. Dear Leslie, I am awfully sorry I did not write for over a week. I had been very busy. Enna, my youngest sister, has got the German Measles. One of our men was taken away with it, the Doctor said it will go all through the house.

Dear Leslie, Mam had another letter from Mick this morning. He said that the end of the war is very near. He was twenty-two on the fifteenth of last month and he has been a prisoner two years and a half on the twenty ninth of last month, poor fellow. Dear Leslie, we are having awfully hot weather here, it is too hot to do anything. Did you see that Sgt of the Irish Guards yet?

I don't think there is any more news. Mam and Dad send you their best respects and hope to see you soon, so I will close with fondest and dearest love and lots of kisses to my own dearest sweetheart Leslie, from your ever loving and true Phine.

XXXXXXXXXXXXXXXXXXXXXXXX

3rd March 1917

My own dearest Leslie

I received your letter dated the 27th. I was very pleased to hear from you, also to hear you are still quite well as it leaves myself at present. Dear Leslie, it was funny it was a fortnight yesterday when I had your last letter and then to have come yesterday.

Dear Leslie, Mam and I went to the Cpls dance of the Irish Guards last night. It was very nice, it was nicer than the Sgt dance last week and was not quite so late. We got home about three o'clock, roll on when we can go to the Grenadiers. I am afraid it will be a long time yet. Dear, I had three dances with three Irish Guard Officers. Dear Leslie, it said in yesterday's paper that they want young women to go out to France. I wish I could go, you must be over twenty and under forty.

Dear Leslie, I don't think there is any more news. Mam and Dad send you their best respects and hope to see you soon, so I will close with fondest and dearest love to my own darling Leslie, from your ever loving and true Phine.

4th March

My own darling Phine

I received your letter dated the 24th, and was glad to hear from you. I am so sorry I cannot find time to write you oftener, but I am so awfully busy. I got rid of the Draft and another arrived next morning. I hardly know which way to turn. I am running about and writing from morning to night.

I am glad to hear you went to the dance, but what is the use of going if you do not enjoy it? You want to have a good time, never mind about thinking of me, whilst you are there. I expect you will have enough of me when I come home for good. Roll on, I should just like to have another dance, especially on St Patrick's Day. I often think of the one at the Hall, it seems ages ago now. It will be 3 years, and most of the time still I think we are going to see the end soon now. There are big things happening up the line.

There is one thing I want to ask you. I should very much like for you to send the ring out to me, as my leave seems to be a long way off yet. Anyhow while I am here at the Base I think if you register it in a letter I should receive it quite safe, you cannot register a parcel I know, but a small thing like a ring would go by letter post alright. Of course, if you think it is not safe I will wait till I come home.

Well I think this is all this time, I will write again as soon as possible, but do not be angry if it is a long time, as for once in my life I have got work to do, and you know how terrible that is to me.

Well, I will close now, so once again au revoir, with best wishes to your Mam and Dad, hoping they are in the best of health, and fondest and dearest love and kisses to my own darling sweetheart Phine, from your ever loving Leslie.

XXXX

10th March 1917

My own dearest Leslie

Just a line hoping you are still quite well as it leaves myself at present. Dear Leslie, I don't suppose you will get your leave now, I think it is a shame don't you? It is twelve months now since you were home, I think it is time you came home for good. Dear Leslie, when I went to the first Sgts dance of the Irish Guards there was a tall fair Sgt asked Mam could I go out with him, but Mam said no he was too late. Dear, I wish you was home so you could go as well, but I suppose you could not dance with your bad knee.

Dear Leslie, I am getting fed up of this blessed old war. Dear, I don't think there is any more news now. Mam and Dad send you their best respects and hope to see you soon. I will close with fondest and dearest love and lots of kisses to my own darling sweetheart Leslie, from your ever loving and true Phine.
XXXXXXXXXXXXXXXXXXXXXX

17th March 1917

My own darling Phine

I received your letters dated the 3rd and the 10th and was very glad to hear from you.

My word, I shall have to look out, now you are going to the dances. I can see myself losing you yet. I am just trying to picture you now at the St Patrick's Dance. It is about half past two, I have seen a Draft off and am waiting for one to come in at any moment from England. This is the second night running I have been up, last night we had the Zepps very near and had to turn out, but we did not see them. I was going to a concert tonight at the Ulster Divisions Sgts Mess, but had to stay in on account of the draft coming. You must write and tell me about the dance, did Mabel go, and I wonder if that Sgt you spoke of was there? There is one arrived here tonight from England with a draft, who is tall and very fair, I was wondering if it was him or not.

Well I see the War is progressing very well, we have had excellent news tonight, Bapaume is fallen and we have advanced all along the line. Of course you will know by the time you have this letter. Roll on, I can see the War finishing this year yet. I hope so, I am properly fed up and longing to get back, it is over a year now since I was home.

Well I will close now darling, I am nearly falling asleep, so au revoir, with best wishes to your Mam and Dad, and fondest and dearest love to my own darling sweetheart Phine, from your ever loving and true Leslie. XXXXXXXXXXXXXXXXXXXXXX.

My own dearest Leslie

I received your letter yesterday morning dated the 4th. I was very pleased to hear from you. Mam had a letter from Bruce yesterday and he said he has made up again with his young lady. He said they are very busy down there, they are even working on Sundays.

Dear Leslie, Mam and I went down the Station last night to see the wounded come in. There was twenty-one poor fellows, they did look bad. Mam gave them a packet of cigarettes each.

Dear Leslie, I don't think there is any more news now. Mam and Dad send you their best respects and hope to see you soon, so I will close with fondest and dearest love and tons of kisses to my own darling Leslie, from your ever loving and true Phine.

XXXXXXXXXXXXXXXXXXXXXX.

P.S. Dear Leslie, I hope you will like the ring.

23rd March 1917

My own dearest Phine

I received the registered letter quite safe and I like the ring very much, it fits just right. I received it just after I wrote my last letter. I am sorry I did not let you know before, but there is so much to be done here. You must think awful things of me, not writing to you more often, but I hope the War will be over soon now.

We are still having cold weather here, it snowed very hard last night. I am glad I am at the Base whilst the weather is bad. When the weather changes, I shall ask to go up again, and take part in the big advance.

I have not heard from home for over a month now, but I suppose they are alright, or I should have soon heard.

Did you go to the dance on St Patrick's Day? The Irish Guards kept it up here, and they all received their shamrock on parade to wear on their caps.

I was glad to hear Bruce had made it up with his girl again, I suppose he feels a lot better now, poor chap. He has not wrote me for some time now.

Have you heard from Mick lately? I hope he is still well and sticking it.

Well this is about all this time darling, so I will close, thanking you again for the ring, with best wishes to your Mam and Dad and fondest and dearest love to my own darling sweetheart Phine, from your ever loving and true Leslie.

31st March 1917

My own dearest Leslie

I received your letter yesterday dated the 23rd. I was very pleased to hear from you. Dear Leslie, I am pleased you liked the ring. Bruce said it would not fit you. Dear, you said in your last letter when the fine weather came you would ask to go up and take part in the big part in the big advance. I think you are best off where you are. Mam has not heard from Mick for several months now, poor fellow, I expect he is fed up.

Dear Leslie, I don't think that there is any more news now. Mam and Dad send you their best respects so I will close with fondest and dearest love and lots of kisses to my own darling sweetheart Leslie, from your ever loving and true Phine.

XXXXXXXXXXXXXXXX

P.S. EXCUSE SCRIBBLE AS I AM IN A HURRY.

3rd April 1917

My own darling Phine

I received your two letters dated the 23rd and 27th and was so glad to hear from you. I am sorry I do not write you more often, but I have so little time now.

I suppose you have received my letter, I received the ring alright, I thought you would have had it, before you wrote your last letter.

You are having quite a glad time lately from what I can see of it, making your monthly trips to London and seeing the latest revues at the theatres. I hope you enjoy yourself, I wish I could be there with you. I don't suppose it will be very long now though. We are still having cold weather and plenty of snow, I shall be glad when the warm weather comes, it is not very nice in tents this time of year.

I have got to finish this short letter at once, there is a boat going out and there will not be another for two or three days. So once again au revoir. With best of wishes to your Mam and Dad and fondest and dearest love to my own darling sweetheart Phine, from your ever loving and true Leslie.

XXXXXXXXX

13th April 1917

My own dearest Leslie

Just a line hoping you are quite well as it leaves myself at present. Dear Leslie, I think the Ball is coming off today week of the 13th. Mam had a letter from Bruce one day last week and when he went back off leave he left his belt in the train. Mam goes up to your Mother's nearly every week, they are all quite well.

Dear Leslie, one-day last week I was walking out in the garden and I stood on a rusty nail. My foot was awfully sore, I could not walk on it for two or three days. It is nearly better now dear.

Will you get your leave if you go up to the Batt? I think they ought to send you home for good, it is over a year since you last were home, roll on when the War is over so we can have our big party. I expect poor Mick is fed up, he has been a prisoner for two years and a half on the 29th of last month.

My dear Leslie, I don't think there is any more news. Mam and Dad send you their best respects so I will close with fondest and dearest love and lots of kisses to my own darling sweetheart Leslie, from your ever loving and true Phine.

XXXXXXXXXX

14th April 1917

My own dearest Leslie

Just a line hoping you are quite well.

Dear Leslie, my foot is still a bit sore so I can't go to the Ball tonight, and Mam had to go to London with Freddy today, because he is going to work in the signal box at Shenfield Station, so Mam thought she might as well spend the day there. I expect

Mabel will be disappointed.

Dear Leslie, roll on when we can go to the Grenadiers dances. I suppose it will be a long while yet. Look at America, she is preparing for a two-year War and it has been on nearly three so that will be five.

Dear Leslie, I wish you were in England, it seems years since I have seen you dear. Dad had two days' holidays last week, he went to London. Mam and Madgie went with him to the Lyceum Theatre to see "seven days' leave". They said it was very good. Dear Leslie, I lost my brooch last Sunday night going up Warley. I thought I would never see it any more so I had some bills printed and the Police gave them to some of the shops. As soon as the word was put out on Wednesday a young girl who I knew found it and brought it to me last night. I could have cried when I found I had lost it, I would not like to lose it for anything.

Dear Leslie, I don't think there is any more news now. Mam and Dad send you their best respects, so I will close with fondest and dearest love and lots of kisses to my own dearest sweetheart Leslie, from your ever loving and true Phine.

XXXXXXXXXXXXXXXXXXXXXXXX

19th April 1917

My own dearest Leslie
Just a line hoping you are quite well as it leaves myself at present. Dear Leslie, Mam had a letter from Mick this morning. He is still quite well and he wanted to know if I was married and how many children had I got. If not, who is she engaged to, he said I knew it is not myself of course, but with this awful disfigurement of mine I hardly think I will have the pleasure in doing so, he said never mind better alive with a disfigurement than under the Belgium soil, where many of my poor comrades lay today. He said he has not received a letter from Mother for a long time while Mam sends a letter every week.

My dearest Leslie, we are having some awful cold and wet weather, it is enough to give anybody the pip. Dear, I don't think there is any more news now, so I will close with fondest and dearest love and tons of kisses to my own darling sweetheart Leslie, from your ever loving and true Phine.

XXXXXXXXXXXXXXXX

20th April 1917

My own darling Phine
I have received your last two letters quite safe, I feel quite ashamed not having wrote to you before, it is the same old yarn, so much work to do with the drafts arriving and then going up the line. I have not been out of the Camp for over two months. I am writing from Reveille[4] to "lights-out" practically, and when I do get a minute to spare I feel too fed up to write a letter.

I was very sorry to hear that your foot was so bad. I hope you will soon be better with it. I expect you and Mabel were disappointed at not being able to go to the

Ball, still never mind dearest we will make up for all this lost time when the War is ended. I don't think it will be long, although America is preparing for a two-year War. Don't forget America is the country of Bluff and Swank, it is ourselves that will end the War.

You say you wish I was in England, so do I darling but it cannot be helped, the leave is stopped at present, and there are many out here who have not had leave for a longer time than I.

I am glad I have a lot to do here, when I have nothing to do, I just sit and think of you and all the loved ones at home, and then get miserable. But I always console myself with the times to come with my dear sweetheart Phine.

I was glad to hear you found your Brooch again, it was lucky you put the bills out, or you may never have found it.

I had a letter this morning from Mother and she tells me she is working in the Post Office as a sorter with my cousin Jenny. I also had another letter addressed to "Brave Soldier somewhere in France". From what I can make of it, my cousin put my address on it in the bottom corner, and of course I opened it. It is from a lady whether old or young I could not say, and it just wishes whoever receives it the best of luck, and says she has no one out here fighting, so feels compelled to thank someone out here so I opened it. I suppose I must answer it, I suppose you will not mind dearest, but I think it is the only thing I can do. I don't know whether Jenny (and of course Mother is in on it) sent it, as a compliment, being a brave soldier, or as a joke, because I am stuck down here at the Base. But I think it is because I am a Brave Soldier. I suppose your Mam will say that is more Swank from the Guards.

I thought you would mention about my last letter not having any kisses in. The reason is because when I was writing it, there were several inquisitive persons in my tent wanting to know who I was writing to. So I told them it was strictly business and then sealed it up, as they were waiting for me to put some crosses on.

Well I will conclude now dear as I must get a letter off to Mother and it is nearly nine o'clock. Give my best wishes and best respects to your Mam and Dad, hoping they are quite well, and fondest and dearest love and lots of kisses to my own darling sweetheart Phine, from your ever loving and true Leslie.

XXXXXXXXXXXXXXX

P.S. These are what are owing from my last letter dear.
XXXXXXXXXXX

27th April 1917

My own dearest Leslie

I received your letter yesterday dated the 20th. I was very pleased to hear you are still quite well as it leaves myself my foot is better now. Dear Leslie, there was a draft of Irish Guards went out to the Front last Sunday, there was a Sgt went out with them who I know. He said he would try and find you if he could, he has gone to Le Havre, he is very dark and has been wounded three times, his name is Connolly. Dear Leslie, I was just wondering what was the matter. I thought perhaps you had gone up to the firing line and did not have time to write, still never mind you made up for lost time. Dear Leslie, I am going to the Corps dance of the Irish Guards tonight, it starts at eight and finishes at five in the morning, it is the best dance dear Leslie. I don't think there is any more news now. Mam and Dad send you their best respects and hope to see you soon, so I will close with fondest and dearest love and lots of kisses to my own darling sweetheart Leslie, from your ever loving and true Phine.

XXXXXXXXXXXXXXXXXXXXXXXXXXXXXXXXXXXXXXXXXXXX XXXXXXXXXXXXXXXXXXXXX

30th April 1917

My own dearest Leslie
I received your card dated the 27th. I was very pleased to hear you are still quite well as it leaves myself at present.

Dear Leslie, Mam and I went up to see your Mother last Saturday and Bruce also came up on leave from Saturday until tonight. Mam came back on Sunday and I stopped until Monday night. Bruce and I got home about twelve o'clock then he went back today. Dear Leslie, your Mam and Dad, Mabel, Bruce and I went to see "The Better Ole"[5] Monday night after seven thirty and came out at quarter past ten, then we caught the six minutes past eleven train home. The Play was lovely. I was thinking of you, what you had to go through.

My dearest Leslie, I was wishing it was you home on leave, did you know that Bruce is going out to France with the next draft? He expects to go next month.

Dear Leslie, I don't think there is any more news at present, so I will close with fondest and dearest love and tons of kisses to my own darling sweetheart Leslie, from your ever loving and true Phine.

XXXXXXXXXXXXXXX

May 1917

My own dearest Leslie
Just a line hoping to find you in the best of health as it leaves myself at present. Dear Leslie, I am just as bad off as you are, I don't get a minute to spare, we are busy spring cleaning. My dearest Leslie, it seems years since I have seen you, we won't know you when you come home, if you stop out there until the war is over, I wish you were home for good. I am getting fed up of the blessed old war.

It is Dad's birthday on Thursday, he will be forty-three, and it was my little sister's birthday last Monday, she was two.

Dear Leslie, have you seen that Sgt of the Irish Guards yet? I don't think there is any more news now dear. Mam and Dad send you their best respects and hope to see you soon, so I will close as I am just off to bed. I have been washing all day long so I am tired. Fondest dearest love to my own darling sweetheart Leslie, from your ever loving and true Phine.

XXXXXXXXXXXXXXXXXXXXXXXXXXXXXXXXXXXXXXXXXXXX XXXXXX

12th May 1917

My own dearest Leslie

Just a line hoping to find you in the best of health as it leaves myself at present. Dear Leslie, I feel awfully lonely and miserable, I have been thinking all sorts of things about you this last fortnight because I have not heard from you. The last letter I had was dated the 20th of April. I hope you have not forgotten me dear. I wait at the door every morning and night for the post when I find there are not letters I feel I could sit down and cry.

Dear Leslie, I wish the blessed old war was over so you could get home for good. I sat at the window yesterday evening watching the fellows going by with their young ladies. I felt worse than ever then.

My dearest Leslie, I don't think there is any more news, so I will close with fondest and dearest love and lots of kisses to my own darling sweetheart Leslie, from your ever loving and true Phine.

XXXX

17th May 1917

My dearest Leslie

I received your letter on Tuesday dated the 8th . I was very pleased to hear from you and you are still quite well, it was just a week coming. Mam also has a letter from Sgt Connolly of the Irish Guards.

It was funny, he sent his letter on the 8th, the same as you, and they both came on Tuesday, he said they are down resting for a while.

Dear Leslie, Enna is better. The Doctor said she only had it slight, nobody has caught it. Mam had another card from Mick and nearly every bit of it was crossed out.

Dear Leslie, excuse this short letter as I have got eight shirts to button hole and they go in tomorrow dear, so I will close with fondest and dearest love and lots of kisses to my own darling sweetheart Leslie, I am your ever loving Phine.

XXXXX

Guards Division Base Depot
Le Havre B.E.F
17th May 1917

My own dearest Phine

I received your letter of the 8th, and also the one of the 12th, which I received yesterday. I felt such a brute when I read your last letter, I know how you feel when you do not have a letter from me. I am so sorry but I am so awfully busy here, and fed up with the place, still I know I am to blame and I feel ashamed of myself for not writing you more often, but I will do so.

I felt quite hurt when you ask me if I have forgotten you, I think of you a hundred times a day, and simply long for the time when I forget you dear I shall forget everything in this world, and I hope that will be a good long time yet.

I wish I could be at home with you dearest, I feel quite sad to hear that you are miserable. Oh roll on this blessed War, so we can all get home again I hope it will not be long now.

Well dearest, I have been called five times since I started to write these few lines, and now I have a big parade on, more men going up the line, so I must close.

I will write you as often as possible, but if I don't for a time you will know I am very busy, but I will be thinking of you still, so cheer up my sweetheart, and wait for better days.

With best wishes to your Mam and Dad and I hope they are in the best of health, and fondest and dearest love to my own darling Phine, from your ever loving and <u>always</u> true Leslie.

XXXXXXXXXXXXX

26ᵗʰ May 1917

My own dearest Leslie

I received your letter dated the 17ᵗʰ, also received one yesterday dated 21ˢᵗ. I was very pleased to hear from you, also to hear you are still quite well. Dear Leslie, I was very sorry that my letter upset you, still never mind. Mam said wait till the War is over when all the poor lads come home and poor Mick, that will be the day. Mam is going to have the party over in the Summerset Hall.

Dear Leslie, Mam had a letter from Mabel about a fortnight ago, your Mother and Father are quite well then. Mabel is working in the telephone service now, she said she likes it better than dressmaking.

My darling Leslie, Freddy thanks you very much for the badges. He said he will drop you a few lines, he is working on the railway now. Dear Leslie, we knew Sgt Connolly through going to the Sgts Dances. I have had several dances with him, he is a nice fellow. He has been wounded three times, this makes the fourth time he has been out, he has only gone out for commission this time. Dear Leslie, as I am writing this letter there is another draft of Irish Guards going out, it makes you miserable when you hear the band play. My dearest Leslie, I don't think there is any more news at present. Mam and Dad send you their best respects and hoping to see you soon. Dear, it is fourteen months since you have been home, still never mind, roll on for a good time when the blessed War is over. I must close now because I have six shirts to make by dinner time, with fondest and dearest love and tons of kisses to my own darling sweetheart Leslie, from your ever loving Phine.

XXXXXXXXXXXXXXXXXXXXXXXXXXXXXXXXXXXXXXXXXXXXX
XXXXXXXXXXXXXXXXXXXXX

27th May 1917

My own dearest Leslie

Just a line hoping you are quite well as it leaves myself at present. Dear Leslie, we have got five of my Dad's sisters and two sister-in-laws coming down from London tomorrow for the day. It was Mona's birthday yesterday, she was four years old. My dear Leslie, did you hear about the Air Raid we had last Friday afternoon? Some of the people heard it quite plain, but we did not hear anything of it until Saturday. Then there was a bit in the paper about it.[6]

Dear Leslie, I don't think there is any more news present. Mam and Dad send you their best respects and hope to see you soon, so I will close with fondest and dearest love and lots of kisses to my own darling sweetheart Leslie, from your ever loving and true Phine.

XXXXXXXX

P.S. Dear Leslie, excuse this short letter.

1st June 1917

My own dearest Phine

I received your letter of the 26th and was pleased to hear you are all quite well.

So, we are going back to have the tea party in Somerset Hall, I think it would be better in the Old Tin Hut, just for old times' sake.

I have just received another letter of yours dated the 27th. I did not think Mona was four years old, it seems only a week or so ago when she was a baby, but I suppose she is a big girl now.

It was a lovely day here yesterday and I managed to go out on the river for a couple of hours. Two or three of us went right up into the country, it was grand just like being in good old England.

We are just beginning to get busy again, another 300 have just arrived from Warley. I expect you see them coming. I expect the next big push is coming off soon, the one that is going to end the War I hope. I think it is about time it ended, don't you darling?

I have put another couple of badges in this letter for Freddy, they were on the shoulder straps, a Coldstream, Scots, and Irish Guards. I hope he is getting on well with his work, and that he likes it.

Well I will close now dear, I cannot write letters, I am an awful dud at it, I will save it all up and tell you when I come home. Give my best respects and wishes to your Mam and Dad and fondest and dearest love and lots of kisses to my own darling sweetheart Phine, from your ever loving and true Leslie.

XXXXXXXXXXXXX

2ⁿᵈ June 1917

My own dearest Leslie

I received your letter yesterday. I was very pleased to hear from you, also to hear you are still quite well as it leaves myself at present. Dear Leslie, Mam had a postcard from Mick this morning and he said that they are allowed to go out for a walk on Sundays. He asked Mam to send him some khaki shirts and a couple of green ties, but must send them to his depot, then they will send them on to Mick. Dear Leslie, we had an awful storm here the other night, it brought all the seeds out of the ground. Dear Leslie, there was five hundred and fifty men who went from here this morning to the Front and three hundred went to Ireland.

Dear Leslie, I don't think there is any more news at present. Mam and Dad send you their best respects and hope to see you soon, so I will close with fondest and dearest and lots of kisses to my own darling Leslie, from your ever loving and true Phine.

XXXXXXXXXXXXXX

10ᵗʰ June 1917

My own dearest Leslie

I received your letter yesterday, I was very pleased to hear from you, also to hear you are still quite well as it leaves myself at present. Dear Leslie, Mam went up to London to your Mother's last Sunday. She missed the eleven o'clock train so she had to go back and stop the night, then she went over to my aunties on the Monday because your Mother had to go to work, so Mam had a nice weekend.

Dear Leslie, we had eighteen German aeroplanes over here the other day, one came over our house, it was like a bird in the sky.

Dear Leslie, while Mam was in London there was a Sgt in the Coldstream Guards went to your Mother's, but Mam did not see him because she was out with Mabel. Dear Leslie, I don't think there is any more news at present. Mam and Dad send you their best respects and hope to see you soon, so I will close with fondest and dearest love and lots of kisses to my own darling Leslie, from your ever loving and true Phine.

XXXXXXXXXX

13ᵗʰ June 1917

My own dearest Leslie

Just a line hoping you are quite well as it leaves myself at present. Dear Leslie, we have been out of Barracks three years yesterday. Mam had another letter from Mick, he said he did not receive any of Mam's letters. Dear Leslie, have you heard from Bruce lately? It's a long time since Mam heard from him.

Freddy thanks you very much for the badges. I don't think there is any more news now. I am tired, I have been washing all day long, so I will close with fondest and dearest love and lots of kisses to my own darling Leslie, from your ever loving and true Phine.

XXXXXXXXXXXXX

26th June 1917

My own dearest Leslie

Just a line hoping you are quite well as it leaves myself at present. Dear Leslie, there is another draft of Irish Guards going who we know, he said he will try and find you, his name is Readman.

Dear Leslie, I don't think there is any more news now. Mam and Dad send you their best respects and hope to see you soon, so I will close with fondest and dearest love and lots of kisses to my own dearest sweetheart Leslie, from your ever loving and true Phine.

XXXXXXX

Guards Base Depot
Le Havre B.E.F
27th June 1917

My own dearest Phine

I have received your last letter and was glad to hear you are still well, and quite safe after the air raids. I suppose you are getting quite used to them now.

I have been rather busy again just lately, we had six hundred men, but they have gone up now. These were four hundred arrived from Warley this morning, the place is never empty for long. I should not think there are many Irish Guards at home now after the lot they have sent out. By the way I suppose you have not heard weather Sgt Connolly obtained his commission or not, nobody here knows yet.

I was glad to hear Bruce had been promoted to Corporal, I hope he keeps it and receives the other stripe. I have just wrote him a letter. He has been grousing to Mother because I have not wrote him for some months now.

I have just met my cousin out here in the next camp, he is a driver R.F.A.[7] You know who I mean, my cousin Jenny's brother who lives at Stoke Newington. I am wondering if Bruce will be the next one out. I should like to have him here, but for my Father and Mother's sake I would rather he stayed at home until he is old enough of course and then it is his duty to come.

I have enclosed another badge for Fred, but I suppose he is getting too big for collecting badges now that he goes out to work. How does he like his place? Getting along nicely I hope?

We are having tremendous rainstorms lately. I thought my tent would be battered in this afternoon with the force of the rain. I am in rather a fortunate position down the lines into my tent I found several things floating around.

Well dearest I will close now, I am hoping to be able to come home soon, they have started with men who are 18 months without a leave and there are a good many yet, but still it will come round soon. I would give anything for a leave now, I feel as fed up all this time, darling. If it was not for you Phine dear, I should not care how long the War lasted.

Well I must close now, give my best wishes and respects to your Mam and Dad, hoping they are both in the best of health, and all my fondest love and kisses to my own darling sweetheart Phine, from your ever loving and true Leslie.

XXXX

1st July 1917

My own dearest Leslie

Just a line hoping you are quite well as it leaves myself. Dear Leslie, I have not had a letter since the 14th of last month. Mam had a letter from Mick and he said he has not had a letter from Mam for a long time, yet he gets all my letters. He said that I picked a man of rank and he hopes you are keeping well. I expect Mam writes to Mick about the War and our people will not pass them on.

Dear Leslie, I don't think you get all my letters because I have wrote and told you lots of things and you have not answered them. Dear Leslie, I don't think there is any more news now. Mam and Dad send you their best respects and hope to see you soon, so I will close with fondest and dearest love and lots of kisses to my own darling Leslie, from your ever loving and true Phine.

XXXXXXXXXXXXXXXXXXXXXXXXXXXXXXXXXXXXXXXXXX
XX

4th July 1917

My own dearest Leslie

I received your letter this morning dated the 27th. I was very pleased to hear from you, also to hear you are still quite well. Dear Leslie, I wish you get home for good. When Mam goes to the Pictures at night I feel so miserable as anything. I will be glad when it is all over, I will be glad when you come home on leave dear, but it is when you are going back, it is a year and four months since you were on leave. I should think poor Mick is fed up with it, he has been a prisoner two years and 9 months.

Dear Leslie, Dad heard that the Irish Guards were leaving Warley and the Canadians are coming in their place. Dear Leslie, I don't think there is any more news. Mam and Dad send you their best respects and hope to see you soon, so I will close with fondest and dearest love and lots of kisses to my own darling sweetheart Leslie, from your ever loving and true Phine.

XXXXXXXXXXXXXX

5th July 1917

My own darling Phine

I have received your letter of the 26th and also one of the 1st. I have been in doubt whether to answer your letter, because I have been expecting to go up the line any day. No doubt when you receive this one I shall already be up with the batt. I am glad to hear you are quite well.

I have seen Sgt Readman, he spoke to me the day after he came. I have not seen him to speak to since as they are out of camp training all day long.

I am glad to hear Mick is still alright, thank him for me for his kind wishes. I hope it will not be so long now before he is free again. I don't think the War is going to last much longer now. I have always thought and told the chaps out here that it would be over about January 1918, and I still think it is possible now.

What makes you think I do not get your letters dear? Have you wrote and asked me something special that I have not answered or what is it? I cannot think of anything I have missed answering, and I am almost sure I get all your letters, there is very few get lost.

Well I think this is all this time, give my best respects to your Mam and Dad, and fondest and dearest love and heaps of kisses to my own darling Sweetheart, from your always loving and true Leslie.

XXXXXXXXXXXXXXXXXXXXXXXX

8ᵗʰ July 1917

My own dearest Phine

Just a line to let you know I am still on the land of the living. I have enclosed a photo I had taken last week; I am wondering what you will think of it. We happened to be passing the shop, and as I was expecting to go up the line we went in. The chap with me is an old friend who was in my Company before the War, the one standing is my friend, and the other is myself. You can see what a rough time I am having, I look quite bad don't you think?

Sgt Readman is still here. I expect he will be going up some time this week. It is probable that I shall go at the same time just to finish the War off by January.

Well I will write again soon, give my best respects to your Mam and Dad, and fondest and dearest love to my own darling sweetheart, from your always loving and true Leslie.

XXXXXXXXXX

P.S. Shall be glad when I can give you these crosses personally, and not have to put them on paper.

13ᵗʰ July 1917

My own dearest Leslie

I received your letter this morning dated the 3ʳᵈ. I was very pleased to hear from you, also to hear you are still quite well as it leaves myself at present. Dear Leslie, your letter has been nine days coming. I was wondering if anything had happened to you.

My Darling Leslie, I am sending you this photo, this is the only one I have got. I am going to have them taken again because the plate is all spots. Mrs Mann, the lady who took them, said she had to throw away hundreds of plates this last fortnight, so I will send you one of those when they are finished, that's if you are not home. It will be a fortnight before they are done and I will not be able to have them taken until Saturday or Sunday because I start work tonight.

Dear Leslie, I don't think there is any more news at present. Mam and Dad send you their best respects and hope to see you soon, so I will close with fondest and dearest love and lots of kisses to my own darling sweetheart Leslie, from your ever loving and true Phine.

XXXXXXXXXXXX

15th July 1917

My own dearest Leslie

Just a line hoping you are quite well as it leaves myself at present. Dear Leslie, Mother and I went to a dance last Thursday up in the town hall, do you know where that is, it is in the middle of the town it has a big clock outside. I did not care for it and they kept on dancing with the same girls. I had all the dances with Mam, she likes dancing with me because I can take gent.

My dearest, I don't think there is any more news now. Mam and Dad send you their best respects and hope to see you soon, so I will close with fondest and dearest love and lots of kisses to my own darling Leslie, from your ever loving true Phine.

XXXXXXXXXXXXXXXXXXXXXXXXXX

Phine started work as a munitionette at a factory in Brentwood. Before the War, the factory – W. J. and C. T. Burgess – made agricultural mowers, but had switched to making munitions.

20th July 1917

My own dearest Leslie

I received your letter yesterday dated the 11th. I was very pleased to hear from you, also to hear you are still quite well. I am very sorry dear that I did not write before, I have been so tired this week. I start days today, Monday I have to be there at seven until half past six at night. Dear Leslie, my Dad's brother came home from France last Monday, he came to see us yesterday.

We have started today to make eighteen-pound shells, the others were thirteen.

My dearest Leslie, I had a nice gold chain from your Mother yesterday morning, it is very pretty. Dear Leslie, I don't think there is any more news at present. Mam and Dad send you their respects and hope to see you soon, so I will close with fondest and dearest love and lots of kisses to my own darling sweetheart Leslie, from your ever loving and true Phine.

XXXXXXXXXXXX

Leslie was back with the Battalion which was in the Ypres sector, preparing for the big push. This was to become the Third battle of Ypres, known as Passchendaele.

24th July 1917

My own dearest Phine

I received your letter of the 12th, it was forwarded to from the Base yesterday. I was glad to hear from you and to know you are quite well. I must say you are not very flattering about my photo, fancy saying I look thirty-four and am not half the age I was, you wait till I come on leave in about a month's time, you will see how well I look, and I am twice as fat as I was, everyone tells me so.

My dear Phine, you must get that silly idea out of your head that I am not coming back. Trust in God, that is all one can do, but spare me from this awful War, to my loved ones at home, and to return to you, my darling Phine. Don't worry, if your people at home could see things out here you would be very confident of the War ending very soon. It will not last much longer now, and then I shall be coming for that "somebody's heart" I have captured. I received the card, it is very nice, and the words are good.

Well I must close now dearest, give my best respects to your Mam and Dad, hoping they are quite well, and fondest and dearest love and tons of kisses to my own darling sweetheart Phine, from your ever loving and true Leslie.

XXXXXXXXX

P.S. I am watching the men go on leave and I reckon that it will take me about a month's time, if nothing occurs to stop it.

Roll on, I am longing and longing every day to see you, it seems awfully long time since I saw you last, Les.

XXXX

2nd August 1917

My own dearest Leslie

Just a line hoping you are quite well as it leaves myself at present. Mam had two cards from Mick this morning he said he is still alive and kicking. Dear Leslie, we are getting a week's holiday next week for August. Dear Leslie, I am looking forward for when you get your leave. I wish you was coming home for good. I don't think the War will be over this year, because we have got enough thirteen-pound shells to last this year, then we are going to make eighteen pound shells.[8]

Dear Leslie, I don't think there is any more news at present. Mam and Dad send you their best respects and hope to see you soon, so I will close with fondest and dearest love and lots of kisses to my own darling sweetheart Leslie, from your ever loving and true Phine.

XXXXXXXXXXXXXXX

No. 4. Coy
1ˢᵗ Batt Gren GRDS
3ʳᵈ August 1917

My own dearest Phine

I have received your letters alright, but have had no time to write before. No doubt you know the reason now by the papers, we had a big part in the great push. I am glad to say I have come through alright with the help of God.

We had beastly weather and it hampered us a bit, we should have gone much further if it had not rained so. It has not stopped now, when it does no doubt we shall be off again. We are up to our knees in mud and water, owing to the ground being churned up with the shells. There is no doubt we have old Fritz properly beaten now, it will not be long now before the War ends.

I am very glad to hear you are doing your bit in the Munitions Factory. I hope you like the work alright. You say it is hard, do not overdo yourself, especially on night work, but from what I remember, you are quite strong enough, at least you used to be with me.

I think the photo of your sisters is very good. My word, they have grown, I would not have known them, especially Enna. Don't forget to send me one of yours when you get them.

Well I will write again in a day or two when we are settled down, we are not in very select surroundings just at present, so I will say au revoir.

Give my best respects to your Mam and Dad and fondest and dearest love to my own darling sweetheart Phine, from your ever loving and true Leslie.

XXXX

P.S. It is getting near for my leave, but I cannot say exactly when yet, Les.

Passchendaele consisted of a number of battles between July and November. It was a Commonwealth-led offensive in the Ypres–Flanders sector. The battle was one of the most bloody battles of the War and was hampered by persistent rain and artillery shelling, which turned the battlefield into a quagmire.

7ᵗʰ August 1917

My own dearest Leslie

Just a line hoping you are quite well as it leaves myself at present. Dear Leslie, I am looking forward for when you come home. I expect you will be home in another week or two, it seems years since I have seen you.

Dear Leslie, do you know if it is right that Sgt Readman is killed? One of the Sgt of the Irish Guards told Mam so.

Dear Leslie, I don't think there is any more news at present. Mam and Dad send you their best respects and hope to see you soon, so I will close with fondest and dearest love and lots of kisses to my own darling sweetheart Leslie, from your ever loving and true Phine.

XXXXXXXXXXXXXXXX

8th August 1917

My own dearest Leslie
I received your letter this morning dated the 2nd and a card yesterday. I was very pleased to hear from you, also to hear you are still quite well. Dear Leslie, I am awfully sorry I did not write, but I have been busy this last two or three weeks. Dear Leslie, there was a Sgt of the Irish Guards buried his wife today, they have only been married a year. She left a baby a month old, poor little thing. Mam and I went to see her buried, the poor fellow was crying like anything, then Mam started crying then I started. It seemed a shame to leave a dear little baby like that.

Dear Leslie, I don't think there is any more news now. Mam and Dad send you their best respects, so I will close with fondest and dearest love to my own darling Leslie, from your ever loving and true Phine.

XXXXXXXXXXXXXXXXXX

11th August 1917

My own dearest Phine
I received your letter of the 2nd and was glad to hear from you again. I could not write before as we have been in the trenches, but are out again now for a short rest. We are glad of it too, as we have been having rather a warm time lately.

Glad to hear you are having a week's holiday. I should like to be on leave at the time, but I shall have to wait a bit longer yet, as they are not going on leave very quick and there are a few in front of me yet. Will you be able to get any time off when I come on leave? I expect you will be working on day shifts then.

You do not want to think that by the number of shells you are making the War is going to last a long time dear. If you could only see how many are fired a day out here, you would wonder how the supply is kept up. The shell holes literally touch one another for miles and miles, the ground is honeycombed with them.[9]

I am glad to hear Mick is still well and kicking, I expect he is kicking over being in captivity so long. Still the end will soon be here now.

Well I will close now dearest, hoping to hear from you soon, with best wishes and respects to your Mam and Dad, hoping they still continue in the best of health, and fondest and dearest love to my own darling sweetheart Phine, from your ever loving and true Leslie.

XXXXXXXXXXXXXX

1st September 1917

My own dear Leslie
Just a line hoping you are quite well as it leaves myself at present. Dear Leslie, I wish you had your leave last week, because I had hardly anything to do. I was standing still for three days but now I am as busy as I can be. I am making tubes which fit inside the shells, there are thousands to be done because all the 13 pounder shells

must be all cleared out before the 18 pounders ones are started. I have to make fifty an hour, they are like a great long gas pipe. I have to cut them the length of the shell and then make the tube so it screws into like a cup which is fixed into the bottom of the shell. Dear Leslie, I expect you will be home next week. I don't think there is any more news now dear, so I will close with fondest and dearest love and tons of kisses to my own sweetheart Leslie, from your ever loving and true Phine.

XXXXXXXXXXXX

Leslie finally got his third leave home. On his return, he was soon back to trench life with the Battalion in the Ypres sector.

18th September 1917

My own darling Leslie

Just a line hoping you got back safe. Mam and I got home just after four. Dear Leslie, you know I wrote a letter to Pat, when I got home there was a letter from him. He said he has got a young lady in London, she is Irish. He said he would like her to come down for a day, he also said he is getting married very shortly and he wants me to go to the wedding.

Dear Leslie, I went to work after all. I was tired as anything after I had been standing a little while. I have been in bed all day long, now I am just off again. My dearest Leslie, I don't think there is any more news now. Mam and Dad send you their best respects and hope you will soon be home for good, so I will close with fondest and dearest love and tons of kisses to my own darling sweetheart Leslie, from your ever loving and true Phine.

XXXXXXXXXX

20th September 1917

My own dearest Leslie

Just a line hoping you are quite well. Dear Leslie, Monday night when I went to work I was sick twice and I did not do anything all night long. Tuesday I felt a bit better, but when I got to work I was sick again so they sent me home. I felt better last night. Dear Leslie, one of the girls at our place knows Sgt Driver's wife and she told the girl that Sgt Cox was coming home from France to see her, her husband wrote and told her.

Dear Leslie, I had to have a cry when you went back. If the train did not go out when it did I would have cried on the station, but I tried to keep it back. I don't think there is any more news now dear, so I will close with fondest and dearest love and tons of kisses to my own darling sweetheart Leslie, from your ever loving and true Phine.

XXXXXXXXXXXXXXXXXXXXXX

23rd September 1917

My own dearest Leslie

I received your letter yesterday morning. I was very pleased to hear from you, also to hear you got back safe. Dear Leslie, Mam and I went up to London to your Mam's yesterday and they made us stop there until about half past nine, so we did not come back until this morning. Mam took me up there because I was miserable. I am going to see the Doctor because I have got an awful feeling in my chest, your Mam said it is the work it does not agree with me, the oil that I put on my machine gets on my chest.

Dear Leslie, roll on when this blessed old War is over when you come home for good. (With God's help.) Dear Leslie, I don't think there is any more news at present. Mam and Dad send you their best respects, so I will close with fondest and dearest love and tons of kisses to my own darling sweetheart Leslie, from your ever loving and true Phine.

XXXXXXXXXXXXXXXXXXXXXXXXXXXXXXXXXXXXXXXXXX
P.S. I am just off to work, Phine.
XXXXXX

24th September 1917

My own darling Phine

I received your letter dated the 18th and was pleased to hear from you.
I knew you would be very tired on that Monday night after sitting up so late Sunday, fancy it is a week ago since I started back, the time soon rolls on, roll on when it is all over.

I am on guard writing this letter and I have just received your letter dated the 20th. I was very sorry to hear you was sick on Monday night and again on Tuesday. I hope you are quite alright again and able to do your work. It was the late hours we kept during that week and only about 3 hours' sleep Sunday night, poor Phine you must have been thoroughly tired out and done up.

I think it is rather a good job I do not get leave more often if it upsets you like that. Still roll on the next time I come home and may it be to stop for good. I felt like having a howl myself that day, it was rather a good job the train did go sudden, although I rather resented it at the time, not being able to say goodbye, or au revoir, I mean properly.

Yes, I explained to Sgt Driver how I did not go around to see his wife, I should like to have done, but I would not go until he had wrote her and let her know, and of course we were in London then till I come back.

Well dear, today I start my tenth year in the Army. What a lot has happened in these nine years, nearly three years of it out here. I never thought I should be out here when I went to enlist nine years ago. It does not seem so long though, although I am an old soldier compared with the recruits we get nowadays.

Well Phine dearest, I will close now. Give my best wishes to your Mam and Dad and fondest dearest love and tons of kisses to my own darling sweetheart Phine, from your always loving and ever true Leslie.

XXXXXXXXXXXXXXXXXXXXXXXXXXXXXXXXXXXXXXXXXXXXX
XXXXXXXXXXXXXX

P.S. Did you put a stamp on your last letter dear? There was no stamp on and the post mark was incomplete, so if you put one on, it must have fell off whilst in the post box. Still I received it quite alright and there was no delay in it coming. With love, Les.

XXXXXX

29th September 1917

My own darling Leslie

Just a line trusting you are still quite well as it leaves myself at present. Dear Leslie, I thought our last day had come last night. We had another air raid last night, but they did not get to London, they were beaten back, but we got it instead. They dropped five aerial torpedoes[10] on Shenfield Common and our works shook like anything.

Dear Leslie, I have only had one letter from you since you have been back, I have written five. I am wondering if anything is wrong. I had such an awful dream about you again last night, dear.

My darling Leslie, we have got my Uncle Pat's young lady coming down to see us. Mam had a letter from him the other day. I don't think there is any more news now. Mam and Dad send you their best respects, so I will close with fondest and dearest love and tons of kisses to my own darling sweetheart Leslie, from your ever loving and true Phine.

XXXXXXXXXXXXXXXX

P.S. Dear Leslie, excuse this letter as I am in a hurry dear. Hoping to hear from you soon.

XXXXXXXXXXXXXXXXXXXXXXXXXXXXXXXXXXXXXXXXXXX

4th October 1917

My own dearest Leslie

Just a line trusting you are quite well as it leaves myself at present. Dear Leslie, what do you think of the raids? Mam went up to London last Monday morning to see if Dad's sisters were alrightt and when she got there nearly all the houses in the street are blown down to the ground. She was frightened out of her life. My dear Leslie, I have only had one letter since you have been gone back. I expect you are busy, but just drop a field card dear just to know you are alright. Dear Leslie, Mam had a letter from Mick this morning, he said he is still alive and kicking. I don't think there is any more news, so I will close with fondest and dearest love and tons of kisses to my own darling sweetheart Leslie, from your ever loving and true Phine.

XXXXXXXXXXXXXXXXXXX.

4ᵗʰ October 1917

My own darling Phine

I received your letter dated the 29ᵗʰ and was glad to hear from you. I cannot understand you only receiving one of my letters because I have written five since I have been back and this one makes the sixth.

I did not know you had had another air-raid. Mother told me they had one last Monday. We do not know here, we cannot get a paper here at all, so we have no news. It was rather unfortunate for you that the planes were driven back from London, especially as they dropped the bombs on your part of the world.

I think that was rather spiteful of them, just because they could not get rid of them in London.

You did not mention anything about seeing the Doctor. Are you feeling alright? You said you were quite well, I hope so anyhow.

What makes you dream such awful things about me dear? If you keep on dreaming something is going to happen to me, you will make me have the wind up. Don't worry sweetheart, as I have said before I have faith in God and with his help I shall get through this lot alright.

Well I am awfully busy this week dear as I am in waiting, so I will close. With best wishes to your Mam and Dad, and fondest and dearest love and tons of kisses to my own darling sweetheart Phine, from your always loving and true Leslie.

XXXXXXXXXXXXXXXX

6ᵗʰ October 1917

My own dearest Phine

Just a few lines to let you know I am quite well and still alive. I had a letter from Mother today and she told me you and your Mam had been to London because you wanted cheering up a bit. I wish I could slipover to London each time I wanted cheering up, but I think Brentwood would be far better than London.

I hope you are quite well, have you been to the Doctors yet, because you have quite frightened me since you told me about those pains you suffer from. I do hope they are nothing serious.

We are feeling the effects of the coming winter, it is very cold and plenty of rain every day, still I think I shall be able to manage through it all right, with the help of God.

We are doing awfully well out here at present, I can see the end of the war in sight now, roll on when it does end, because, tell your Mam I have not forgotten that party she has promised when it is all over.

Well dearest I will close now, what news I would like to tell you is forbidden by the censor, and I am an awful letter writer at the best of the times, so I will close now, wishing your Mam and Dad the best of health also my best respects, and fondest and dearest love to my own darling sweetheart Phine and tons of kisses, from your ever loving and true Leslie.

XXXXXXXXXXXXXXXX

11ᵗʰ October 1917

My own dearest Leslie

I received you letter yesterday dated the 4ᵗʰ. I was very pleased to hear from you, also to hear you are still quite well. Dear Leslie, I went to see the Doctor, he said I had got indigestion but I feel ever so much better now, thank God.

Dear Leslie, you said you had a letter without a stamp. I expect it came off in the post.

Mam had another letter from Pat the other day, also one from poor Mick. He is still quite well. Dear Leslie,I don't think there is any more news at present. Mam and Dad send you their best respects and hope to see you soon, so I will close with fondest and dearest love and lots of kisses to my own darling sweetheart Leslie, from your ever loving and true Phine.

XXXXXXXXXXXXXXXXXXXXXXXXXXXXXXX.

Leslie describes the conditions of the final stages of the Battle of Passchendaele

15ᵗʰ October 1917

My own dearest Phine

I received your two letters dated the 4ᵗʰ and 7ᵗʰ and was awfully pleased to hear from you and to hear you had all survived the air raids. They are really getting most serious. They make us chaps out here worry about the safety of those at home, nearly as bad as you worry for us out here.

I am sorry I have not answered your letters before, but perhaps you have seen in the papers we have been at old Fritz again, but thank God, I came out of it safely once more. I feel quite confident when we are in action now, I know the Lord protects me safely out of this awful War back to you, my darling.

We have had some awful weather, the mud in the trenches was up to our knees, it literally sucked one into it but I was not troubled, I was uncomfortable at times.

Well I will make this a short letter dearest, as I want to catch the mail and I know you will be wondering why I have not wrote you before now, it is over a week I believe.

Give my best respects to your Mam and Dad and fondest and dearest love and tons of kisses to my own darling sweetheart Phine, from your ever loving and true Leslie.

XXXXXXXXXXXXXXXXXXX

16th October 1917

My own dearest Leslie

Just a line hoping you are quite well as it leaves myself at present. Mam had another card from Mick yesterday.

My dearest Leslie, I am sending you these few cigarettes. I won them up at our works, there is four girls go in for it. Mr Leross our charge hand has the cigarettes. Then we have to guess a number on the cigarette card, the one who wins them have to pay 1 half and the others have to pay 1d.

Dear Leslie, I am quite well again now. I will be glad when this blessed old War is all over so that you can come home for good dear. Dear Leslie, I don't think there is any more news at present. I am worse than you at letter writing, so I will close with fondest and dearest love and tons of kisses to my own darling sweetheart Leslie, from your ever loving and true Phine.

XXXXXXXXXXXXXXXXXXX

18th October 1917

My own dearest Leslie

Just a line hoping you are quite well as it leaves myself at present. Dear Leslie, the dances have started, Mam and I are going to a dance in the Gymnasium on Saturday in aid of the Red Cross, it starts at half past seven and finishes at twelve. I wish you was home dear so you could go as well. Dear Leslie, we are going to start our eighteen pound shells after Christmas. Dear Leslie, do you think that the war will be over by Christmas? A lot of people here think it will. I don't think there is any more news now. Mam and Dad send you their best respects and hope to see you soon, so I will close with fondest and dearest love and tons of kisses to my own darling Leslie, from your ever loving and true Phine.

XXXXXXXXXXXXXXXX

22nd October 1917

My own dearest Leslie

I received your letter this morning dated the _____I was very pleased to hear from you, also to hear you are still quite well.

Dear Leslie, I went to the Irish Guards dance last night. It was lovely, there was all the Irish Guards Officers' wives and a lot of Red Cross nurses. Dear Leslie, I hope you do not mind me going to the dances, I said to Mam I don't think it is right that I should go while you are out there fighting for us.

Mam had another letter from Uncle Pat this morning, he said he is still alive and kicking so I suppose he has been in that last battle.

Dear Leslie, I don't think there is any more news at present. Mam and Dad send you their best respects, so I will close with fondest and dearest love and tons of kisses to my own darling sweetheart, from your ever loving and true Phine.

XXXXXXXXXXXXXXXXXXXXXXXXXXXXXXXXXXXXXXXXXXX

26th October 1917

My own dearest Phine

I received your letter dated the 18th and was glad to hear you are still well. I am sorry I have not had a chance to answer before now but we have been having a busy time this last day or two, and when we have had any spare time I was too tired to write.

I hope you enjoyed yourself at the dance on Saturday, I should like to have been there with you, still there will be plenty of time after the War is over.

You will have to teach me all the new dances and the old ones as well, I am afraid. I have nearly forgotten them all now, except those few we were doing when I was on leave. Write and tell me about the dance, and whether you got off or not.

We were near the Irish Guards today. I looked out for Readman but could not see him. I asked a Corporal where he was, he told me he had been reported wounded in the last action we were in. He did not know if it was serious or not. Connolly is in the other Batt. I think so, I do not know how he is. I see the Irish did well last time, a Sgt and Private both won the V.C.[11]

You have asked me a funny question dear when you want to know if the War will be over by Christmas. I should like to think so dearest, but honestly speaking I do not think it will. There is certainly a chance of it doing so, but I think it will last a few more months yet. So, keep on working at those 18 pound shells, and we shall soon finish it off.

Well I will close now dear, give my best respects to your Mam and Dad, and fondest and dearest love and tons of kisses to my one and only darling sweetheart Phine, from your ever loving and true Leslie.

XXXX

Leslie was awarded the Military Medal. This was no ordinary medal, it was quite the opposite. It was awarded to Armed Forces personnel for their acts of 'bravery in the field', extraordinary acts of courage and bravery in the face of war. Unfortunately, there are no records that tell us what Leslie undertook to be awarded the medal.

26th October 1917

My own dearest Leslie

I received your two letters dated the 15th and 21st I was very pleased to hear from you, also to hear you are still quite well as it leaves myself at present.

Dear Leslie, what did you do to be mentioned in the dispatches? I thought you said you would not do anything, only what you was told to do. I suppose it was a case that you had to do it. That is only my fun.

Dear Leslie, Sgt Driver's wife knows that he is wounded, she knew about a week ago.

Do you know dear if that is right about Sgt Readman, we heard he is killed? Dear Leslie, we have got to get 20,583 13 pound shells done by the end of November, then we are going to start the eighteen pound shells.

The Irish Guards are starting their dances the eighth of next month. Dear Leslie, I don't think there is any more news at present. Mam and Dad send you their best respects, so I will close with fondest and dearest love and tons of kisses to my own darling sweetheart Leslie, from your ever loving and true Phine.

XXXXXXXX

29th October 1917

My own dearest Leslie

Just a line trusting you are quite well as it leaves myself at present. Dear Leslie, I had my photo taken yesterday, I have had it taken with my hat and coat on. I wonder if they will come out all right this time, the last one I had taken was an awful thing. Dear Leslie, I am on a different job now. I am filling the shell and weighing them up, I am only doing that while they alter my machine.

Dear Leslie, I had plenty of chances at the dance last Saturday, but I would not take them, because I will never find anyone better than you dear. The fellows never trouble me when I go to a dance. I am thinking of you all the time and wishing it was you I was dancing with instead of an Irish Guard.

Dear Leslie, I had such a funny dream last night. I dreamt I was marrying a German. I don't think there is any more news at present. Mam and Dad send you their best respects, so I will close with fondest and dearest love and tons of kisses to my own darling sweetheart Leslie, from your ever loving and true Phine.

XXXXXXXXXXXXXXXXXXXX

P.S. Dear Leslie I am very sorry I did not write before, but I am busy now I have to work until half past eight at night now and I feel too tired to do anything when I get home, that is long hours standing all the time, from Phine.

XXXXXXX

5th November 1917

My own dearest Leslie
I received your letter this morning dated the 1st. I was very pleased to hear from you, also to hear you are still quite well.

Dear Leslie, don't you think it is sad about poor Readman? He was a nice fellow, don't you think so?

I expect Bruce will be up on leave this week or next. I wish it was you dear, it doesn't seem as though you have been home on leave, it seems a year since I have seen you. I wish you could get home for good. I am getting tired of everything. Dear Leslie, Mam had a letter from Pat one day last week. He said he expects his leave in January and he is going to get married then to an Irish girl in London.

Dear Leslie, I don't think there is any more news at present. Mam and Dad send you their best respects and hope to see you soon, so I will close with fondest and dearest love and tons of kisses to my own darling sweetheart Leslie, from your ever loving and true Phine.

XXXXXXXXXXXX

On 20th November 1917, the British started an offensive on the Hindenburg line at Cambrai. By using the newly designed tank in vast numbers they managed to break through the German lines, although in the end this was a short-lived success.

21st November 1917

My own dearest Leslie
Just a line hoping you are quite well as it leaves myself at present. Dear Leslie, I went to work Friday as usual, I worked up till dinner time, then Mr Butcher said you better go home and come to work tonight, so I am on nights now. Bruce came down on Saturday about quarter to twelve then I went back with him in the afternoon and stopped until Tuesday afternoon. Bruce took me all over the west end to look at the shops, we went to two theatres.

Dear Leslie, Bruce he has got an idea that you are coming home for a while, I hope you do. Dear Leslie, they are all pleased you have got the Medal. Dear Leslie, I don't think there is any more news at present, so I will close with fondest and dearest love and tons of kisses to my own darling sweetheart, from your ever loving and true Phine.

XXXXXXX

22nd November 1917

My own dearest Phine

I received your letter of the 15th and I was very glad to hear from you and to hear you are quite well. I received the photo and I think it is absolutely "Tres-bon" as the French people say. I think it's very good and exactly like you. It makes me wish I was on leave again. I suppose it is because you are wearing that white felt hat. I like you best of all in that, although you do not know my favourite colour. I saw you once in it, but you have not worn it since. Of course I do not mean the colour of your hat, but the colour of your dress. It was at one of the dances, but perhaps you remember.

I am waiting for the time when I can see you dressed again like that. Roll on the end of this War. I do not think it will be long now after the glorious news we have just received. No doubt you will have heard all about it by the time you receive this letter.

I think it is the best news we have had since the War started. Of course you can bet your life that we are in it. Although for myself I am having a rest for a short while.

That is the reason your letters will take longer to reach me because I am not with the Battalion. All these men who have been out a certain time and have done good work have been sent back for a time and I am the fortunate one to be sent in charge of them. Your letters go to the Batt, and are sent on here afterwards, which take two or three days. That is the reason I have not wrote you before because I have been travelling to this place and we have only just settled down. So, do not be angry or worried because you have not heard from me before this.

You seem to be very busy nowadays making the shells, but I think the day is coming soon where there will be no more shells to make. We are very elated and happy over our last success and everyone is sure the War will be soon over.

Well I will close now dearest, give my best respects and kind wishes to your Mam and Dad and fondest and dearest love and hundreds of kisses to my own darling sweetheart Phine, from your ever loving and true Leslie.
XXXXXXXXXXXXXXXXXXXXXXXXXXXX

26th November 1917

My own dearest Leslie

I received your letter yesterday dated the 14th. I was very pleased to hear from you, also to hear you are still quite well.

My dear Leslie, Mam had a letter from Bruce yesterday. He said he enjoyed his leave very much, he also said he will write to you as soon as he gets time, he must write to let you know his address because he has moved again. He is staying at Chilsedon near Swindon.

Dear Leslie, I wish they would send you home for winter, it is so cold enough here and I am inside all the time, so I don't know what it must be like out there. We had some snow here this morning.

My dearest Leslie, there is a Cpl dance of the Irish Guards on Thursday but I am not going because I am on nights, but there is another Sgt Dance on Thursday. Mabel is coming down to the Cpls because I am not going.

Dear Leslie, I don't think there is any more news at present. Mam and Dad send you their best respects and hope to see you again soon, so I will close with fondest and dearest love and tons of kisses to my own darling sweetheart Leslie, from your ever loving and true Phine.

XXXXXXXXXX

29th November 1917

My own dearest Leslie

I received your letter yesterday dated the 22nd. I was very pleased to hear from you, also to hear you are still quite well as it leaves myself at present.

Dear Leslie, was it a pink silk dress? I don't remember any other one, pink is old maid's colour, but is my favourite colour. When I went to the last Irish Guards dance I danced with a fellow by the name of Parish. He said he knows you well, he said he knows you was stationed at Aldershot, he said he was in the same room as you was.

Dear Leslie, I am making myself busy now, I don't get much time to spare, because I am busy making things for the bottom drawer.

My darling Leslie, I don't think there is any more news now. Mam and Dad send you their best respects, so I will close with fondest and dearest love and tons of kisses to my own darling Leslie, from your ever loving and true Phine.

XXXXXXXXXX

P.S. Excuse pencil because I am writing this letter at work.

30th November 1917

My own dearest Phine

I received your letter dated the 21st and was very pleased to hear from you again. I was pleased to hear you had been up to London with Bruce. I hope you enjoyed yourself during the weekend.

I have not heard from him for a long while now, still I suppose he is quite alright. I wonder what makes him think I am coming home for a while. I cannot think what has put that idea into his head. I shall not be home again until next March at the earliest. The leave is a lot quicker now you know, we send four or five every night.

Have you read in the papers how our division has been swiping old Fritz about? I think it is great, although the fighting was very stiff. I cannot help thinking how lucky I am to get through every time. I thank God every time, and I hope he protects me to the end.

I do so want to come back again to you sweetheart. I think of you every hour. I was very surprised today, I received a letter from one of my old school-masters congratulating me on getting the medal. I wondered who on earth the letter was from at first. Anyone would think I had done something wonderful because I have got that blessed old medal. I shall think a lot more of the 1914 bronze star that they are going to give us now. I expect Mick will be proud as well when he receives his. There will not be very many about to wear them.

Well Phine dearest, I will close now. Give my best wishes and respects to your Mam and Dad and fondest and dearest love and tons of kisses to my own darling sweetheart Phine, from your ever loving and true Leslie.

XXX

2nd December 1917

My own dearest Leslie
I received your letter, I was very pleased to hear from you, also to hear you are still quite well as it leaves myself at present.

Dear Leslie, I went to another dance last night. It was a practice dance like they used to have down Harmony Hall in peace time. Miss Everand was there, she used to go out with a very tall dark Sgt of the Grenadiers. He was killed, she is pretty tall and fair. Dear Leslie, there is a fancy dress dance in the Town Hall on Tuesday, I can't go because I am on nights. The Irish Guards are having a big night on the 13th of this month in aid of the prisoners of War. I am going to that, I will be on days then. I have only got another week of nights .What I don't like about the Irish Guards dances is there is a lot of fellows,I hate dancing with them. Last time I went I danced with eight Officers. They dance different to what the Tommys do, I wish you was home dear so you could go as well.

Dear Leslie, Bruce said he would write to you when he got time.

I don't think there is any more news at present. Mam and Dad send you their best respects, so I will close with fondest and dearest love and tons of kisses to my own darling Leslie, from your ever loving and true Phine.

XXXXXXXX

7th December 1917

My own dearest Leslie
I received your letter yesterday dated the 30th. I was very pleased to hear from you, also to hear you are quite well as it leaves myself at present.

Dear Leslie, we had another air raid last night. We left off work at quarter to three until half past six, we had quite a long rest, we only had a quarter of a hours work, we left at a quarter to seven.

Dear Leslie, Mabel is coming down to the Irish Guards dance next Thursday. It is a big night. You must excuse this short letter as I am just off to work.

So I will close, Mam and Dad send you their best respects and hope to see you soon, so I will close with fondest and dearest love and tons of kisses to my own darling Leslie, from your ever loving and true Phine.

XXXXXXXXXX

10th December 1917

My own dearest Leslie

Just a line hoping you are quite well as it leaves myself at present. Dear Leslie, Christmas will soon be here now. We are only having two days' holiday, Christmas day and Boxing day.

We have finished our thousand eighteen-pound shells, we ought to have them done by the end of last month, but we had such a lot of the others to do and we had a lot back from Woolwich with loose cups so they all had to be refilled again. Dear Leslie, did I tell you I was on a new machine? It is called the drill, it is the largest machine in the shop. I have to make pockets in the bottom of the shell, first I rough pocket, then finish pocket, rough shoulder and finish shoulder. I have to put the same shell in four times and each time a different tube. Dear Leslie, I wish you was home for Christmas.

Dear Leslie, I don't think there is any more news. Mam and Dad send you their best respects, so I will close with fondest and dearest love and tons of kisses to my own darling Leslie, from your ever loving and true Phine.

XXXXXXXX

Dear Leslie, excuse the dirty paper, I am writing these lines at work. Phine.

14th December 1917

My own dearest Phine

I have just received your letter dated the 2nd Dec, it has taken 12 days to reach me. I thought I was never going to hear from you again, it seemed years instead of days waiting for your letter. I have not had any letter from home yet. I cannot quite understand why it is. It seems funny because I have had your letters forwarded on, but none from Mother, and it is over five weeks since I heard last.

I am glad to hear you are still enjoying yourself at the dances. I cannot remember the Miss Everard you spoke of or the Sgt she went out with. Still as I have told you before there was only one girl I ever knew or worried about at Brentwood. I did not know there were any more there.

I suppose you went to the Irish Guards dance last night. I hope you had a jolly good time there, write and tell me about it.

Why is it you do not like dancing with the Officers? How is it they dance different than a Tommy, do they dance better or worse? I should feel something if eight Officers danced with me.

You say you wished I was home so that I could go. If I did, I should bar Officers and everybody from dancing with you, and then perhaps you would not enjoy half so much, as perhaps it is better for me to be out here. Don't flare up at me, as I am only joking.

When Bruce wrote me he seemed quite upset and troubled, because the day you went back, he said you lost the train and that it was his fault. He thought you would get into trouble because you would not get to work in time. I hope everything was alright, I presume it was, as you did not mention anything about it.

Well I will close darling, as we are moving early in the morning and I have a lot to get ready, and pack up. My address will still be Guards Reinforcement Batt.

Well au revoir dearest, give my best wishes and kind respects to your Mam and Dad and fondest and dearest love and tons of kisses to my own darling sweetheart Phine, from your ever loving and true Leslie.

XXXXXXXXXXXXXX

21st December 1917

My own dearest Leslie

I received your letter this evening dated the 14th Dec. I was very pleased to hear from you, also to hear you are quite well as it leaves myself at present. My darling, I expect you will call me a flirt. I went to another dance last night, the Cpls of the Irish Guards. It was very nice there, but there always seems as though somebody is missing. They are just like the Grenadiers want to be, but of course they are not so jolly as they were in peace time. Sgt Brown is a lad, he is full of life. He said he knows you dear and also the Drum Major of the Irish Guards. He said he was staying in a hotel in Paris and you had two days' leave and went and stayed in the same hotel.

My dearest Leslie, if you expect your next leave in March you might be able to go to Saint Patrick's Ball.

Dear Leslie, I don't think there is any more news now at present. Mam and Dad send you their best respects again, wishing you a happy Christmas, so I will close with fondest and dearest love and tons of kisses to my own darling sweetheart Leslie, from your ever loving and true Phine.

XXXXXXXXXXX

24th December 1917

My own dearest Leslie

Just a line hoping you are quite well as it leaves myself at present.

Dear Leslie, Mam and I have been thinking what to get for your birthday. I don't know whatever to get, what would you like? Or is there anything you want? Write back and let me know so I will be able to get it in time.

Dear Leslie, we are having a miserable Christmas this year. Poor old Prince died yesterday. I expect he died of old age. Mam don't half miss him, she had a cry and so did Freddy.

My darling Leslie, I don't think there is any more news at present. Mam and Dad send you their best respects, so I will close with fondest and dearest love and tons of kisses to my own darling sweetheart Leslie, from your ever loving and true Phine.

P.S. Dear Leslie, hope you have a happy Christmas, Phine.

XXXXX

27th December 1917

My own dearest Phine

I received your letter of the 19th and also your Xmas card. I received them just after dinner on Xmas day. I was awfully pleased with it, it is very nice. I am sorry I could not get one to send you. Still we can make up for it after the rotten old War is over. We had a very good time at Xmas, but I believe Xmas was very quietly kept up in England.

You asked me if I knew a Sgt Brown of the Irish Guards. I do not think I do, I cannot recollect the name, why do you ask? Do you know him at all?

I read about that nurse being killed whilst on leave from France. Her name was Bates. They must have been awfully near, to drop bombs on Shenfield Common.[12]

I see there is going to be an enquiry why no warning was given when the aeroplanes were coming. I should like to have seen your friend and you trotting home that day. Why do the people in England always run when the raiders come over?

Well I will close now dearest. I have not improved at letter writing. I am still a bad hand at the game. Give my best respects to your Mam and Dad and best wishes for a happy and prosperous new year and the same to my own darling sweetheart Phine with fondest and dearest love and tons of kisses, from your ever loving and true Leslie.

XXXX

My own darling Leslie

I received your letter yesterday I was also pleased to hear from you, also to hear you are still quite well.

Dear Leslie, I went to R.E.[13] dance last night, it was very nice. Mam had another letter from Mick this morning, he is quite well, he is still wishing to come home soon.

Dear Leslie, I will make this a short letter because I am dead tired and I did not get home till one, it must have been half past one or quarter to two before we got to bed, then I was up again at half past five. So I will close now dear with fondest and dearest love and tons of kisses to my own darling sweetheart Leslie, from your ever loving Phine.

XXXXXXXXXXXXXXXXXXXXXXXXXXXXXXXXXXXXXXXXXX
XXXXX

28th December 1917

My own dearest Leslie

I received your two letters this morning dated the 20th and the 23rd. I was very pleased to hear from you, also to hear you are still quite well as it leaves myself at present.

My dearest Leslie, Mam and I went to the R.E. dance on Boxing night, it was very nice up there, it was held in the Ilford works Inn, Woodman Road, near the

Barracks. I expect you remember it.

They had a Concert to begin with, it lasted about an hour and a half, then there was a whist drive and then three hours' dancing. It was twenty past one when we got home. I know one of the R.E., he is a nice fellow, it is like speaking to Bruce. He is only eighteen. I had several dances with him and then we got talking and I told him I had got a young man so he said "BH" have you, as though he was surprised, I expected he thought he was going to hang his hat up.

Dear Leslie, I hope you will like this card I have enclosed.

Mam and I had a card from Bruce Christmas morning. He sent me such a saucy one, it is a photo of a young girl with her hair in one plait and a little red hat on the side of her head and she looks so saucy.

Dear Leslie, I don't think there is any more news at present. Mam and Dad send you their best respects and wish you a happy new year, so I will close with fondest and dearest love and tons of kisses to my own darling sweetheart Leslie, from your ever loving and true Phine.

XXXXXXXXX

My dear Leslie, I will be glad when this blessed old war is over and we can go to the dances together again. Phine.

XXXX

29th December 1917

My own dearest Phine

I received your letter yesterday dated the 21st and was glad to hear you are still quite well.

Why should I call you a flirt because you went to the Cpls dance? I am pleased you go, to enjoy yourself, there is no need to be miserable because there is a war on. Go to as many as you like, as long as you do not get off with anybody else.

I do not know who Sgt Brown is, you tell me that he says he knows me, but I am sure he must be mistaken my dear.

I don't quite understand your letter, you say that he says he knows me and he knows the Drum Major, do you mean the Drum Major knows me? The Drum Major at Warley is named Fitzgerald, and I have never spoken to him. The only one I know well is named Smith and I think he is still out here with the 2nd Irish Guards, as Drum Major.

I am sure there is a mistake somewhere, because one of them (I do not know if you mean Sgt Brown or the Drum Major) says he met me on a two day leave in Paris and that I stayed in the same hotel. Well my dearest I have only been to Paris once in my life and that was in 1914, after I had been wounded and was going back to the Bn. You know darling that if I had been there at all on leave, I should certainly wrote or told you something about it. So, you see dear that he must be mistaken or has taken me for somebody else.

Yes, dear, it would be fine if I could manage to get home on leave for the St Patrick's Ball. We must wait and see what happens, the war might be finished by then, one never knows.

A man in my hut who lives in the Old Kent Road has just received a letter from home and he tells me they bombed around our way on Xmas eve and caused a large amount of damage. I suppose they are alright at home, but it makes a chap worry till he hears if everything is alright.

We have beastly cold weather out here at present, it snows every night, and freezes terribly. Still we manage to keep warm alright, and sit and wish the war was over.

Well I will close now dearest, give my respects to your Mam and Dad, and fondest and dearest love and tons of kisses to my own darling sweetheart Phine, from ever yours loving and true Leslie.

XXXXXXXXXXXX

31st December 1917

My own dearest Phine

I received your letter of the 24th yesterday and was glad to hear you are still well. You ask me what I would like for a birthday present, well really dearest I know you would like to give me something, but do not worry about it, there is nothing at all that I require, just send me a letter, that is all I want.

If you want to get anything, buy something for that bottom drawer of yours.

Besides I am not going to have any more birthdays, I shall be getting old if I do. I only feel about 17 or 18 and here I am nearly 25, I think I shall remain at 24 for a few years yet.

I am so sorry to hear poor old Prince is dead, no wonder Mam and Freddy cried, he was a lovable dog, I liked him very much.

How is Mick going on? Have you heard from him lately? I have been wondering if he will be among those prisoners who are being transported to Switzerland. I have heard that all those who have been there since the beginning are going, but I do not know if it only applies to the civilians or not.

Well my darling, I must conclude to get this letter off tonight. Do not trouble about a present, just a few lines from you is all I want.

Give my best wishes to your Mam and Dad, and hopes for a prosperous and happy new year and fondest and dearest love and tons of kisses to the best girl in the world, my own darling Phine, from your ever loving and true Leslie.

XXXXXXXX

Notes 1917

1.   On Friday 19th January, a TNT factory in Silvertown London exploded causing 73 deaths and injuring over 400 people.
2.   Bruce was promoted to Corporal.
3.   On 1st February 1917, Germany put into place unrestricted submarine warfare. This meant that all enemy shipping was to be destroyed, including civilian.
4.   Reveille – armed forces wake-up call using a bugle or drum.
5.   *The Better 'Ole'* – was a theatre version of the wartime humour cartoons, produced by the famous war cartoonist Captain Bruce Bairnsfather.
6.   25th May 1917, 23 German Gotha bomber aeroplanes were sent on a mission to bomb London, but due to cloud cover they had to change the target location to Folkestone, ending in 95 civilians being killed.
7.   R.F.A. – Royal Field Artillery.
8.   13-pounder and 18-pounder shells – name given to the ordnance fired by mobile artillery field guns.
9.   Leslie describes the Passchendaele Boesinghe battlefield, Belgium.
10.   Aerial torpedoes – a mortar bomb equipped with fins, dropped from an aircraft.
11.   John Moyney VC and Thomas Woodcock VC from the Irish Guards were both awarded Victoria Crosses for their bravery in battle.
12.   British Red Cross Voluntary Aid Detachment nurse Madeline Elsie Bates.
13.   R.E. – Royal Engineers.

Thoughts of home 1918

My own dearest Leslie

I just received your letter dated the 27th. I was very pleased to hear from you, also to hear you are still quite well.

Dear Leslie, we had some bad news yesterday. Do you know my uncle Arthur died on Christmas Eve? He died of smallpox, he is out in Egypt. Mam went up yesterday to see my aunty, she is awfully upset, she has only got one child.

Bruce got four days leave for the new year, he came down here Sunday night and stopped until last night. There was a Irish Guards dance on Monday and we took Bruce, he got on fine. I took him round five or six times, so did Mother. It was very nice there.

Dear Leslie, I don't think there is any more news at present. Mam and Dad send you their best respects and hope to see you soon, so I will close with fondest and dearest love and tons of kisses to my own sweetheart Leslie, from your ever loving and true Phine.

XXXXXXXXXXXXXXXXX

4th January 1918

My own dearest Leslie

I received your two letters this morning when I came home from work, dated the 29th and the 31st of last month. I was very pleased to hear from you, also to hear you are still quite well as it leaves myself at present.

Dear Leslie, Mam had a card from Mick one day last week dated the 15th. He said he is still alive and kicking and hopes for a soon Liberation.

Dear Leslie, fancy we heard of three deaths in a week. My Uncle Arthur and then my Dad's sister's husband's cousin, and Prince. My dearest, I don't think there is any more news at present. Mam and Dad send you their best respects and hope to see you soon, so I will close with fondest and dearest love and tons of kisses to my own darling sweetheart Leslie, from your ever loving and true Phine.

XXXXXXXXXXXXX

14th January 1918

My own dearest Leslie

Just a line hoping you are quite well as it leaves myself at present. My dearest Leslie, have you received the letter and card I sent you for your birthday? It is a fortnight today since I had a letter from you, it seems months. I am just beginning to worry, been as I had that card to say that you have joined the Batt. I wish it was all over, the papers don't look very bright. Dear Leslie, what do you think of it, do you think it will last much longer?

My dearest Leslie, Mam went to the Irish Guards dance last Thursday by herself because I am on nights, and who do you think she met up there? Poor old Sgt Connolly, but he is a Sgt Major. Now Mam said he has been over to Ireland on fortnights leave, he came over to England Wednesday night and stopped at Warley Barracks Thursday and he went to France from here Sunday morning.

Dear Leslie, I don't think there is any more news at present, so I will close with fondest and dearest love and tons of kisses to my own darling sweetheart Leslie, from your ever loving and true Phine.

XXXXXXXXXX

My darling, excuse pencil as I am just off to work. I wish I was just going up to see you in Barracks. I expect I will one day, but that day is a long way off yet.

23rd January 1918

My own dearest Leslie

I received your letter yesterday. I was very pleased to hear from you, also to hear you are still quite well as it leaves myself at present. Dear Leslie, you don't know how pleased I was when I got that letter, it was just three weeks since I heard from you last when I had the letter yesterday. I thought perhaps you had been wounded and could not write. Dear Leslie, Mam met Payne in town one day last week, he told her he is home for good, lucky fellow. Sgt Driver is also home for ten days' sick leave, I will be glad when you come home again on ten days' leave.

My dearest Leslie, Mam had a letter from Mabel yesterday, she is coming down tomorrow to the Sgts dance of the Irish Guards, so I will get the night off. I asked for it last night and they said I can have it. Dear Leslie, we have not heard from Bruce since he went back off his new year's leave, I expect he is busy.

My own dearest Leslie, I don't think there is any more news at present, so I will close. Mam and Dad send you their best respects and hope to see you soon, to my own darling sweetheart Leslie, from your ever loving and true Phine.

XXXXXXX

25th January 1918

My own dearest Phine

Just a line or two to let you know I am quite well and in the best of health.

I have not heard from you for over a week, I hope you are not punishing me because I had to keep you waiting for a letter. Still I knew you would not do that.

We are off up to the trenches for another sixteen days,[1] so do not worry darling if you do not hear from me during that time. It is practically impossible to get a letter off, whilst we are up there, but if it can be managed I will write you, if it is only a field postcard, to let you know how I am going on.

I have not time to write more darling, as we are just off up the line, so au revoir, with best wishes to your Mam and Dad, and fondest and dearest love and tons of kisses to my own darling sweetheart Phine, from your loving and true Leslie.

XXXX

27th January 1918

My own dearest Leslie

I received your letter this morning dated the 14th. I was very pleased to hear from you, also to hear you are still quite well as it leaves myself at present.

Dear Leslie, the dance was not very nice last Thursday up at the Irish Guards, there was hardly any Gents, there was twice as many ladies as there was Gents.

My own dearest Leslie, I had a letter from Mick this morning dated the 15th of Dec. He said he hopes that you are still A.1. He also sends his best respects and hopes to see you soon, he also asked me to state in my next letter your name and what Regt you are in, so I have sent your address.

Dear Leslie, I went up the town on Saturday afternoon with my two little sisters and I met Sgt Payne. It is the first time I have seen him for over two years. Hadn't he altered? He looks a man about forty.

My dear Leslie, I don't think there is any more news at present. Mam and Dad send you their best respects and hope to see you soon, so I will close with fondest and dearest love and tons of kisses to my own darling sweetheart Leslie, from your ever loving and true Phine.

XXXXXXXX

P.S. Dear Leslie, Mick asked me to send him a photo if I had got one. I have only got one, that is the last one you sent me, shall I send him that one?

XXXX

31st January 1918

My own dearest Phine

I have received your letter of the 23rd, and was pleased to hear you are well.

I am writing this letter in answer, but I do not know when I shall be able to post it. But with a bit of luck I may be able to get it sent out of the trenches tonight.

I expect you were wondering what had happened when you did not hear for three weeks. I thought you would be thinking I was wounded or something.

Yes, I heard about Payne going home. He is rather fortunate, still he is medically unfit, and I would rather stay out here longer and come home fit and well than be home now and be unfit. I heard from Sgt Driver when he was in Hospital, I am glad to hear he is well again to be about. I think they ought to keep him at home a bit now, this makes the third time he has been wounded.

You say you will be glad when I come home on leave again, so shall I dearest. It is creeping round to my turn again. They are not sending so many now but I think it should be by May at the latest.

From what I can see of it, Mabel is taking to the glad life going to all the dances. I thought she was too staid and prim for dancing. Does she go mad in the "Rancers" like Bruce does, I wonder? Write and let me know whether you have a good time, but I expect you will. When you see Mabel next time you might jog her memory and tell her she has still got a brother out here who'd like to have a line or two from her. I know it is up to me to write first, but time and circumstance do not allow at present.

I see in the paper dated the 29th that you have had another air raid over Essex and London, I am glad they brought one down. I hope there are no casualties, it does not say if there were any.[2]

Well I will close now dearest, I hope I can get this letter off in a day or two. Give my best wishes to your Mam and Dad, and fondest and dearest love and tons of kisses to my own darling Phine, yours ever loving and true Les.

XXXXXXXXXXXXXXXXXXXXXXXXXXXXXXXXXXXXXXXXXXX

P.S. Excuse paper, this is all I have in the trenches with me. Les.

XXXXXXXXX

3rd February 1918

My own dearest Leslie

I received your letter this morning dated the 25th of last month. I was very pleased to hear you are still quite well as it leaves me at present.

Dear Leslie. fancy you thinking that I am finishing with you. I would not do such a thing, you have a cause not to write, I have not, when I am on nights I only write one a week and one on Sundays, because by the time I get home in the morning it is about quarter to eight then I have my breakfast then I feel too tired to do anything. I am starting days tomorrow, I won't be sorry neither. I hate nights how I like them when I first went there, but you get so tired and fed up with everything.

My own dearest Leslie,by the time you get this letter you will nearly have done your sixteen days in the trenches, because your last letter took ten days to come.

Mother and I are going to a dance of the Irish Guards on Thursday. I wish you was coming, still never mind I hope you will get your leave soon so that you can go to one.

My dear Leslie, I don't think there's any more news at present. Mam and Dad send you their best respects and hope to see you soon, so I will close with fondest and dearest love and tons of kisses to my own darling sweetheart Leslie, from your ever loving and true Phine.

P.S. Dear Leslie, I have enclosed Mick's last letter. Phine.

6th February 1918

My own dearest Phine

I received your letter dated the 27th, and was so pleased to hear from you, I hope you are still safe and well after the air raids. I had a postcard from Mother and she tells me they are all quite safe. It is a bit too rough the way old Fritz carries on. I don't mind going in the trenches, but I always start worrying when I read that the planes have been over London and Essex. I am always wondering how you are.

I am glad to hear Mick is still quite well. Thank him for me for his kind wishes and I sincerely hope it is not very long before we shall be able to meet. I would a thousand times rather be where I am than where he is, it must be simply rotten for him, roll on when it is all over.

You can please yourself Phine dearest, whether you send him my photo or not, I am going to have it taken again when we come out of the trenches, and perhaps it will be better than the one you have got. Still you do as you wish I have got another one of those I had taken at the Base, you can have it if you like, but perhaps you will not want it as you said I looked like an old man of forty in one of your letters.

You must have given both Mabel and Bruce a good time at the dances, I have had letters from both of them, saying what good times they have had, and how they enjoyed themselves. I hope it will not be long before I can go to the dances with you all. The only dance I know now is the "French Crawl", and I am pretty good at that, keeping well down to dodge old Fritz's souvenirs.

Well I will close now darling, I will write again before we come out of the trenches if possible. Give my best wishes to your Mam and Dad and fondest and dearest love and hundreds of kisses to my own dearest sweetheart Phine, from your ever loving and true Les.

XXXXXXXXXXXXXXXXXXXX

6th February 1918

My dearest Leslie

I received your letter yesterday dated the 31st of last month. I was pleased to hear from you, also to hear you are still quite well as it leaves myself at present.

My dearest Leslie, I hope you get your leave before May, because I would like you to go to an Irish Guards dance. I think the dances end in March or April. Dear Leslie, I had a letter from my Uncle Pat yesterday asking how you was and poor Mick, he also said he expects his leave shortly. It will be nice if you both get your leaves together.

We are getting short of shells up at our works. I am doing mines now, and they started yesterday to make Mowing Machines, that is what they used to make before.

Dear Leslie, I don't think there is any more news at present. Mam and Dad send you their best respects and hope to see you soon, so I will close with fondest and dearest love and tons of kisses to my own darling sweetheart Leslie, from your ever loving and true Phine.

XXXXXXX

10th February 1918

My own dearest Leslie

I received your three cards, I was very pleased to hear from you, also to hear you are still quite well as it leaves myself at present.

Dear Leslie, Mam and I did not go to the dance last Thursday because it was put off on account of General French was coming down from London, then he did not come after all. I think it is going to be on Wednesday or Thursday.

I had another letter from my Uncle Pat last Friday, asking if we had heard from Mick. He said he has an idea that he will be amongst these exchanged prisoners, I expect that's not his luck because he is not disabled.[3]

My dearest Leslie, I think the end of the War is coming near now because our foreman told me that he thinks they will soon close down because they have not enough shells, they have sacked about thirty girls. I expect as soon as these mines are finished I will get the sack too.

My dearest Leslie, I don't think there is any more news at present. Mam and Dad send you their best respects and hope to see you soon, so I will close with fondest and dearest love and tons of kisses to my own darling sweetheart Leslie, from your ever loving and true Phine.

XXXXXXXXXXXXXXXXXXXXXXXX

12th February 1918

My own dearest Leslie

I received your letter and card this evening when I came home from work, I was very pleased to hear from you, also to hear you are still quite well as it leaves myself at present.

Dear Leslie, I will wait for the photo until you have it taken by yourself as you say you look older than twenty five, but you don't look forty, that was my Father when I said that. I was taken for twenty two last Saturday and the person would not believe I was only eighteen.

There was a new moon yesterday so I expect we shall have old Fritzy over here the beginning of next week. They nearly always come the night after the full moon. I was on nights last time they came.

Yes, I did think Bruce did enjoy himself at the dance because he was laughing the whole time he was there. We have not heard from him since he went back off his new year's leave.

Dear Leslie, I hope you get your leave before the dances finish. It is just about four years since we both went to a dance together.

My dear own dearest Leslie, I don't think there is any more news at present, Mam and Dad send you their best respects and hope to see you soon, so I will close with fondest and dearest love and tons of kisses to my own darling sweetheart Leslie, from your ever loving and true Phine.

XXXXXXX

19th February 1918

My own dearest Leslie

I received your letters this evening dated the 12th, 13th. I was very pleased to hear from you, also to hear you are still quite well as it leaves myself at present.

Dear Leslie, just as I begin this letter the gas hooter went for an air raid.

The guns are banging like anything. Mam and Dad are in London, they went this morning while I was at work. I did not know they had gone, not until I came home from work this evening.

We are having lovely weather here, only it is so cold it was enough to freeze any one yesterday and today.

Dear Leslie, there is about 5 or 6 more dances then St Patrick's ball, there is a big Batt dance tonight. I wish you was coming, still never mind I expect the day will come when we can go together.

My dearest Leslie, I wish the same as you that the kisses were real instead of in paper.

I do not think there is any more news at present, so I will close with fondest and dearest love and tons of kisses to my own darling Leslie, from your ever loving and true Phine.

XXXXXXXXX

P.S. Excuse this short letter, I am like you and no good at writing love letters. Phine

XXXX

How long can this War go on?

21st February 1918

My own dearest Leslie

Just a line hoping you are quite well as it leaves myself at present.

Dear Leslie, I think I told you in my last letter that I was going to a Batt dance of the Irish Guards last Tuesday, but I did not go after all, they have put it off again, that makes the third time. There was to have been a Cpls dance tonight, they have put that off too. They are afraid there will be an air raid, then if there was one the Gents would have to leave the dance room and the ladies would be frightened out of their lives. We had a raid Saturday, Sunday and Monday last weekend, the full moon is on Monday so I expect we shall have them all next week. They don't trouble me, I always go to bed. Last Sunday when the raid was on I never heard a sound of it. Mam said the guns were making a terrible noise.

My dearest Leslie, I have been up at the Munitions works seven months on Saturday the 23rd. I did not think I had been up there all that time. I expect I shall be up there another two sevens before the war is over.

Dear Leslie, I am worse than ever like you for writing love letters, I can never think what to put in them. I should think you must laugh at times when you read my letters dear, still never mind we must look forward to the time when you come home, then there will not be so many letters to write.

My darling Leslie, I don't think there is any more news at present. Mam and Dad send you their best respects and hope to see you soon, so I will close with fondest and dearest love and tons of kisses to my own darling sweetheart Leslie, from your ever loving and true Phine.

XXXXXXXXXXXXXX

25th February 1918

My own dearest Phine

I suppose you are wondering again why I have not written, and also if anything has happened.

Still I am glad to say I am quite alright and in the best of health. We have just finished a long spell in the trenches, and I had no chance of writing you, not even a field card. The Batt has gone in for another spell, the last before we go back for a rest, but I am lucky and have been left back this time.

I have plenty of work to do however, taking the Company's rations up etc. I am doing the Quartermasters Sgts work, but it is better than being in the trenches.

I have received your four letters of the 6th, 10th, 12th and 19th and am glad to hear you are still quite well. I am awfully sorry I could not answer them before.

I have not had my photo taken yet as we are not near enough to the Town, but as soon as we get there, which will be when the Batt arrives out of the line, I will have it done. I hope it will be a bit better than the other I had taken.

You were not far wrong when you said you expected an air raid with the new moon. I saw in the paper that they had been over again. Did you see anything of them?

Well I will close now darling. I will write you again soon, now that I am not handicapped by being in the trenches. Give my best wishes to your Mam and Dad and fondest and dearest love and hundreds of kisses to my own darling sweetheart Phine from your ever always loving and ever true Leslie.

XXXXXXXXX

26th February 1918

My dear Leslie

Just a line hoping you are quite well as it leaves myself at present.

Dear Leslie, Mam had a card from Mick this morning. He said that we are allowed to send him one parcel in three months then we must not send eatables, he just asked for shaving brush and soap, toothbrush and powder. Have you had a letter from Mick yet dear? I have sent him your address. I have not had an answer to that letter yet so I don't know if the censor has passed it or not.

My own dearest Leslie, this is my last week on days. I go on nights on Monday. I dread going on nights, I come home from work in the morning, have my breakfast then I go to bed until half past four or five and when I get up I feel as disagreeable as anything, everything seems to get in my way.

You said in your last letter dear that you are going to reduce the leave to ten days from the first of March, they might have waited until you had your leave.

Dear Leslie, I don't think there is any more news at present. Mam and Dad send you their best respects and hope to see you soon, so I will close with fondest and dearest love and tons of kisses to my own darling sweetheart Leslie, from your ever loving and true Phine.

XXXXXXX

3rd March 1918

My own dearest Leslie

Just a line trusting you are quite well as it leaves myself at present.

Dear Leslie, I told you in my last letter that I was going on nights on Monday, but that is all, after now we are to keep on days because there is not enough work for all of us girls on nights.

Dear Leslie, Mam and I are going to a dance on Monday night up at the Irish Guards. I don't suppose there will be many more dances now. I wish you was having your leave dear so that you could come to one of the Irish Guards dances.

We are starting to make mine parts up at our work soon, a part that they call the horn. They are about twenty of them. The horns are fixed on the outside of the mine and as soon as the ship touches one of these the mine explodes.

Dear Leslie, have you heard from Bruce lately? Mam has not heard from him since he went back off leave. I expect he is too busy learning how to dance.

My dearest Leslie, just about four years since we went to a dance together. I expect it will be another two more years yet. I shall be getting quite an old woman, in two years' time I shall be nearly twenty-one.

Dear Leslie, I don't think there is any more news at present. Mam and Dad send you their best respects and hope to see you soon, so I will close with fondest and dearest love and tons of kisses to my own darling sweetheart Leslie, from your ever loving and true Phine.

XXXXXXXXXX

5th March 1918

My own dearest Phine

I received your two letters dated the 21st and 26th and was glad to hear you are quite well.

Yes, it hardly seems seven months since you went to work on the Munitions, you are very cheerful saying you expect it to last another two sevens. Are you trying to cheer me up or what?

You amused me when you said you go to bed when there is an air raid on. I think it a jolly good plan, you would make a typical Soldier dearest, but then of course you are a Soldier's daughter, so that explains it.

No Phine dear, I have not heard from Mick. I should very much like to hear from him if he is allowed to write. I thought his letters which he wrote were limited, in that case he would naturally write to you or your Mam. If he is allowed to write more, he will probably drop me a few lines.

That is a new order I suppose, cutting down the parcels to one in three months and not allowing eatables to be sent. Just what one might expect though from such a nice sociable nation like the Germans.

You have been disappointed in the dances lately, owing to the air raids, have they had them yet? If not, I suppose you will not be able to go now you are starting nights again. That will be rather unfortunate for you.

I am sorry you have got fed up with nights. I suppose that is the time when you think it will last another two seven months. I can quite sympathise with you, I know what it is working all night. I am just the same when we are in the trenches. Never mind dearest, it will be over soon, and we can make up for it all.

Well I will close now dear, give my best wishes to your Mam and Dad, hoping to hear from you soon, (I do not laugh over your love letters sweetheart, they are too precious to me) with fondest and dearest love and hundreds of kisses to my own darling sweetheart Phine, from your ever loving and ever true Leslie.

XXXXXX

6th March 1918

My own dearest Leslie
I received your letter last night dated the 26th. I was very pleased to hear from you, also to hear you are still quite well as it leaves myself at present.

Dear Leslie, I was just beginning to wonder if there was anything happened to you, because it was just on a fortnight since I heard from you.

My dearest Leslie, I wish you was home for next week, the Sgts are giving special invites for a big dance next week, the Irish guards are having sports on Saturday week, then on the following Monday they are having St Patrick's Ball. I should love you to be here for that week. I said to Mam today I feel I don't want to go because I don't think it is right I should go while you are out there fighting. When I go to the dances there always seems the day will come sometime when we can go together.

Dear Leslie, I don't think there is any more news at present. Mam and Dad send you their respects and hope to see you soon, so I will close with fondest and dearest love and tons of kisses to my own darling sweetheart Leslie, from your ever loving and true Phine.

XXXXXXX

8th March 1918

My own dearest Phine
I have received your letter dated the 3rd this afternoon and was pleased to hear you are still well.

I expect you are very glad now you have not to go on night work. I am pleased because I thought it might be too much for you and cause you to break down, especially as you were fed up with it as well.

I am awfully disappointed I shall not be able to go to one of the dances with you. Still it cannot be helped, we shall make up for it all when this lot is over.

In the ordinary course of wants I should just about be coming on leave now, but for some unknown reason or mistake our Battalion is a long way behind in the granting of leaves. They are making enquiries, so in a few days we expect to be sending about ten a day instead of the one or two we are sending now. Some of the other Battalions are months ahead of us and chaps who were on leave after me have been home again since. Still the old saying, better late than never.

No dearest, I have not heard from Bruce lately, but I had one letter, the one I told you about, in which he mentioned how he enjoyed the dances and everybody went mad in the Rancers. He sent me some brotherly advice, which I found I had to accept, although he is younger than I, and at the same time he mentioned he was very busy and had a lot of correspondence to answer. I do not suppose I shall hear from him until I answer his last letter.

What a dear pessimist you are, fancy saying you expect the War to last another two years. I shall begin to think you actually do want it to last a long time soon. You say you will be quite an old woman in two years' time, I hope it will not offend you, (in fact I do not care whether it does) what I am going to tell you, but you are not a <u>young woman</u> yet, so keep your pecker up sweetheart, the War cannot last for ever.

I hope you had a jolly time at the dance on Monday, how will they manage about St Patrick's Ball? I see the 17th falls on a Sunday (you see I have been working it out, wondering whether I should be lucky enough to be with you on that day), will they have it on the Saturday? I expect it will so as to give the dancers a chance to get over it on Sunday.

You must write and tell me all about it, I shall be thinking about you and wondering if you are having a good time.

Roll on, they were happy days, but I know there are better ones to come soon.

Well I must close now dearest, it is very late, and lights out have gone some time ago, so good night, with best wishes to your Mam and Dad, and fondest and dearest love and tons of kisses to my own darling sweetheart Phine, from always yours ever loving and true Leslie.

XXXXXX

17th March 1918

My own dearest Leslie

Just a line hoping you are quite well as it leaves myself at present.

Dear Leslie, I went to St Patrick's ball last Thursday, it was lovely there and I enjoyed myself, but I would enjoy it ever so much better if you had been there. Dad, Mam and I went to the Irish Guards sports yesterday afternoon, it was awfully nice there, it was like old times. As I was going up the Barracks Road I thought to myself I wish I was only fourteen and was going up to meet you dear.

Dear Leslie, I had another letter from my uncle Pat last Friday, he told me to ask you if you could get a pass and go and see him if you are anywhere near where he is, he said they are more likely to give you the pass because you are Sgt.

My own dearest Leslie, I don't think there is any more news at present. Mam and Dad send you their best respects and hope to see you soon, so I will close with fondest and dearest love and tons of kisses to my own darling sweetheart Leslie, from your ever loving and true Phine.

XXXXXX

20th March 1918

My own dearest Leslie

Just a line trusting you are quite well as it leaves myself at present.

I went to the dance on Monday, it was awfully nice there. I nearly got off with a Cpl. He was only nineteen, then when I told him I was engaged he never said anything. I expect he thought he better not.

Dear Leslie, I had my fortune told again yesterday in my tea cup. I was told that I was going to a strange Church to a grand wedding. The young lady who told me showed me the bride and two little children holding her train. I said to Mam that it must be my uncles Pat's wedding, because that is the only one I know of. She also told me that the young man was pretty tall, my uncle Pat is rather tall, he stands about five ten or eleven.

My dearest Leslie, I am looking forward to when you come home. I am anxious to see you once again. It seems a long time since I have seen you.

Dear Leslie, I don't think there is any more news at present. Mam and Dad send you their best respects and hope to see you soon, so I will close with fondest and dearest love and tons of kisses to my own darling sweetheart Leslie, from your ever loving and true Phine.

XXXXXXX

25th March 1918

My own dearest Leslie

Just a line trusting you are quite well as it leaves myself at present. Dear Leslie, I am very sorry to keep you waiting for a letter. I have been very busy this week, I had to work from seven in the morning until eight at night and Saturday afternoon and all day today Sunday. I have just come home from work, it is now half past six, and I have also got to work until eight all next week. By the time I get home it is half past eight so I don't get much time to myself. I don't mind working all those hours and every day in the week because I know it is to help to win the war.

My dearest Leslie, what do you think of the war? Don't you think it is getting awful? When Mam read the paper yesterday she sat and cried over it. I expect you was in this last attack[4] was you dear. I think it is very near time they sent you home for good.

Dear Leslie, when the foreman asked me to stop Friday I said I did not mind stopping, so he said don't stop if you have a boy to meet. I said I have no boy to meet. I thought to myself I only wish I had you to meet every night dear, still I expect we have got our day to come if God only spares you dear.

I don't think there is any more news at present so I will close with fondest and dearest love and tons of kisses to my own darling sweetheart Leslie, from your ever loving and true Phine.

XXX XXXXX

With best love to my dear Leslie.

28th March 1918

My own dearest Leslie

I received your letter last night dated the 21st. I was very pleased to hear from you, also to hear you are still quite well as it leaves myself at present.

Dear Leslie, you must excuse me not writing so often as I have got to work overtime last night and the night before I worked up until 10 o'clock. We have also got to work through the Easter Holidays. Still I don't mind, some of the girls grumble.

My dearest Leslie, have you heard anything about your leave? I expect it will be later on account of this big push. There is a big draft of Irish Guards going out on Sunday. They say that the Guards have been cut up terrible.

My darling Leslie, will make this a short letter. I will write to you again tomorrow night when I come home from work.

So I will close with fondest and dearest love and tons of kisses to my own darling sweetheart Leslie from your ever loving and true Phine.

XXXXXXXXXXX

4th April 1918

My own dearest Phine

No doubt you are wondering how I am, not having wrote you for such a long time, but we are having about the fondest time of our lives just at present, and not a minute to spare to write letters. I have sent a few field cards to let you know I am alright, and I am afraid you must be content with those, dearest, until this big push simmers down a bit. We never had our month's rest, only two days, before old Fritz was trying his hand on, and back we had to come. This is about the twelfth day,[5] and we are dead beat and tired out, but hope to go back for a short rest in a couple of days. There is not a bit of truth in that yarn that we have been out cut up terribly. We have had casualties certainly but he has not pushed us back a yard, except where we had to drop back on our own to conform with the remainder of the line, although he has attacked us and tried hard to get through.

I have received your four letters alright dated the 17th, 20th, 25th and 28th, but as you can understand, I had no chance to answer them.

I am glad you enjoyed the Ball on St Patrick's day. I thought about you being there and hoped you were enjoying yourself. I think we will be able to go the next one together. I hope so anyhow, because I am beginning to "Bob" a bit on these Cpls, who try to hang their hats up to you.

You said you were wishing you were only fourteen again and on the way up to Barracks to meet me. Well yes they were grand times, the best I have ever had, but I would not care for them again and go through this War afterwards. I don't think I could ever stick another War after this awful lot. Still I don't suppose there will ever be another like this.

When we get settled down again I will certainly get a pass to go and see Pat if he is anywhere near. It is rather unfortunate for him the leave being stopped, he will have to postpone his wedding. You will have to have your fortune told again and see when the wedding is coming off. Then that I shall be coming on leave myself. This big push has upset all the leave arrangements. Still never mind dearest we have it to come. Roll on the last long leave, when we shall not come back to France anymore. You will be able to tell your foreman then that you <u>have got a</u> boy to meet and he won't let you work overtime.

I suppose you are tired out having to work such long hours and every day of the week. Still keep it "up" dearest, if you only knew how much we depend upon and require it out here, I am sure your girls would not grumble, in fact they would be willing to work night and day. It is hard times having to give up the Easter Holidays, but if we do not get the shells and munitions we shall not win. Do not worry about writing a letter my darling when you are so tired, just drop an ordinary postcard, the same as my field cards, just to let me know you are still well, that is all I want to know.

It won't be long now when we will not have letters to write, with the help of God. Well I will close now darling, I will write you again the first appointment I have, which will be in about three days' time. Give my best wishes to your Mam and Dad, hoping they are enjoying the best of health, and fondest and dearest love and hundreds of kisses to my own dear sweetheart Phine, from your ever loving and always true Leslie.

P.S. Don't forget, sweetheart, just a postcard when you are so very tired, if you write a letter now I shall be angry. A letter now and again will do.

6th April 1918

My own dearest Leslie

I received your card this evening when I came home from work. I am very pleased to hear you are still quite well. What do you think of the War, dear? Don't you it is getting awful? I only had Easter Monday for our holidays this year. I had to work all day Good Friday and all day Saturday.

My dearest Leslie, when I came home from work in the evening and I see our girls meet their boys I often wish that you was at home so that I could meet you, still I expect we have got our day to come if God spares you. Dear Leslie, you remember Sgt Connolly? We heard last week that he was killed.

I don't think there is any more news at present. Mam and Dad send you their best respects and hope to see you soon, so I will close with fondest and dearest love and tons of kisses to my own dearest Leslie, from your ever loving and true Phine.

XXXXXXXXXXXXXXXXXXXXXXXXXXXXXXXXXXXXXXXXXX

10th April 1918

My own dearest Leslie

I received your letter this evening dated the 4th April, I was very pleased to have a letter from you, also to hear you are still quite well. I said to Mam this evening when I received your letter I think it is a shame that I only send you just a few lines and you send me five or six pages and you are out there and have not got a minute to spare. I am no hand, dear, at writing love letters, I can never think what to put in them. Still I expect there is an excuse because I am only young yet.

My dearest Leslie, I don't suppose you will get your leave in May now as you said in your letter that the push has put all the leaves off. I was looking forward to you coming home in May. Dear sweetheart, as I sit writing this letter I can imagine you sitting in the trenches up to your neck in mud, you ought to try and swing the leg as they call it and try and get home for good. I should love you to be home in England, you have been out in France just about three years and a half.

My dearest Leslie, I don't think there is any more news at present, I left off work a bit early tonight so that I could write you a letter so I will close as it is getting late and want to wash my hair tonight.

Mam and Dad send you their best respects and hope to see you soon. To my own darling sweetheart Leslie from your ever loving and true Phine.

XXXXXXXXXXXXXXXXXXXXXXXXXX

Roll on dear, when we have these kisses real.

12th April 1918

My own dearest Leslie

Just a line hoping you are quite well as it leaves myself at present dear.

My dear Leslie, I should like you to have your photo taken just as you come out of the trenches, just for a novelty.

There is no fear of me getting off with the Cpls now, because they have all gone to France. They went Easter Sunday, poor fellows, I think it is a shame.

Dear Leslie, there is nobody that will take your place, if anything happened to you I should never love another boy like I do you. What do you think of the War, dear? Do you think it will last much longer? We have not heard from Mick or Pat for quite a long time now.

Dear Leslie, I don't think there is any more news at present. Mam and Dad send you their best respects and hope to see you soon, so I will close with fondest and dearest love and tons of kisses to my own darling sweetheart, your ever loving and true Phine.

XXXXXXXXX

16th April 1918

My own dearest Leslie

I received your card last night dated the 10th. I was very pleased to hear you are still quite well, I also received your letter dated the 7th last Saturday.

Dear Leslie, if we get three or four days holiday for I think I shall go up and see your Mother. I have not been to London since you was home on leave, that was last Sept.

Have you heard from Bruce lately? Mam has not had a line from him since he went back off leave last January. Is he still in the same place?

Dear Leslie, I am pleased in a way now because I work overtime, the dances have finished and I have nowhere to go of a evening only to the Pictures and I don't like them.

My dearest Leslie, I don't think there is any more news at present. Mam and Dad send you their best respects and hope to see you soon, so I will close with fondest and dearest love and tons of kisses to my own darling sweetheart Leslie, from your ever loving and true Phine.

XXXXXXXXXXXXXX

20th April 1918

My own dearest Phine

At last I have been able to settle down in quiet for a few days and so be able to answer your letters.

I have received your last three letters of the 6th, 10th and 12th and was so glad to hear from you sweetheart, and to know you are quite well.

I was sorry to hear Sgt Connolly had been killed, he was a nice fellow. He was married too, was he not? You asked me if I knew a Sgt Hill, yes I remember him at the Base. I think I have seen him since.

Well dearest, I shall be glad when the War is over. We had a rotten time last time up. Still they say the War will be over this year. Then you will not have to see your girls meeting their boys every night and wishing you was doing the same. I often wonder whether you will not see me too much and get fed up with the sight of me. Also we shall not have to write so many letters. Letter writing always has me guessing, I never can think what to write about, especially as we are not allowed to write about what we are all doing out here.

Yes, darling, the leave question has been squashed altogether, it has been stopped over a month now. Still today I heard they were going to start again in a day or two, so perhaps we may see one another again very soon now. Do not rely upon it, however, as it is only a rumour I have heard, it is not official.

What an idea Phine, wanting a photo of me just as I come out of the trenches, I should not dream of sending you one ever if I want to lose my best girl, I am not so handsome at the best of times, as goodness knows what you would think if you see me coming out of the line. Don't forget you have only seen me when I am on my best behaviour, "all dressed up and nowhere to go".

Yes, I suppose all the Cpls have left the Barracks now, we have had a lot come from Chelsea, they say there are hardly any left at home now. The Barracks are quite empty.

When I read your letter and you said nobody could take my place, I loved you more than ever, if it was possible, because truly speaking sweetheart I am awfully jealous of my girl, and there is nobody in this world could take your place. Ever since the night I first see you at the Cpls first dance I have loved you.

Well dearest, I will close now and will write you again in a day or two, give my best respects to your Mam and Dad and fondest and dearest love to your own sweet self from, your ever loving and true Leslie.

XXXXXXXXXXXXXXXXXXXXXXXXXXXXXXXXXXXXXXXXXXXXXXXX
XXXXXXXXXXXXXXX

Sadly, James Connolly Lance Sergeant 6452 of the Irish Guards died on 23rd March 1918.

22nd April 1918

My own dearest Leslie

I received your card this evening when I came home from work dated the 17th. I was very pleased to hear you are alive and kicking.

Dear Leslie, we had a field card from poor Mick yesterday. He is moved to a different place and he is also in Hospital, but he don't say what is the matter with him. Mam thinks he is starved, and he also asked Mam to send him some cigarettes, so Mam does not know what to do because she is not allowed to send him a parcel of any sort now.

My dearest Leslie, I have only got work five days a week now, because we can get our work done in five days instead of six, we got to get so many mines out in a week and when they are done we have got nothing to do. They have given us ninety two boxes to do in a day and each box contains four mines, it is like being down the seaside playing in the sand. We fill the boxes with black sand, it makes your hands awful, all the palm of my hands are splitting, still never mind it is all to win the War, that is nothing to what you and your poor comrades have to go through to save our lives dear.

My own dearest Leslie, I don't think there is any more news at present. Mam and Dad send you their best respects and hope to see you soon, so I will close with fondest and dearest love and tons of kisses to my own darling sweetheart Leslie, from your ever loving and true Phine.

XXXXXXXX

With best love, Phine.

XXX

My own dearest Leslie

Just a line hoping you are quite well as it leaves myself at present. Dear Leslie, we are having awful weather here, it has been raining for three or four days, we had snow last Tuesday and it was terrible cold.

We had a letter from one of my married aunties today to say that she has moved to Sidcup in Kent, that is the one that's husband is discharged from the Army.

Dear Leslie, is there any W.A.A.C.[6] girls where you are? They seem to be doing good work out there. We have got a lot stationed here at Warley Barracks. I was longing for May to come dear, because I was looking forward to you coming home on leave, but I don't suppose you will get it now.

My dearest Leslie, I don't think there is any more news at present. Mam and Dad send you their best respects and hope to see you soon, so I will close with fondest and dearest love and tons of kisses to my own darling sweetheart Leslie, from your ever loving and true Phine.

XXXXXXXXXXXXXXXXXXXXXXXXXXXXXXXXXXXXXXXXXXXXX
XXXXXXXX

24th April 1918

My own dearest Phine

Just a few lines to let you know I am still in the best of health.

We have had a short rest and are back again, but quite cheerful and happy. I received, your two letters dated the 10th and 18th and was glad to hear you are quite well dearest.

Yes, certainly go up to London when you get your holidays, it is a long time since you have been there, last September. I wish I could be there with you. I have heard that the Base is starting again shortly, I hope it does.

I have not heard from Bruce for some time now, but I heard from Mother that he is still in Hospital with Impetigo but expects to be out very shortly now.

No Phine, there are no W.A.A.C. here where we are. There are nobody, only soldiers and shell ruined houses,[7] they are at the Bases I believe. I remember seeing two or three at Boulogne when I was going on leave.

Why do you ask, are you thinking of coming out? Or are you afraid I might get off with one of them?

No those pieces in the papers about the dances and concerts they give do not affect the soldiers who are fighting, only those employed at the bases.

I have enclosed that cutting from the newspaper that I meant to have sent before with one of my letters, I thought I put it in.

Well dear I will close now, I will write again the first chance I get. Give my best wishes to your Mam and Dad and fondest and dearest love and hundreds of kisses to my own darling Phine, from your ever loving and true Leslie.

XXXXXXXXXXX

25th April 1918

My own dearest Leslie

Just a line hoping you are well as it leaves myself at present.

Dear Leslie, I received your card yesterday dated the 17th. Mam went up to London last Monday to see your Mother and stopped there until Tuesday. Do you know Bruce is in Hospital with a sore face? Your Mother said that you had the very same thing when you was in Wellington Barracks. Dear Leslie, do you think you will get your leave next month?

I don't think there is any more news at present. Mam and Dad send their best respects and hope to see you soon, so I will close with fondest and dearest love and tons of kisses to my own darling sweetheart Leslie, from your ever loving and true Phine.

XXX

Phine wears the trousers

2nd May 1918

My own dearest Leslie

I received your letter dated the 24th April. I was very pleased to hear from you, also to hear you are still quite well as it leaves myself at present. My dearest Leslie, you will be pleased to hear that I am wearing trousers at my work. I have been wearing them for a month now, but I did not like telling you before. Mam told your Mother when we went up there last week, your Mam said she would like me to have my photo taken in them, what do you think dear?

Dear Leslie, I have also received a field card this evening dated the 28th April.

My dearest Leslie, it was Enna's birthday yesterday, she is three. It is my Dad's the 10th and Mona's 26th, she will be five.

Well dear Leslie, I don't think there is any more news at present. Mam and Dad send you their best respects and hope to see you soon, so I will close with fondest and dearest love and tons of kisses to my own dearest Leslie, from your ever loving and true Phine.

XXXXXXXXXX

4th May 1918

My own dearest Phine

I have received your last two letters of the 22nd and 20th and you must excuse me not answering them before. I have been pretty bad for a few days and once or twice thought it would be a case of Hospital. However they let me rest in my dug out and told me I need not do any duty, as with a good rest and some medicine I soon pulled round again and am quite fit again now.

I am awfully sorry to hear Mick is in Hospital. Probably your Mam is right when she says he is starved, they certainly do not treat them properly. Never mind dear, we shall have the dirty curs beaten soon. Things do not look very bright at present but we have got them alright.

I am glad you do not have to work so long now, only working five days a week gives you plenty of time to rest. I am sure you would have knocked yourself up if you had continued working so hard and doing overtime.

Well it seems that some of the units have started leave again, but it has not reached us yet, so perhaps with a bit of luck I shall be seeing you again soon. I hope so dearest because I do so want to be with you again. Roll on this blessed old War and may it finish soon.

Well I must close now sweetheart. I will write again at the first opportunity. Give my best respects and kind wishes to your Mam and Dad and fondest and dearest love and hundreds of kisses to my own darling Phine, from your always loving and ever true Leslie.

XXXX

11th May 1918

My own dearest Leslie

I received your letter this morning dated the 4th of May. I was very pleased to hear from you, I am very sorry to hear you have not been well. Dear Leslie, I thought there was something the matter with you because Mam dreamt of you the other night. Do you remember when you was wounded Mam dreamt of you two or three nights before we heard? Dad said he thinks that they ought to send you home and all the poor fellows who have been out there since the beginning.

Dear Leslie, if the War is another year they will take my brother for the Army. He will be seventeen the 10th of November. Mam was always wishing I was a boy before the War, but she don't now.

My own dearest Leslie, I was just thinking I have only seen you dear twenty-seven days in three years and a half. We will all go mad when the War is over, it has been on nearly four years. Dear Leslie, was it October when you went out to France? My darling Leslie, I don't think there is any more news at present. Mam and Dad send you their best respects and hope to see you soon, so I will close with fondest and dearest love and tons of kisses to my own darling sweetheart boy, from your ever loving and true Phine.

XXXXXX

P.S. Roll on dear when we will not have to put these crosses on paper. Phine.

XXXXXXXXXX

5th May 1918

My own dearest Leslie
Just a line hoping you are quite well as it leaves myself at present. I received your field card yesterday dated the 30th. I also had a field card from my uncle Pat dated the 29th so I was quite alright then.

Dear Leslie, I have been engaged two years this month, it does not seem as long as that to me, does it to you dear? Mam read in today's paper that the Grenadiers have been in big bayonets charge.

Dear Leslie, I was dreaming I was out in France last night with Bruce and Mam was dreaming about you. She dreamt that you was her young man. My own dear Leslie, I don't think there is any more news at present. Mam and Dad send you their best respects and hope to see you soon, so I will close with fondest and dearest love and tons of kisses to my own darling sweetheart Leslie, from your ever loving and true Phine.

XXXXXXX

7th May 1918

My own dearest Leslie
Just a line hoping you are quite well as it leaves myself at present.
Dear Leslie, I don't suppose you have heard, they have rationed us in gas now. Mam is only allowed 10/- worth in six weeks, that works out about 3d a day, that is no good, she puts in five pence to cook the dinner.[8]

Dear Leslie, my Dad will be 44 on Friday. I told him he was getting quite old.

I took my two little sisters out last evening and some old lady stopped me and said are those two little children of yours, she thought they were mine, and when I told her my age she would not believe, she said she quite thought I was twenty five, or six.

Dear Leslie, I don't think there is any news at present. Mam and Dad send you their best respects and hope to see you soon, so I will close with fondest and dearest love and tons of kisses to my own darling sweetheart Leslie, from your ever loving and true Phine.

XXXXX

13th May 1918

My own dearest Leslie
I received your letter this morning dated the 9th. I also had your letter and card yesterday. Dear Leslie, I was very pleased to hear from you, also to hear you are quite well as it leaves myself at present.

Dear Leslie, the reason I did not tell you that I was wearing trousers is because I thought it was not nice for girls to wear them. I am going to have my photo taken on Sunday, I expect you will die with laughing Bruce saw me in them when he came up on leave, he came home with me Monday night and stopped until Tuesday dinner. I thought he was going back in the morning or else he would not have seen me.

My dearest Leslie, when you come home on leave you must come and see what sort of work I do.

Dear Leslie, I don't think there is any more news at present. Mam and Dad send you their best respects and hope to see you soon, so I will close with fondest and dearest love and tons of kisses to my own darling sweetheart Leslie, from your ever loving and true Phine.

XXXXXXXXXX

19th May 1918

My own dearest Phine

I received your letter yesterday dated the 11th and was pleased to hear from you, and to hear you are quite well.

We are having a fairly quiet time at present waiting for old Bill to come over again. I don't suppose he will be long now, as the weather is lovely now. It is just like summer in the afternoon, it is too hot to move.

I just heard someone say he thought it was Whit Sunday today. I would like to be in dear old blighty now. I should want to be there for good though. I don't want to come back here again. Still I suppose the day will not be long now dearest, as you say we shall all go mad. I know I shall, I intend to, I am going to have the time of my life when this old War is over.

Yes dear, it does not seem much only seeing one another for twenty seven days in 3 years and 7 months. It was on the 5th October when we sailed from Southampton.

You said your Mam does not wish you were a boy now. I agree with her most decidedly. I should never have known you at all. Just fancy how awful that would have been.

I was quite surprised to know Freddy would be 17 in November. I don't think it will take him to come out here though. It will just about have ended by the time he is 18.

I am expecting Bruce out any day now, and I think I shall try and claim him into our regiment when he comes if it is possible. I should like to have him with me.

Well Phine dearest, it is getting dark now and our work commences then, everybody comes to life at night, so I must close.

Give my best respects to your Mam and Dad, and fondest and dearest love to my own dear sweetheart Phine, from your ever loving and true Leslie.

XXXXXXXXXXX
XXXXXXXXXX

P.S. I keep a note of all these kisses, do you think I can have them all when I come home? I think it is some <u>millions</u> now, Les.

XXXX

23rd May 1918

My own dearest Leslie

I have received your letter this Monday dated the 19th. I was pleased to hear from you, also to hear you are quite well again, I also received a card dated the 13th. Mam had a letter from Sgt Brown, he said he hopes to be home for the dances next season.

Dear Leslie, if I had been a boy you would have fell in line with another girl. I think

I shall have to get all your letters and count all the crosses. I am afraid I should be three or four days counting them. Fancy dear asking if you can have those kisses when you come home, you can have as many as you want, but I was afraid you would not want nothing else to do while you was home, you would soon wish you was back in France in your dug out by the coke fire.

Dear Leslie, I suppose you heard about the air raid we had last Sunday night. It was awful, they say it is the worst one we have had, the guns were going off terrible.[9] I don't know what it must be like out in France, it would drive me silly, although I should like to go out to France to see what it is like out there and come back again.

My own dearest Leslie, I don't think there is any more news at present. Mam and Dad send you their best respects and hope to see you soon, so I will close with fondest and dearest love and tons of kisses to my own darling sweetheart Leslie, from your ever loving and true Phine.

XXXXXXXXXXXXXXXXX

26th May 1918

My own dearest Leslie

I received your letter this morning dated the 22nd. I was very pleased to hear from you, also to hear you are still quite well as it leaves myself at present.

Dear Leslie, I expect you would be shy if you saw me in my trousers, but I hope you will never see me in them because I am just as shy as you are.

Bruce saw me in them when he was on leave and he did laugh.

Dear Leslie, the raid was awful last Sunday night. Mam said that the guns were going off terrible. Mam called me when they were getting near, I got up and put my clothes on and then laid on the bed and went fast to sleep so I did not hear anything of it. They don't trouble me now, I am getting quite used to them now, so is Mam.

Dear Leslie, Mona is five today. I don't think there is any more news at present dear. Mam and Dad send you their best respects and hope to see you soon, so I will close with fondest and dearest love and tons of kisses to my own darling sweetheart Leslie, from your ever loving and true Phine.

P.S. I am having my photo taken tomorrow, Phine.

XX

28th May 1918

My own dearest Leslie

I received your field card yesterday dated the 22nd. I was pleased to hear you are quite well as it leaves myself at present. Dear Leslie, I had my photo taken yesterday evening. I wonder if they will come out alright. I will have them on Saturday so I will send you one Saturday night. I am only having a half a dozen done, one for Mick, Pat, your Mam and one for you dear. I expect you will be shocked when you see it, you will not have nothing to do with me then because I don't think it is nice for girls to wear trousers, do you dear? When Bruce was up on leave, I told him I thought I would have my photo taken so I must send him one if I may dear, then I will have one for myself.

My dearest Leslie, I have enclosed a slip of paper. Don't you think it is from a British prisoner of war? Have you heard Germany is starving?

I don't think there is any more news at present, so I will close with fondest and dearest love and tons of kisses to my darling sweetheart boy, from your ever loving and true Phine.

XXX

P.S. Dearest, I do wish you was home for good so I could give you these crosses, Phine.

XXX

P.S. Dear Leslie, keep the slip of paper. Phine.

XXX

31st May 1918

My own dearest Leslie

Just a line hoping you are quite well as it leaves myself at present.

Dear Leslie, fancy old Fritzy bombing a Hospital in France. There was some wounded came in yesterday afternoon. Mam went down to see them, they were the fellows that was in that Hospital.[10] She heard one of the wounded say that another three months will finish the War. I said to Mam let's hope it does.

Dear Leslie, Mam has not heard from Mick for several weeks now, she is beginning to worry. I don't think there is any more news at present. Mam and Dad send you their best respects and hope to see you soon, so I will close with fondest and dearest love and tons of kisses to my own darling sweetheart Leslie, from your ever loving and true Phine.

XXXXXXXXXXXXXXXX

2nd June 1918

My own dearest Leslie

Just a line hoping you are quite well as it leaves myself at present.

Dear Leslie, what do you think of the War now? I think it is getting terrible, the Germans are only 45 miles from Paris.[11] I have just written a letter to your Mother and sent her a photo. I have also sent one to Pat. What do you think of it, dear? Don't you think I have come out awful? It is my face what spoils it. Mam said that the other part is very nice, still it is not my fault, it is my misfortune dear Leslie, if I had not told you, I would not have sent you one.

My dear Leslie, I always feel miserable on Sundays. I often wished I had to work weekends in a way, because I sit down and think all sorts of things. I often feel I should cry. I am longing for the time to come dear when you will come down weekends or I will go up to London.

My dearest Leslie, I don't think there is any more news at present. Mam and Dad send you their best respects and hope to see you soon, so I will close with fondest and dearest love and tons of kisses to my own darling sweetheart Leslie, from your ever loving and true Phine.

XXXXXXXXXXXXX

2nd June 1918

My own dearest Phine

I received your letter dated the 26th and was pleased to hear you are still in the best.

I am afraid that this last attack of old Fritzys has put the stopper on any leave now, at least for the present, although a few have gone. Still I do not think they will continue with it, still they say these big attacks point to the end of the War, quite a lot seem to think it will end this year. Let us hope it does, so we may have the days of peace again.

I have just had your letter of the 28th handed to me. I am rather interested about your photo, as you remark dear I expect I shall be awfully shocked, but as for having nothing more to do with you, well I am sure that could never happen dear.

Send one to Bruce if you like sweetheart, but you want to watch him, he has quite a collection of girls' photos, he showed me a dozen or more when I was on leave and he told me he loves them all.

The slip you sent me was rather interesting, it is clever. I hope the message he sends is true, we might then see some signs of peace. According to the papers there is a big movement on foot for the exchange of prisoners of War, so perhaps you may have the pleasure of having Mick home soon. I am sure it's time he did, I think I should have gone mad after all these years.

Well I must close now dearest. Give my best wishes to your Mam and Dad and fondest and dearest love and hundreds of kisses to my one and only dearest girl, from your ever loving and true Leslie.
XXXXXXXXXXXXXXXXXXXXXXXXXXXXXXXXXXXXXXXXXXXXXX
XXXX.

4th June 1918

My own dearest Leslie

I received your field card this evening. I was very pleased to hear from you, also to hear you are quite well as it leaves myself at present.

Dear sweetheart, I have just written a letter and sent one of my photos to Mick. I wonder if they will pass it. I hope they do, we have not heard from him since we had that card to say he was in Hospital. I have been worrying what was the matter until I got your card this evening.

Dear Leslie, excuse this short letter as I am awfully tired. Mam and Dad send you their best respects and hope to see you soon, so I will close with fondest and dearest love and tons of kisses to my own darling sweetheart boy, from your ever loving and true Phine.
XXXXXXXXX

9th June 1918

My own dearest Leslie

I received your two letters also a field card, I was very pleased to hear from you, also to hear you are still quite well as it leaves myself at present.

Dear Leslie, Mam had a field card from Sgt Lerowin, he is still quite well.

My dearest Leslie, Bruce has come up on leave again, so I am writing this letter at your Mother's. I wish you was here dear. I have got three weeks off holiday, all our girls are stood off for three weeks, so Bruce has got his leave just in time. He said when he gets back he expects to go to France any day. I was saying to Mam the other day it would be nice if you got your leave now.

Dear Leslie, Mam was dreaming about you Friday night. She dreamt that you had got your leave and did not come near me. I went off with another fellow and spent the fourteen days with him, then Mam said she made me sit down and write you a letter to chuck you up. I sent your ring and everything back, and then yesterday morning we had a letter to say Bruce was coming down.

My own darling sweetheart, I wish you was here today. I don't think there is any more news at present so I will close with fondest and dearest love and tons of kisses to my own darling sweetheart boy, from your ever loving and true Phine.

XXXXXXXXXXXXXXXXXXXXXXXXX

13th June 1918

My own dearest Phine

I received your letter of the 2nd and also the photo and also your letter of the 4th. It is pretty good but not as good as the last photo you had taken. It does not look as I picture you. You are certainly ten times prettier than the last photo shows. I shall be glad when I do not have to look at photos, and have the original there instead.

Still I was not shocked so I shall still continue to hang my hat up to you.

We are out of the line at present after six weeks of it and we are training pretty stiff and do not get much time. We have just returned from a field day[12] and I feel as tired as anything.

The leave seems as far off as ever. They are still going, but oh as awfully slow. Goodness knows when it will come again. Still we cannot expect too much just now whilst Fritz is making his big push. I expect it will not properly start until the winter months are here.

It seems strange that you have not heard from Mick so long. I wonder if he is very ill. I hope not and that also you will soon receive news of him.

Well Phine dearest I will close now. Give my best respects to your Mam and Dad and fondest and dearest love and hundreds of kisses to my own darling sweetheart girl, from your ever loving and true Leslie.

XXXXX

14th June 1918

My own dearest Leslie

I received your letter yesterday dated the 7th. I was very pleased to hear from you, also to hear you are quite well as it leaves myself.

Dear Leslie, I came back from London yesterday dinner time. I enjoyed myself very much, but I would have enjoyed myself much better dear if you had been there. Dearest

Leslie, I feel as miserable as anything, I will be glad to get back to work. Madam Oills told my fortune, she told me that I was going into a government place and I was going to have lots of money in about three or four weeks' time and lots of other little things but I could not remember them.

Bruce is now going out with a W.A.A.C., her name is Betty.

My own dearest, I don't think there is any more news at present. Mam and Dad send you their best respects and hope to see you soon, so I will close with fondest and dearest love and tons of kisses to my own darling sweetheart boy, from your ever loving and true Phine.

XXXXXXXXXXXXXXXX

17th June 1918

My own dearest Leslie

I received your card this morning dated the 14th. I was very pleased to hear from you, also to hear you are quite well as it leaves myself at present.

My dearest, I been helping Mam to do the washing so I am tired. While I was in London I went to Norwood and came back on the top of the bus. I caught a cold, so I am writing this letter in bed. I know you will call me lazy.

Dear Leslie, I expect you will see Bruce out there very soon now. He said when he gets out there, you will come home. He said they only want one Cox to push old Fritz back.

Mam has not heard from Mick yet, perhaps they will exchange him. I hope they do.

Dear Leslie, I don't think there is any more news at present. Mam and Dad send you their best respects and hope to see you soon, so I will close with fondest and dearest love and tons of kisses to my own darling sweetheart boy, from your ever loving and true Phine.

XXXXXXXXXXXXXX

P.S. Dear Leslie, excuse this letter because I feel tired. Colds always make one feel bad in the evening time, it is only half past eight and I am in bed. Phine.

XXXXXX.

19th June 1918

My own dearest Leslie

Just a line hoping you are quite well as it leaves myself at present

I had a funny dream last night dear, I dreamt your Mother, my Mother and myself was in a big ship on our way to France. I don't know what we were going there for, just as we were going to land I woke up.

Dear Leslie, I heard the other day that the War would last another four years yet. If so dear you will not be able to stick it at all that time. All the poor men now who have been out there since the beginning will be eaten up with all sort of pains. Still never mind, don't matter how you come home. I shall do all I can for you, not like a young girl I know, her young man got wounded in the foot and when he come to England he had to have his foot off. Then when he wrote and told her she threw him up. Don't you think she ought to be ashamed to say so? If that was me I should love the fellow all the more if it was possible. I am looking forward for when the blessed old War is over, looking forward to you dear coming down weekends.

Dear Leslie, I don't think there is any more news at present. Mam and Dad send you their best respects and hope to see you soon, so I will close with fondest and dearest love and tons of kisses to my own darling sweetheart boy, from your ever loving and true Phine.
XXXXXXXXX

Leslie came home after serving three years and 258 days abroad.
When Leslie came back from the Front, he carried on with soldiering in the Grenadier Guards. While being transferred to the 2nd Battalion he was stationed at Aldershot Barracks in Hampshire. Meanwhile, Phine was still working hard at the munitions factory and looking forward to their wedding day.

5th (Res) Grenadier Gds.
Chelsea Barracks
S.W.1
4th July 1918

My own dearest Phine
I found one of your letters dated the 17th waiting for me when I returned to Barracks last Monday. It had been to France, then to Caterham and eventually Chelsea.

I am still at Chelsea and up to the present it seems probable that I shall remain here. I may go off any day to one of the Camps, either Brighton or Epsom, but I am not certain yet.

If I do go to one of those places it will be rather too far to come down next weekend, so if it is convenient for your Mam I shall come down this weekend. Still I know I have that standing invitation to come when I like and to what I like. Besides I must come dear because it must be two or three months since I saw you last, or is it two or three days?

I shall come on Saturday with that train that arrives about half past five.

If I do not come by that train you will know that I am on Guard on Sunday, which would prevent me from coming.

I am having a very easy time, just walking around to see how things are done, which just suits me for the present.

Well I have got to get to Barracks now, it is nearly eleven o'clock so I must say goodnight, with best wishes to your Mam and Dad and fondest and dearest love to my own darling girl, from your ever loving and true Leslie.
XXXXXXX

21ˢᵗ July 1918

My own dearest Leslie

I received your letter on Friday I was very pleased to hear from you.

Dear Leslie, I told Mam what we were talking about last Sunday, you know what it was, and she asked had we said yes, what did we get engaged for, we might as well and save the money. I am delighted Mam and Dad said yes because I am like you, don't want to wait any longer.

I am ready dear when you like, you said you was ready, all I have got to do is to have my dress made, and to get a costume to go away in, I have got everything else.

My own dearest Leslie, I have felt very miserable this weekend because you were not down here. I miss you more than ever if you were in France, it seems weeks since I saw you last.

I am starting down the foundry tomorrow making mines again, so I won't go on nights now.

I don't think there is any more news at present, Mam and Dad send you their best respects, so I will close with fondest and dearest love and tons of kisses to my own darling sweetheart Leslie, from your ever loving and true Phine.

XXXXXXX

P.S. Dear Leslie, I hope you come down next weekend.

XXXX

5ᵗʰ Grenadier Gds
Chelsea Bks
London S.W.
24ᵗʰ July 1918

My own dearest Phine

I received your letter of the 21ˢᵗ and was so pleased to hear from you.

I was coming down this weekend but my Father has written me and asked me to come down to Crowthorne. He seems so anxious for me to go that I do not like to disappoint him. He wants us both to go down on Sunday evening.

I was thinking that now you work at the foundry you will have Saturday off, so perhaps you would come up Friday evening if possible as Mother wants to have a chat to us about our arrangements for the future. We are only kids in this matter so we must obtain all the advice our parents can give us.

I am glad you will not be on nights again, I did not like the idea of you having to do two months of it.

I know how you felt last weekend sweetheart, I was like it myself. I was awfully miserable, although I was awfully busy and did not have much time for thoughts.

It seemed to me ages since I saw you, it is far worse than being in France and right away.

Well dearest, let me know if you are coming up and what day. If you let me know the time of your train I will be there to meet you.

I have told Father that we are going down with the 2:00 from Waterloo on Saturday. If we cannot catch it I will telegraph him.

Well I will close now with all my fondest and dearest love and kisses (and best wishes to your Mam and Dad), from your ever loving and true Leslie.

XXXXXXXXXXXXXXXXXXXXXXXXXXXXXXXXXXXXXX

30th July 1918

My own dearest Leslie

Just a line to let you know I arrived back safe.

Dear Leslie, I did not feel so very tired yesterday. Last evening about quarter to six my Foreman came up to me and begged me to stop overtime, so I stopped until quarter past eight.

My dearest Leslie, I have thought it over. I think we might as well have those two rooms of your Mother's. We might not be able to get two more rooms like those near Chelsea Barracks dear. Mam was wild with me because I did not stop yesterday morning, she said she thought it was a shame to bring you out of bed so early in the morning. I was thinking of you too dear, but I did not know what to do.

My darling, I don't think there is any more news at present, so I will close hoping to see you Sunday, try and get the weekend off if you can dear. Dad will be at the Palace Saturday night so will be able to talk to Mother then you will not blush.

To my own darling sweetheart boy, from your ever loving and true Phine.

XXXXX

17th August 1918

My own dearest sweetheart

I received your letter this evening from Aldershot. I also had your other letter saying how you enjoyed yourself last Sunday. I wish I had been there, still I did not feel very lonely last weekend because one of my aunties came down last Sunday afternoon. I kept on saying to Mam Sunday morning, that I had got an idea Leslie will be down this afternoon and when I heard the knock I thought it was you, but I was disappointed. My auntie stayed here until yesterday, she went up with Mother, so I am all on my own this weekend. If I had known for sure you was coming up to London last Sunday I would have gone up. Dear sweetheart, I was looking forward to see you this weekend but when I had your letter Wednesday dinner time, I did not eat any dinner I could have sat down and cried.

Mam said to me I thought you did not miss Leslie, of course that started me off. I did not do hardly any work that afternoon. Sweetheart, it seems such a long while since I saw you last dear, yet it is only a fortnight. My dear sweetheart I have got a wedding present already, what my auntie brought me who was staying here last week.

My own dearest sweetheart, I don't think there is any more news at present. Mam and Dad send you their best respects so I will close with fondest and dearest love and tons of kisses to my own dearest sweetheart, from your always loving and true Phine.

XXXXX

P.S. Dear, I did not write before, I was waiting to get a letter from Aldershot. Phine.

XXX

19th August 1918

My own dearest sweetheart

Just a line hoping you are quite well as it leaves myself at present.

Dear sweetheart, I am going to London on Saturday to see the Registrar and to be fitted for my wedding dress, so if you can get this weekend off I will stay in London until the evening, then you and I sweetheart can come down here if you will, because Mam and Dad want to see you.

I had a lovely bunch of flowers given to me this morning by Grace for my birthday. I told her on Friday that it was my birthday, but I never thought any more about it until she gave me the roses this morning. Fancy me, sweetheart, nineteen. I said to Mam that I am going back when I am twenty, it seem to me only the other day I was a young Flapper with my hair down.

Well dearest sweetheart, I don't think there is any more news at present. Hoping to see you on Saturday, try and get the weekend dearest, it will be nearly three weeks since I saw you last. Well I will close now with fondest and dearest love and tons of kisses to my own darling sweetheart Leslie, from your ever loving and true Phine.

XXXX XXXXXXXXX

XXXXXXXXX

XXXXXXX

XXXXXXXX

P.S. Dear, hope to see you on Saturday, I will not torment you like I did last time.

1st September 1918

My own dearest sweetheart

I received your letter dated 28th on Friday, I was pleased you got back on time.

Dear Leslie, I should not trouble about getting two rooms, one will do for the time being, if you can get a pretty large one.

Dear sweetheart, the twenty first will soon be here now, you said in your letter you feel a trifle nervous, I am afraid I shall be worse than nervous that day, I expect we shall soon get over it dearest.

I am going to London this Saturday to be fitted for my dress. I was thinking dearest about going down to see you on Sunday morning early but it is too far.

My dearest Leslie, I don't think there is any more news at present. Mam and Dad send you their best respects so I close with fondest and dearest love and tons of kisses to my own darling sweetheart Leslie, from your ever loving and true Phine.

XXXXXX

3rd September 1918

My own dearest sweetheart

Just a line hoping you are quite well as it leaves myself at present.

I wrote and asked my uncle Pat if he could get a leave to come to the wedding. I wonder if he can. There are a lot of men coming home on leave at present, there were five weddings in Brentwood last week and there is two more on Saturday. They were all Soldiers. Fancy sweetheart, only another two weeks and I shall be an old married woman.

I am afraid dearest I shall be awfully nervous that day, still I expect I shall get over it. Are you getting ten days dear? I hope you are.

I don't think there is any more news at present. Mam and Dad send you their best respects so I will close with fondest and dearest love and tons of kisses to my own sweetheart Leslie, from your ever loving and always true Phine.

XXXXXXX

9th September 1918

My own dearest sweetheart

Just a line hoping you are quite well as it leaves myself at present.

Dear Leslie, the 21st is getting near now. I am leaving my work on Friday, they are sorry I am leaving.

I expect I shall see you Wednesday week. I hope they will give you ten days, dear Leslie. I went to London on Saturday and stopped there until Sunday night, I got home about half past nine. I see Ethel and Jenny on Saturday and they teased me like anything.

Dear Leslie, I don't think there is any more news at present so I will close hoping to see you soon, to my own darling sweetheart Leslie, from your ever loving and true Phine.

XXX

Phine is preparing for her big day and has decided to leave her work, so her work friends are very sorry to see her leave.

The old War will be over soon

Leslie and Phine finally tied the knot on 21st September 1918. They had a wedding reception with relatives and friends and then went on to their honeymoon in Bath in the county of Somerset.

Mr and Mrs Cox returned from their honeymoon and moved in to Leslie's mother's house in London, as she had a floor she could rent them at a reasonable cost. Leslie was still based at the Aldershot Barracks, so could only go home to see Phine on occasional weekends when possible.

29th September 1918

My own dearest Wife

I received your letter last night and was so surprised and pleased to hear from you so soon.

I am very lucky getting home on Friday night. The train I should have caught was cancelled and I had to run for that one which took me to Woking. When I reached Woking there was no other train until half past ten and I was supposed to be in by 10 o'clock. Luckily however there were so many for Aldershot that they run a special train, and I reached the Barracks just in time after half past ten. Of course, really, I was absent but as luck happened the Sergeant of the Guard was my dear old best man Jock and of course everything was alright.

What an awful dream to have dearest, for goodness sake do not have any more like that, the old War will be over soon. Have you read the papers today? The news is absolutely great.

My dearest Phine, I was like you on Friday night, I could not get to sleep for hours thinking of you. I missed you terribly. Still dearest God is with us and some day very soon we shall be together for always. You must be brave sweetheart, there are hundreds like us parted through this awful War. I am sure you can be brave, you are a Soldier's Daughter and a Soldier's Wife.

I shall come up and see you the very first chance I get. I hope you are quite happy dear, if there is anything you want let me know at once. Enclosed you will find a £1. Will you give it to your Mam when you see her again? It is what I owe her for the beer we had last Saturday.

Let me know when you write next time if you have received your ring paper for your separation money. It should be 30/- a week and if you are not receiving it I can make enquires and back them up. I am afraid you will have to be economical dearest, it is not much money in these days, but you know a Soldier is not overpaid at any time.

I have enclosed another 10/-, you will find it handy. I forgot to tell you dearest the rent for our rooms is 7/- a week, so the 10/- will cover that for you. Don't be shy dearest about paying Mother, she knows all about it. If there is anything you want she will see to it for you, because she told me she thinks of you and loves you as if you were a daughter of hers.

Well darling I must close now. I have an awful amount of work to get finished by tomorrow morning, so good night sweetheart, give my love to all at home, with fondest and dearest love and hundreds of kisses to my own dearest Wife, from your ever loving and true Husband.

XXXXXXXXXXXXXXXXXXXXXXXXXXXXXXXXXXXXXXXXXXXXXXX XXXXX.

10th November 1918

My own dearest Husband

Just a line hoping you are quite well as it leaves myself at present. Dear Leslie, Dad had a letter from Mother yesterday and she said Miss Sutton, a young girl who worked at the same place as I did, has died of the Flu. She had been married about five months, I forget her other name and there was only her Husband there, she has not got any parents. If you get your long weekend dear this week, Mabel is going to a dance on Saturday and she wants you and I to go.

Dear Leslie, your Mother had a letter from Bruce one day last week and he said they have put him out in the tents. He said it is awfully windy.

My dearest Leslie, I don't think there is any more news at present so I will close with fondest and dearest love and tons of kisses to my own dearest Husband, from your ever loving and true Wife.

XXXXXXXX

After all that both civilians and soldiers had suffered during the War, thousands of people died of the Great Influenza epidemic between 1918 and 1919.

The War was nearly at an end and many people were looking forward to the Armistice. Leslie was still stationed at Aldershot and could not get any leave to celebrate the Armistice. Leslie writes to Phine.

November 1918

My darling Wife

I received your letter this afternoon, and was pleased to hear from you. I am sorry you have caught another cold, you must take care of your self, darling, when you go out.

Yes I should like to have been in London when the Armistice was signed. I was hoping to have a bit of apse this weekend, but unfortunately the Coy Sergeant Major has decided to go so I have got to wait again. I am awfully wild about it because I am so sorry to keep disappointing you, but never mind dear, the War will soon be finished and it will not matter about leave then. I shall always be with you, and I thank God I have been spared to say so.

I think I shall leave the Army as soon so I can because I am properly fed up with it.

Well never mind dearest, plenty of good times in store. I expect Mick will be home very shortly now and the times we have planned will all come off.

Well dearest I will close now. Roll on next week. I hope to be up then at all events.

Give my love to all. Fondest and dearest love and tons of kisses to my dearest Wife from your ever loving and true Husband.

XXXXXXX

On 11th November 1918, at the time agreed 11am French time, the Armistice was set in place by France, Great Britain and Germany. This was the agreement to stop fighting which was followed later by the Treaty of Versailles which formally marked the end of the War, on the 28th June 1919.

12th November 1918

My darling Wife

I received your letter this morning and am glad to hear you are still well.

That was rather pathetic that young girl dying with the Flu. Thank God you recovered dearest. I don't know what I should do in her Husband's place. He must be awfully upset.

Yes dear, if I get my long weekend I will go to the dance if you wish, but remember it is years since I danced and I do not know all the latest ones.

Still that does not matter much to you as you would only have one dance with me and the remainder with other fellows. I can be a wallflower.

Well what do you think of the good news yesterday? I hear they all went mad in London. I should like to have been there. Did you go out at all?

Well I will keep all the news till the weekend, dearest. Love to all, fondest and dearest love and hundreds of kisses to my own darling Wife, from your ever loving Husband.

XXXXXX

12th November 1918

My own dearest Husband

I received your letter this morning. I was very pleased to hear from you. How is your cold dear? I hope it is better, mine is not gone yet. I went to see the Lord Mayor's show last Saturday, we went over there about twelve and we got home just about after five. I think I must have caught another cold because it was ever so cold.

Dear Leslie, I hope you get your long weekend this week. You ought to have been in London yesterday, the sights I saw, girls with their hair down their back, drunk as ever they could be, dancing, singing, and there are dozens of flags out, I bought four, two green and two red white and blue. It is not very cheerful for the people who have lost their Husbands. I saw several widows crying yesterday.

My dearest Leslie, I don't think there is any more news at present, so I will close with fondest and dearest love and tons of kisses to my own darling Husband, from your ever loving and true Wife.

XXXXXXX

14th November 1918

My own dearest Husband

I received your letter yesterday, also one this morning. I am awfully disappointed that you are not coming up this weekend and so is Mabel. Mabel said could you get up

Saturday afternoon, if not write back and let me know as soon as you can dear because Mabel has got the tickets, it starts 6:30.

Dear Leslie, there were some prisoners of War come in last night at Liverpool St from Holland, so I expect Mick will soon be home. I went out Tuesday over the West End to see the guns and saw the Queen and Princess Mary. That was the first I have seen them. I was frightened to go out on Monday because lots of the soldiers was getting hold of all the girls and women and kissing them.

My dearest Leslie, I don't think there is any more news at present, so I will close with fondest and dearest love and tons of kisses to my own darling Husband, from your ever loving and true Wife.

XXXXXXX

18th November 1918

My own darling Wife

Just a few lines hoping you are quite well. Did you go to the dance on Saturday or not? I was sorry I could not come but of course orders must be obeyed, and we have only to thank the mad way the people of London carried on last week. I hope they quieten down a bit now so they will cancel the order that stops us from coming to London.

They seemed to have had some fine old times in London celebrating the armistice. We just had the day off and then carried on as usual.

Well roll on Friday dearest, it seems ages since I have seen you. I can just do with a couple of days' rest, we have been so awfully busy lately. How is your cold? Is it any better yet? I have still one in my head, but nothing much.

How is your Dad progressing in his house hunting? Has he had any luck yet? I expect not, with all the accommodation that is required in London now.

Well darling, I will close now, roll on Friday. I am so awfully keen to see you again sweetheart. This weekend has been a nightmare.

I have felt like a fish out of water.

Give my love to all fondest and dearest love and tons of kisses to my own darling Wife, from your ever loving and true Husband.

XXXXXX

Notes 1918

1. Leslie was in the area of Arras, France.
2. The air raid occurred in London on the evening of 28th and 29th of January, killing 67 and injuring 166.
3. Arrangements were made for the severely wounded or disabled P.O.Ws to be sent to neutral countries such as Switzerland, through the Red Cross.
4. On 21st March 1918, the Germans launched a major offensive named Operation Michael. This was their spring offensive. The Germans managed to break the four-year stalemate and were able to push the French and British back. This was the biggest retreat for the British since 1914.
5. The Grenadiers held the front line from strong attacks made by the Germans on their offensive around Arras. Leslie was around in the area of Boisleux-au-Mont, just south of the town of Arras in France.
6. W.A.A.C. – Woman's Army Auxiliary Corps.
7. Leslie is at Villers-au-Bois near Arras, France.
8. Rationing was made compulsory in late 1917 and early 1918 due to German submarines sinking merchant shipping. This also led to the rationing of stocks of gas in Great Britain.
9. On 19th and 20th of May, London and surrounding areas had the largest and final raid in which the Germans used Gotha and Giant Bombers; 49 people killed and over 177 injured.
10. On 19th May 1918, two Canadian hospitals were bombed by German aeroplanes in Étaples in France. Over 60 Canadians were killed and over 70 were wounded.
11. This was part of the German spring offensive which saw Germans come within 50 miles from Paris, but they soon ran out of steam and became exhausted from the advance, causing them to go no further.
12. Field day – military term of a day spent undertaking field exercise manoeuvres.

The final story

Phine and Leslie lived a happy and fulfilling life after the experiences of the Great War. Leslie carried on with his military career with the Grenadier Guards, seeing overseas deployment again in 1922 when the Grenadiers were sent to help with the occupation of Constantinople in Turkey. After serving over a year out in Turkey, Leslie and his Battalion returned to England. Leslie carried on his career working his way up the ranks to finally becoming a Warrant Officer 2nd class, until in 1932, at the age of 38, he decided to leave the army. Between the wars, Phine and Leslie had two daughters, Yvonne (my grandmother) and Beryl. They enjoyed family life, while Phine was a housewife busy bringing up their daughters.

In the late 1930s, World War Two was in its early stages. Leslie, at the age of 47, did his bit again and volunteered for the Royal Artillery which he later amalgamated with the Royal Engineers. He was a member of a team operating a mobile search light, helping to stop the Nazis bombing England. Leslie, Phine and their daughters moved to the village of Crowthorne in Berkshire – where for many years they had visited and enjoyed holidays visiting Leslie's relatives – and settled into the country life.

Leslie's brother, Bruce, eventually went and fought at the Front in France in 1918 at the Battle of Amiens, where he was wounded. After a long time recovering in hospital from his wounds, in 1920 he then went on to join the Metropolitan Police serving as a Constable until his retirement 37 years later.

Phine's Uncle Mick did finally come back from the horrific conditions of the prison camps, but sadly died in 1921 at the young age of 26. As for Uncle Pat, he returned home safely after all those years of fighting.

The Grenadiers were still a large part of Leslie's life, staying in regular contact with his old pals from the Regiment and belonging to the Grenadiers Association. He went to social events and also dinner parties held in London. In 1961, Leslie died, leaving Phine and the family devastated.

Phine managed to make the most of her life and lived as happily as possible, despite losing Leslie and both of her daughters to illness. Phine finally passed away at the age of 77 in 1976.

I would like to dedicate this book to Leslie, Phine
and their friends who are mentioned
in the letters who did not return.

1st Battalion Grenadier Guards
15470 Lance Corporal C.E Gransden died 29th October 1914 Age 21
13549 Sergeant B. East died 31st October 1914 Age 25
13982 Corporal J.W Pickering died 7th November 1914 Age unknown

Irish Guards
6452 Lance Sergeant J. Connolly died 23rd March 1918

The Queen's Regiment
Uncle Mick returned but died from his wounds
L/9747 Drummer M. Gooley died 13th May 1921 Age 26
And to the other soldiers who have been mentioned, but unfortunately
their regiment numbers and rank could not be traced.

Forget-Me-Not